IRAQ
A Journey of
Hope and Peace

Peggy Faw Gish

D0369312

*"Love in action is a harsh
and dreadful thing,
compared to love in dreams."*

—*Dorothy Day, popularizing a saying by
Fyodor Dostoyevski*

IRAQ
A Journey of
Hope and Peace

Peggy Faw Gish

A Christian Peacemaker Teams Publication

Foreword by Kathy Kelly

Herald Press

Scottdale, Pennsylvania
Waterloo, Ontario

Library of Congress Cataloging-in-Publication Data
Iraq : a journey of hope and peace / Peggy Gish.
   p. cm.
ISBN 0-8361-9287-7 (pbk. : alk. paper)
1. Iraq War, 2003. 2. Gish, Peggy—Diaries. 3. Christian Peace
Maker Teams. I. Title.
DS79.76.G57 2004
956.7044'3—dc22

                                                    2004012045

Unless otherwise noted, Scripture is from the *New Revised Standard Version Bible,* copyright 1989 by the Division of Christian Education of the National Council of the Churches of Christ in the USA, and used by permission.

All photos are courtesy of the author except page 38 by Jane MacKay Wright; pages 49, 111 by Neville Watson; page 261 by Lorna Tyschotup; pages 97, 108 by IPT; and pages 79, 174, 200, 249, 251 by CPT.

Map on page 315 by Noah Beam.

IRAQ
Copyright © 2004 by Herald Press, Scottdale, Pa. 15683
   Released simultaneously in Canada by Herald Press,
   Waterloo, Ont. N2L 6H7. All rights reserved
International Standard Book Number: 0-8361-9287-7
Library of Congress Catalog Card Number: 2004012045
Printed in the United States of America
Cover design by Cathleen Benberg, A Distant Wind
   (www.distantwind.com)
Front cover photo by REUTERS / Ali Abu Shish

10 09 08 07 06 05 04 10 9 8 7 6 5 4 3 2 1

To order or request information, please call
1-800-759-4447 (individuals); 1-800-245-7894 (trade).
Website: www.heraldpress.com

To Art, and the other dedicated and courageous people around the world who put aside their own comfort and safety to turn their love into action for justice and peace.

Contents

Foreword

In the months leading up to the 2003 US led "shock and awe" warfare against Iraq, the global peace movement came closer than ever before to achieving the critical mass necessary to stop a war before it started. Campaigners to end economic sanctions against Iraq had already struggled mightily to educate people about the suffering that afflicted innocent Iraqis, lethally punished by economic siege. Masses of people knew that these sanctions had been used to wage a war that amounted to child sacrifice, claiming hundreds of thousands of children among the civilian victims. Pledge of Resistance campaigns, enlisting participants who agreed to commit civil disobedience in the event of a US attack, built broad international networks. On a smaller scale, the Christian Peacemaker Teams (CPT) combined with Voices in the Wilderness (VITW) to form the Iraq Peace Team (IPT), a project that maintained a presence in Iraq before, during, and after the shock and awe bombing. We aimed to live alongside Iraqi civilians and to bring some measure of comfort to them in the event of a war we wished we could have prevented.

When new rotations of IPT members arrived in Baghdad, we would gather in a large circle for introductions. "I am an organic gardener, and I am a grandmother," Peggy would announce, quite simply. "And I feel called to help prevent this war."

In numerous places of conflict, CPT has demonstrated the ability for unarmed teams to establish a needed witness on behalf of human rights for civilians whom war makers endanger and punish. They have also sparked worldwide concern, through their campaign, while they themselves were under fire, for Iraqi prison detainees caught up in a labyrinth US detention system, whose basic human rights were abysmally abused.

By chronicling CPT and Iraq Peace Team endeavors, Peggy

takes us into the laboratory of peace team experiments and stirs our own social imaginings to consider the further invention of nonviolence. She does so with remarkable patience, sincere inquiry, and honest reporting. We benefit from Peggy's consistently replenished reserves of extraordinary courage. We also learn from her acknowledgments of fear and frustration. She shows us what motivates her to "get in the way" as she follows the way of Jesus, espoused through the gospels and Christian tradition.

Barbara Deming, a kindred spirit of Peggy's, who wrote about peace movement efforts in an earlier generation, carefully analyzed experiences in the civil rights, antiwar, and disarmament movements through a series of essays spanning several decades. Barbara recalls watching a woman on a public bus recoil in disgust at the sight of a newspaper photo that showed Bull Connor's troops aiming fire hoses at children during a Birmingham, Alabama, civil rights demonstration. Conversing with the women, Barbara Deming noted that her fellow passenger could no longer stomach being aligned with the bullying cruelty of leading segregationists. Urging us to strategically design campaigns that will convert the onlookers, Barbara reminds us that if we are to succeed we must become many more than we are now.

CPT steadily prepares growing numbers of long- and short-term team members to create rippling outreach and public witness, advocating nonviolent means to resolve conflicts in campaigns around the globe. Through story telling about CPT efforts in Iraq, Peggy challenges the injustices of warfare, occupation, imprisonment, and economic siege.

Through her personal commitment to simplicity, service, and sharing, she challenges all who learn from her to join in becoming agents of change.

One of the ways we can help prevent a next war is to continually tell the truth about current ones. Peggy Gish has planted a new organic garden in this book.

—*Kathy Kelly*
Voices in the Wilderness
Pekin Federal Prison Camp
June 2004

Preface

Trying to deal with tyrants and oppressive government systems through military might has caused much suffering in the world. And even though military interventions continually fail, they are tried over and over. Peace activists have seen the foolishness in this.

In the 1980s there was a stirring among peace activists and pacifists who were looking for new ways to apply their insights through nonviolent action. Students on college campuses were studying Gandhi, Martin Luther King Jr., and the literary works of Gene Sharp (such as *The Politics of Nonviolent Action*) outlining the methods of nonviolence.

New organizations explored innovative forms of nonviolent intervention in places of tension. Witness for Peace discovered in the 1980s that when they brought a group of North Americans to a particular community in Nicaragua, the violence there stopped, at least temporarily. Peace Brigades International arranged for international activists to accompany human rights workers who had received death threats for their actions. (See *Nonviolent Intervention Across Borders* by Yeshua Moser-Paungsuwan and Thomas Weber [University of Hawaii Press, 2000] for a more thorough description of these groups.)

In 1984, Ron Sider spoke at the Mennonite World Conference in Strasbourg, France, and challenged Christian pacifists, saying that if they are really serious about peacemaking, they need to be willing to take the same risks as soldiers do to work for peace and justice.

Christian Peacemaker Teams (CPT) was formed out of this discussion. By 1992, a series of delegations had been sent to Haiti, Iraq, and the West Bank. This led to developing ongoing teams in these and other places, such as Chiapas, Mexico;

Colombia; Washington, D.C.; and several Native American communities in Canada and the US.

Though my husband, Art, and I were excited by this vision of CPT, we felt tied to family and community commitments and initially didn't see ourselves being part of a team. This changed, however, in 1995, when I went on a CPT delegation to the West Bank. Later that year, Art went there for six weeks and has kept returning each winter since. (See his book, *Hebron Journal*, published in 2001 by Herald Press, for stories of peacemaking in the West Bank.)

We discovered that this was not the work of a few unusually gifted, courageous people, but something that could be done by ordinary people like us, with all our weaknesses.

Very important for helping me do this work has been the patience, love, and support I have received from Art; sons Dale, Daniel, and Joel; daughters-in-law, Debbie and Deborah; and my siblings, Myrna, Linda, Bill, and Verda. I am grateful for the people of New Covenant Fellowship who have challenged, encouraged, and nurtured me, and have been an important part of discerning God's call to me. Thanks to Austin Youmans for his care for the farm and marketing during our trips. And thanks to the many committed and creative CPTers who have gone before me, were with me on the team in Iraq, and have taught me much of what I know about peacemaking.

I am grateful for close friends, such as Trisha Lachman and Helen Horn, who gave me emotional support and kept pushing me to be clear about my calling. Invaluable has been Trisha's help with sending out my writings to friends, family, and the media.

Thanks to the many wonderful people in the People for Justice and Peace group, our local CPT support group, the community of friends at the Monday Lunch, to Kathy Gault for her encouragement and help (particularly with media contacts), and those all over the world whose prayers helped sustained me.

I would not have even begun writing this book without Art's encouragement and support. I'm thankful to Kathy Kelly for her longtime dedication to peace and her work with Voices in the Wilderness to defy the economic sanctions against Iraq by bringing in needed medicines and humanitarian supplies.

Through her contacts and experience in Iraq and her vision and loving leadership, the Iraq Peace Team (IPT) was able to carry out a powerful witness before and during the 2003 war in Iraq. Kathy wrote the foreword to this book from the Pekin Federal Prison Camp where she is serving a three month sentence for civil disobedience at the Western Hemisphere Institute for Society (formerly called the SOA). I also thank Cliff Kindy, a fellow CPTer in Iraq, who strengthened IPT and the CPT Iraq team that followed after the invasion, with creative visionary actions. I cannot begin to mention all the strong and caring team members of IPT and CPT who gave leadership and support to me and our team's work. But I am thankful to each.

I am grateful for the following who helped read and critiqued this manuscript under tight time limits: Art, Trisha Lachman, Chabele Graziani, Nancy Beres, John Thorndike, Jim Philips, Cliff Kindy, Gene Stoltzfus, and Rob Miller. Thanks to ACEnet for computer services and its helpful staff. Also thank you to Sarah Kehrberg and Levi Miller of Herald Press for their help and support.

Beyond all those supportive people at home are the countless Iraqi people who have, with some risk, helped us in our work and opened their homes and lives to us in love—we, the strangers coming from the threatening country waging war, and now occupying theirs. There have been many US personnel in Iraq who have been sensitive to the suffering the occupation has caused, as well as international humanitarian and human rights workers also taking risks to help the Iraqis rebuild their lives.

In securing information and opinions of other people (sometimes quoted, sometimes summarized) used in this text, I took extensive notes, asked clarifying questions, and checked with other sources or with other team members who were present during the interviews. In many situations it was not possible to write down the conversations word for word. I often recreated parts or summarized the conversations afterward, as well as my memory served me.

PART 1

Getting in the Way

October 23, 2002—April 4, 2003

*Truly I tell you, just as you did it to one of the least of these
who are members of my family, you did it to me.*
—Jesus, Matthew 25:40

*To save the life of one human being
is to have saved the life of all humanity;
and to take the life of a single human being
is as if to destroy all humanity.*
—Koran 5:32

*Were the whole realm of nature mine
That were an offering far too small
Love so amazing, so divine
Demands my soul, my life, my all!*
—Isaac Watts

CHAPTER 1

Going

There is a story about the teacher who was asked by his disciples, "How can we determine the hour of dawn—when the night ends and the day begins? Is it when from a distance you can distinguish between a dog and a sheep?"

"No," said the teacher.

"Is it when you can distinguish between a fig tree and a grape vine?" asked another.

"No," said the teacher. "It is when you look into the face of another human being and you have enough light to recognize them as your brother or sister. Up until then it is night, and the darkness is still with us."

"In just twenty minutes, we will begin our preparation for landing." These words from the aircraft's loudspeaker jolted me out of my sleep. We would soon be reaching Amman, Jordan, the first step of our journey to Baghdad. Traveling with me were twelve other people from the United States and Canada. This interesting mix of people included teachers, pastors, social workers, a nurse, an archaeologist, a filmmaker, and media specialists, ranging in age from twenty-four to seventy-seven. This was the first Christian Peacemaker Teams (CPT) delegation to Iraq since the first Gulf War. It was Thursday, October 24, 2002, and there was a threat of war.

I was the leader of this delegation, but I had never been to Jordan or Iraq. We had instructions for navigating the airport in Amman and for finding buses or taxis to our hotel, but the closer we got, the more this blurred in my mind. The only one on our delegation who had ever gone to Iraq before was Anne

Montgomery, an energetic seventy-six-year-old religious Sister of the Sacred Heart, former teacher in Harlem, and seasoned peace activist. She had been in Iraq in 1990-91 with the Gulf Peace Team, an international group of peace activists who camped near the Saudi Arabian border to be a peaceful presence between the opposing forces and protest the first Gulf War. Since then she had gone on several trips to Iraq with Voices in the Wilderness and had become a full-time worker with CPT in the West Bank. We would meet Anne in Amman.

Shadowy scenes from the past six months race through my head, reminding me of how I had come on such an incredible journey.

I had become increasingly alarmed that spring, when President Bush began speaking more forcefully about a "regime change" in Iraq, warning us of the threat of Saddam Hussein and his "weapons of mass destruction." Many of us in my Athens, Ohio, People for Justice and Peace group and in organizations all across our nation were concerned and began to discuss what we could do to try to prevent a war or invasion in Iraq. In June, I wrote letters to the editors of our local newspapers. In August, as part of a national campaign, our peace group launched a local Iraq Pledge of Resistance campaign, in which many of us pledged to join with others to engage in public protest invaded Iraq. We had vigils and public forums. To Ohio Congressman Ted Strickland, I wrote, "It would be disastrous to proceed with Bush's plans."

"What would happen if five hundred grandmothers and grandfathers were in Iraq, living among the people and telling our government where they were?" asked Cliff Kindy, a full-time CPTer and longtime friend, as he spelled out his vision to a small group of CPTers. It was early July, at the Church of the Brethren Annual Conference, and the idea sounded intriguing to me. I began telling other people I knew who, like myself, were in that older age bracket.

Voices in the Wilderness (VITW), a Chicago based organization working since 1996 to end the economic and military warfare against the Iraqi people, was also thinking about having an ongoing team in Iraq. CPT decided to join with VITW on this venture to form what became known as the Iraq Peace Team (IPT). On

September 22, 2002, eight people from VITW went to Iraq to establish a base at the Al Fanar Hotel in Baghdad for IPT. Cliff Kindy, the first CPTer, left for Baghdad on October 18, along with Kathy Kelly, director of VITW, and some others. Five days later, fourteen more people, including myself, left for Iraq.

Back in mid-September when it was time for my husband, Art, and me to decide where we, as "reservists," would do our yearly work with CPT in the fall or winter, Art felt called to Hebron in the West Bank, where he had spent two to three months each winter for the past seven years. But I felt a pull to go to Iraq. Art supported me in this decision because we had a common vision for this kind of peacemaking. About a week later I agreed to lead this two-week delegation to Iraq and stay on for four more weeks.

On September 19, Bush sent a proposal to the US Congress, asking them to adopt a resolution to authorize the use of US armed forces against Iraq to bring about a regime change and to hunt for and remove any weapons of mass destruction. On October 16, after Congress passed the resolution, President Bush signed it into law.

Just two weeks before leaving for Iraq, I had been standing in front of a crowd of community people and Ohio University students and faculty gathered around the Athens (Ohio) County Court House steps for a peace rally. "There are no good reasons to go to war with Iraq," I told the crowd, "but beyond all of the political reasons I can give, war is simply wrong. It would mainly be the millions of Iraqi men, women, and children who suffer."

I told of my plans to go to Iraq with the Christian Peacemaker Teams. "I am going because I love my three grand-children, and I want them to grow up and live free and healthy lives. But Iraqi grandparents want the same for their grandchil-dren. And their lives are just as important as the lives of North Americans."

Just before I left on Wednesday morning, October 23, our small community group sang, "Be not afraid. I go before you always; come, follow me, and I will give you rest." They prayed for me and the team. Feelings of pain and grief at leaving Art, my community, and home, mixed with fear of plunging into the unknown, welled up in me as I said good-bye.

It was now almost midnight, and our plane was circling above the Amman, Jordan, airport. I thought of the various visions we had for this venture. Did we know what to expect? Did we really know how to help the Iraqi people or resist a war? We had no idea if or when a war might start. Were we crazy, as many had suggested? It's true, we didn't know what to expect, but we knew what kind of armor we hoped to use—that of truth, faith, and "the readiness that comes from the gospel of peace."

Our plane landed. VITW members Ramsey Kysia, Cathy Breen, and Cynthia Banas greeted us as we went through customs and entered the waiting area. Cathy and Cynthia had arrived earlier and were planning to travel into Iraq with our delegation.

"And you need to know that you might not even get visas to go into Iraq," confided Ramsey, after we all had gotten acquainted and were waiting to get taxis. I didn't believe what I was hearing! We went through all the preparation and agonizing about coming, and now we're told we might not get in.

"It's been difficult getting visas," Ramsey explained. He had been in Iraq off and on over the past two years. "But there is hope that we can get you in. Kathy Kelly will work hard at the Iraqi end. And even if the visas come through, it may not be for two or three days." This dampened the initial exhilaration I had upon arriving. I didn't say anything to the others then. There would be time tomorrow, and we needed the few hours left of the night to sleep.

By 2:30 a.m. we were on our way through the dark countryside and into the modern, well-lit city of Amman, passing large, expensive hotels and beautiful big mosques on our way to the Al Abdali bus depot. Our taxis stopped just across the street in front of a narrow, four-story building. The sign of the Al Monzer Hotel was barely visible.

Hotel workers were there to help pull our luggage into the small, inexpensive hotel, which VITW had been using for several years as a stopping place on their way to Iraq. We were glad to find our rooms and settle in for the night. Some apprehensions lingered about the days ahead, but I was mostly tired and thankful we had made it safely.

~ ~ ~~

"So, what do we do now?" we asked the next day. How could we use this time of being in limbo? At a breakfast meeting, after introductions and team building, we shared our ideas. We would not waste this time in Amman. We planned a short march and candlelight vigil at the United Nations headquarters in Amman and began assigning tasks. The afternoon would be loosely scheduled so committees could work.

We gathered in the early evening for a time of worship. I read from Acts 5:17-39, the story of the disciples being arrested and jailed, released by an angel, then going right back to the temple to preach more. We saw in this story that faithfulness led to bold witness, which often is threatening to institutions of power. People in power are afraid and will try to stop us, but we are called to obey God rather than them. Just as Gamaliel, the leader in that story, said, "If we do this work for our selfish purposes, we will fail," just as those now in power will eventually fail. But if we are a part of a greater movement of God, who is bringing in a new order of justice and peace, we will be part of something that cannot be stopped.

We made time in our meeting for each of us to say something about what had led us to take this trip and what we found challenging. Reasons shared included concerns for the Iraqi people and a strong urge to speak out strongly against war. Many of us hoped our presence would not only support the Iraqi people but also affect the decision about going to war. We also spoke of the fears we and our families had for our safety. Sharing these things seemed to build more trust and openness among us. We also chose team responsibilities, such as coordinating logistics, the trip log, our daily worship times, public actions, and so on. Then we divided up tasks for the next day.

Ramsey briefed us on some history and current conditions in Iraq and on things we could or couldn't do there, either because of cultural sensitivities or government expectations. We would be assigned "minders," men who worked for the Foreign Ministry of Iraq, which had given IPT authorization to be in Iraq. They would not be with us all of the time or set our agenda, but would generally watch over us in Iraq and make arrangements for visiting any institutions and for traveling outside of Baghdad.

We were not to take photographs from our balcony or hotel

windows, and we could take them on the streets only when our minders gave us the okay. We would need to get permission to make visits to families or any institution, such as schools or hospitals. We had to dress modestly and neatly, and the women needed to be careful because friendly gestures toward men might be interpreted as flirting. Men and women don't hug in public in Iraq. We were not to criticize the Iraqi government or its leaders in public or to entertain Iraqis doing that with us, because this could put them or their family in jeopardy. We had to expect to have our actions or words monitored any time we were outside our private rooms. It seemed shockingly restrictive, but we needed to know and prepare for this.

The next morning, two of our group went to the Iraqi Embassy to work on getting visas, which had been applied for a month earlier through CPT and VITW. Meanwhile, others finalized plans for the day's actions.

After gathering in a prayer circle, we went out to the busy street on the other side of Al Abdali bus depot. We spread out in small groups along the hilly street dotted with small shops and businesses and began passing out flyers about who we were and what our purpose was in coming to Iraq. Arabic on one side, English on the other, this flyer became commonly called the "magic sheet" because, when people in Iraq read it, they seemed to open up and become more welcoming to us. We wore the black T-shirts that Cynthia had brought from a New York peace group, with red and white lettering, reading, "War is not the Answer," and our red CPT baseball hats, so we definitely stood out as a group.

People on the street with Jordanian, Palestinian, and even Iraqi backgrounds who knew some English stopped and talked with us about our message. This helped to move us beyond our previous focus on our own group's needs to becoming involved with the local people and culture around us. And we felt connected with the thousands of people in American communities and throughout the world that day (October 26) who were also part of large rallies and marches opposing war.

When we got word that the Jordanian authorities wouldn't give us the permit we needed to have our vigil at the UN offices in Amman that afternoon, because responsible officials were not available on the weekend, we quickly changed plans. We delegated three people and one photographer to go to the UN building to tell reporters we had invited that we wouldn't be able to have the vigil. Our three delegates met a few reporters and police, who said they couldn't be there, but also a small group of Jordanian activists who had come to join us in making a statement against the war.

By evening our group visa for Iraq was granted. We understood that behind the scenes in Baghdad, Kathy Kelly had worked with our minder to push the Foreign Ministry to fax authorization for the visa to the Iraq embassy in Amman. We made reservations for a bus to take us to Baghdad the next morning, gathered food and bottled water, discussed details, and evaluated the day's actions.

It took me a while to get to sleep that night, and I found myself thinking over the events of the past two days. I realized how demanding the job of delegation leader is: overseeing the trip, making quick decisions, delegating responsibilities, troubleshooting, and at times working with difficult group processes. I had also felt stressed because I (and others) were feeling somewhat physically out of whack. I also realized that underneath all these feelings was an underlying fear of what we would face as we proceeded into Iraq. We were all charting new territory. Once more I realized I needed to draw on strength beyond myself.

By ten in the morning, our bus was headed toward Baghdad. Once we got past the urban areas of northeastern Jordan, we got used to a mostly flat, sandy, and rocky desert landscape passing by our windows. From then on we saw occasional Bedouin settlements, herds of sheep and goats, and even some camels. I had time to relax and to think about this amazing journey I was on, who I was, and how I got here.

~ ~ ~

Who am I, a sixty-year-old woman, to think that a small group of us could make any difference in Iraq, against the determination of the most powerful military force on earth and an administration that had no qualms about waging a war?

I had grown up in inner-city Chicago, in a family that believed all killing was wrong. We belonged to the Church of the Brethren, one of the three historic peace churches, along with the Quakers and Mennonites. These churches had carved out a way for young men being drafted to be able to do alternative service as conscientious objectors on religious grounds. Growing up, I saw my own potential for violence and desire for power over others, yet I knew the "right" answers to the questions of war and peace. As a teen, however, I chalked these answers up as weak and impractical.

I had seen racial fights at school in Chicago and the broken window in the house down the street, where someone had thrown in a brick to "welcome" the first black family moving into our neighborhood. I knew a little about bigotry and fear of the "other." It wasn't until I marched and picketed in front of the homes of slum landlords in Chicago and spent the summer of 1968 working in the Poor People's Campaign in Washington, D.C., that I began to understand more about structural violence and its power over society. The war in Vietnam seemed senseless and built on lies. I began to see the deceptiveness of our government leaders and the way they justified aggression around the world.

Dale, Daniel, and Joel, my three sons, are now in their late twenties and mid-thirties and on their own. As they were growing up, Art and I banded together with other families to live communally on a farm, first in Kentucky, then in the hills of southeast Ohio. We saw the hypocrisy of institutional churches and wanted to try to live out a life of love and service on a daily basis.

We chose to live simply in order to put more time and energy into things more important than earning money. We sought to care for the earth and work toward using less of the world's resources. We homeschooled our children through middle school. We took a number of homeless people and people out on parole into our household.

One stepping-stone for me came through a difficult relationship I had with one of our live-ins, Peggy Crosby, a charming, good-hearted woman in her sixties who suffered chronic schizophrenia and manic depression. One day I realized that I was at the breaking point with her. Continuing to relate to her seemed overwhelming and impossible. I couldn't do it anymore; she would have to leave. I felt weak and defeated. I ended up running out into the woods, where I cried and yelled at God.

Something happened to me, however, when I realized I didn't have the love or the strength to keep going with her. Out of desperation I finally told God, "I will keep trying, but only if you change the situation or give me what I need to do it." There was no voice from God, no "opening sky." I still felt the same as I walked back to the house. But I soon realized that I was not only given a new patience and love for Peggy, I was also given a new ability to draw the limits that both she and I needed.

This discovery became the foundation for taking other types of risks, whether it was in dealing with my own places of woundedness or in working for peace and justice. I didn't have to be especially gifted or courageous; I just needed to open myself to the sources of strength beyond my own. I didn't have to pretend to bring about great changes and accomplishments, but just help "water the miracles" that God gives in impossible situations (as Cliff always said in Iraq).

As a Christian community we have had many powerful experiences. Though we failed more than we succeeded in healing hurts, resolving conflicts, loving each other, and building a stable, committed community, we continue to worship together, share our resources, and grow and sell organic vegetables at a local farmers market.

~ ~ ~

This was not the first time I had rallied or spoken out publicly. Back in my college days, I was introduced to public protest in August 1963, when Art and I traveled to Washington, D.C., for the Civil Rights Movement's March on Washington. This inspired us to get more involved, not only in the Civil Rights Movement but also in protesting the Vietnam War and many different peace and justice issues throughout the decades.

Once our youngest son was in public high school, I took a part-time job with a small, grassroots non-profit organization, the Appalachian Peace and Justice Network (APJN). I worked with them for the next eleven years, supporting fledgling peace groups in the area, organizing educational programs, becoming a community mediator, and doing conflict management training with schools, churches, and community groups. All this helped move me beyond the timid, shy, introverted person I was. The boundaries of what I thought I could imagine doing kept pushing further and further out.

A trip to Nicaragua in 1988 with Witness for Peace was my first experience with living in a war zone. We felt the fear of the family we stayed with when they told us to sleep with our heads turned away from the outer wall of the house in case Contras shot at it that night. We were stopped at roadblocks when our bus went through areas of fighting. The horror of war became real and vivid to me. I knew not only in my head it was wrong, I knew it with my whole being. I came back thinking that such things wouldn't happen if every good person said loudly, "No!" I knew that I could no longer let my timidity and fear of speaking be an excuse for not acting boldly.

When I took part in sit-ins and was arrested several times protesting US policies backing Contras and paramilitary thugs in Central America, I was not doing it to rebel; I was acting for people like Dona Digna, a woman whose husband and child had been brutally killed in Nicaragua.

I also began to understand more about the futility of war and of trying to root out evil with violence. The result was always more evil and violence. I began to understand a little of the power of the nonviolent, suffering love Jesus taught and lived. I began to experience that power as I acted and spoke out in spite of my fear. The words I read from Scripture as a child became real, relevant, and alive. Forgiveness and loving one's enemies couldn't be forced or faked, but when it was given through struggle, it brought new strength and freedom.

Trying to deal with tyrants through military might has caused so much suffering in the world and has been a miserable failure. I knew there had to be a better way.

~ ~ ~

At about 2:00 p.m. we got to the border of Iraq. Le Anne Clausen, a full-time CPTer who had worked in the West Bank and could speak some Arabic, helped me take our group's papers to get processed. On the Iraqi side we had to register any computers or cameras our group brought in. Individuals would be expected to have them when they left the country. We didn't experience pressure to pay bribes nor did we have our luggage searched, as others had warned us about, probably because of their respect for our mission.

We all knew that both entering Iraq and buying anything there were illegal according to the economic sanctions on Iraq (UN Resolution 661). Penalties for violating these regulations included up to twelve years in prison or one million dollars in fines. When VITW, a US-based organization working to end the sanctions, was warned by the US State Department not to take medical supplies into Iraq, they wrote back the following, "We will continue our effort to care for the children and families of Iraq. . . . We are governed not by rules that license people to bring aid to people in need, but by compassion."

In Iraq, the two lanes of bumpy Jordanian roads turned into six lanes of smooth, modern highway. Until we got to Ramadi, about a hundred miles west of Baghdad, we saw the same flat, sandy desert, but without any rocks. By that time it was dark. We could see, however, the outline of brick and concrete houses as we passed that city. On both sides of the Euphrates River, lined with palm trees and green garden plots, was the city of Falluja.

Even in the night we could see that Baghdad was a large, spread-out, but somewhat rundown modern city with freeways, statues, and fountains in some of the main intersections. (Later, in the light, we would see the thousands of billboard-size pictures of Saddam Hussein in many poses.) It was exciting to cross the Tigris and head toward the Al Fanar Hotel on the east side.

CHAPTER 2

Learning

"Under the economic sanctions, most hospitals in Iraq have only about ten percent of the medicines they need to treat our patients," Dr. Luay L. Kasha, director of the Al Mansour Pediatric Teaching Hospital in Baghdad, told our delegation on October 28, 2002. He pointed out many ways that the sanctions have contributed to the health crisis in Iraq:

> Only three out of six of the drugs needed to treat children with leukemia are available. In all of Iraq, there are only seven MRI units, with long waiting lists for treatment and only one radiation machine, yet we never refuse patients if we can treat them. Hospitals have not been able to modernize equipment or replace broken equipment. Before the first Gulf War, Iraq had a free "state of the art" medical system. We do not have access to the latest medical journal information and cannot go abroad to medical educational conferences. In all of Iraq there are only 900 ambulances, when there should be 3,000.

Food and medicines had been allowed as imports into Iraq under the "oil for food" programs, we were told, but medicines ended up being on hold for years or not allowed in because they were considered "dual use." About ninety-six percent of these items ordered through the sanctions that were on hold were food or medicines.

The inability to repair sewage and water treatment plants had led to an increase in waterborne diseases. The damaged economic system—due to sanctions—contributed to malnutrition, low birth weight, and weakened immune systems. And complicating all this is that, with the use of depleted uranium

(DU) in weaponry during the first Gulf War, cancers and leukemia had increased four to seven times over the pre-1990 levels in general for Iraq. "Sanctions have been killing us slowly," Kasha said.

Doctors in Basra told us they had charted a 300- to 500-percent increase in cancer there in the first five years after the Gulf War, but then a huge upward spike on the graph in the past three or four years. They also said there were more families in which up to six or seven members had cancer and individuals who had more than one kind of cancer. This pointed to multiple contaminants in their environment. One doctor said, "Iraqis know they are contaminated."

We visited a ward where five or six children were being treated, with their mothers staying with them to care for them. One girl was crying in pain from the injections and IV. A one-year-old boy had bone cancer and had an arm amputated above the elbow, because doctors couldn't give him proper treatments. An eighteen-month-old looked more like a three-month-old. He was weak and listless, a sign of severe malnutrition, and unlikely to recover.

With the help of the doctors we milled around and asked individual mothers about their children. We told them that we were sorry for the problems caused because of our country's actions. In a small way we connected with them on a person-to-person level.

Another day, many of us went to the Al Mustansariya University College of Medicine to hear Dr. Alim Yacoub speak and show his slide presentation about an international research project studying the correlation between the amount of DU left in the soil and water in different parts of Iraq and the higher incidence of cancer, leukemia, and birth malformations.

Our visit to the Amariyah Shelter was even more gripping. On February 14, 1991, during the first Gulf War, the US military fired two missiles that went down into this bomb-shelter through the airshaft. The temperature inside went up to 400 degrees Fahrenheit. About 408 Iraqis, mostly women and children, were killed. We saw pictures of charred bodies and shadows from the vaporized bodies still imprinted on the walls and floor. This reminded us of pictures we had seen of charred bodies from the 1945 Hiroshima and Nagasaki bombings. "And now the US wants to make another war. We can feel it," our guide told us.

Some in our group noticed the similarities between memorials to the dead at the shelter and at Ground Zero after the Twin Towers tragedy of September 11, 2001. How can one witness such horrible destruction of human life and then prepare for another war?

During a medieval English literature class at Baghdad University, the teacher gave us time to ask the students questions. "Are you afraid your studies would be disrupted if a war broke out?" asked one of the delegates. This evoked a variety of responses that showed their pride as Iraqis. "We're not afraid," responded Amer Abdul Zahia, from Basra, "because we are on the side of justice. The Iraqi people are used to it."

Others responses came quickly, "They are invaders, doing it for no reason." "We are facing this situation with courage, because we are Iraqis." The teacher added, "We are going on with our normal life and program. We will not let fear disrupt and dominate our life. Life must go on!"

One professor told us he was taught that the US was a "beacon for all peoples in its values of self-determination, anti-colonialism, prosperity, and democracy. But you are a beacon no more."

Another added, "We see you now as the so-called 'democratic' west that carved up the Ottoman Empire to its own measurements and has continued to impose and depose rulers according to your own whims, disregarding the people who live here. . . . You Americans want us to change our system, but you are incapable of critically questioning your own."

On another afternoon we met with former Iraqi Ambassador to the United Nations Dr. Sa'id Al Mussawi. He was very friendly, personally greeting each one of us. "Iraq was wrong for going into Kuwait in 1990 and has paid a heavy price for it," he admitted to us. "But today the situation is different. For the US to say that 'we don't like your leader' and demand to change it is an insult to every human being. . . . Iraq is cooperating fully with the UN and offered to have delegations of world leaders come right away and examine any place to see for themselves that there are no weapons of mass destruction. The issue for the US is not weapons of mass destruction, or that Iraq is a threat, but the strategic interests of the US."

Mussawi spoke of the hypocrisy of the weapons of mass destruction (WMD) argument the US government used, saying, "The real threat with weapons of mass destruction in the Middle East is Israel." He added, "It would be impossible for Iraq and Al Qaeda to be linked because Al Qaeda considers Iraqis infidels and enemies."

After he spoke, we discussed our work in Iraq and said that we thought it was important to seek peace in nonviolent ways. He responded, "I wish we could." It seemed that he heard us, but either didn't have a vision for what could be done in this situation or felt he had little say over what his country did.

On our way to talk to Mussawi, I had found out that one of our delegation members had been out that morning along the grass and trees near the Tigris River across the street from our hotel and had lifted his binoculars to look at some birds. Very quickly an Iraqi policeman stopped him, took away his binoculars, searched his bag, found in it a National Geographic map of the Middle East, and reported it to Iraqi security authorities. An Iraqi intelligence officer came to Kathy and complained. We were informed that the river area was particularly off limits, because on the other side was one of Saddam Hussein's palaces.

Later we talked with the delegation member who had been apprehended, an avid birdwatcher, who explained what had happened. He was used to having freedom to walk where he wanted and to do what he thought was a harmless activity. "I just didn't think," he said.

We thought it was likely that he would be deported. Kathy was worried that this could even hurt our team's chances of continuing to work in Iraq, but later she was able to apologize to Wada, our minder, and convince him it was innocent short-sightedness. The delegation member stayed, but his binoculars were never returned.

Early on Wednesday morning, October 30, the whole team divided into two groups and headed off to two different parts of the country. I went with the group going to Basra, a seven-hour trip south. The rest traveled north to Mosel.

I was excited about traveling outside Baghdad and about

being able to drive along the countryside and see the more traditional side of Iraqi culture. We passed farms, markets, people working in plots of vegetables, school children on their way to school, and flocks of camels, sheep, and goats. We saw very poor, traditional adobe homes and compounds, yellow Iraqi brick homes, and fancy modern homes. We passed huge brick-making kilns with tall smokestacks and some military bases and guard posts along the way. Our modern highway mostly followed the Tigris River, but snaked around and away at times. Most of the green farmland was along the rivers or its canals.

Around noon we reached the city of Qurna, located at the place where the Tigris and Euphrates Rivers join to form one large river called the Shatt Al Arab, which flows past Basra and south to the Persian Gulf. This area is what has been referred to as "the cradle of civilization," where some believe the Garden of Eden was located. We spent some time walking around at the place where the rivers met, enjoyed the peacefulness of the scene, and watched some people fishing aboard boats floating by. It had a kind of simple beauty, with some green vegetation along the banks, but it was not as one would imagine the Garden of Eden to be. Thousands of years must have changed the landscape considerably.

We got into Basra in time to talk to Chaldean Archbishop Gabril Kassab. As we arrived at the Ephrem Chaldean Church, we heard spirited singing at the end of their Wednesday evening worship service. About fifty members greeted us as they came out of their modern sanctuary. Kassab showed us their small pharmacy. "This is not only for Christians," they told us. "About seventy percent of the medicines are given to Muslims." And then we sat down to visit more with the archbishop. We learned there were one million Christians in Iraq.

"The Iraqi people want peace," he said, "but that is a peace with justice." He thanked us for "coming here to share in our suffering." He talked about the poverty and high rates of cancers and waterborne diseases around Basra, resulting from the 1991 war, and high levels of DU residues in the soil and water.

"The people here have been worried and scared for the past four months about the possibility of war," he continued. "They have been living with bombing raids from the US and UK happening several times a week for the last twelve years. The US instituted no-fly zones in the north and south of Iraq after the Gulf War to protect certain populations disloyal to Saddam Hussein from Iraqi government attacks. Twelve years later, the US and UK continue to bomb in these areas. Ten days ago the Basra airport was bombed four times. Three years ago a bomb, which landed near one of our churches, killed six and injured fifty." Later we found out that in a year and a half, from March 2000 to October 2002, 259 air strikes were recorded in that area, resulting in at least 238 civilian casualties.

When we asked what we and other Americans should do, he answered, "Tell your government to stop the sanctions; they are killing the people. Tell the American people there is no reason for a war, and that the children, who are the image of God, will be hit."

On Thursday, October 31, I woke up thinking about my youngest son, Joel. It was his twenty-ninth birthday. For a while I thought of all my family, my husband and my two other sons, who right now were so far away. I missed them all very much. Leaving them to go on this trip was the thing that tugged at my heart the most.

Marian Solomon, a retired nurse from Ames, Iowa, led our morning worship by sharing some readings. She urged us not to look on the poor in pity or as lacking as persons, but to see the richness and uniqueness in their personhood, culture, natural resources, and connection with others. She said, "Often their lives are richer in the important things of life than those who are wealthy or educated."

At the Iben Ghaswan Hospital, the director, Dr. Janan Hassan, showed us photo albums of babies born with birth malformations associated with radioactivity from depleted uranium. "Before the war we saw practically no birth malformations, maybe two or three a year," she said. "Now it is increasing every year. In 2001, we saw 250 cases, just in this one hospital. It's a crime! Many people, like you, come to see the children, but what good has it done?" Then she expressed anger toward the American government. "Do they think children here are not human beings? Are they animals here? The US fights for oil, not for human beings. There is no benefit for the Iraqi people.

What have our children done to deserve this treatment?"

Visiting the Hamden Sewage Treatment plant in Basra that day was an unsavory experience due not only to the smell but also to the conditions of the plant. Dr. Nory, the head engineer, told us that when the plant was damaged in the Gulf War, it spilled a lake of sewage in Basra, a city of 1.5 million people. "This plant is only operating at less than one half its potential capacity."

We had heard earlier from Carel de Rooy, director of UNICEF in Baghdad, that because of the disrepair of water treatment equipment in Iraq, about half a million tons of raw sewage was dumped into Iraq's water systems daily.

Nory showed us broken and unusable equipment in the plant. Local Iraqi machinists had the skills to repair or recreate some parts, but under sanctions regulations, once a company entered a contract for new parts or service on machinery, all of the work had to be done by companies outside Iraq and chosen by the sanctions committee. This had severely hurt Iraq's economy.

Nory recalled his attempt to arrange a service contract for a machine with a Turkish company with a reputation for reliable work. The approval was delayed, even after repeated appeals. Finally, he was told that the service contract would not be approved unless an American company did it. The picture we saw was of American companies profiting from the war in 1991, destroying the infrastructure, and continuing to profit from building it back up.

At the end of our tour, our group gathered in a semicircle for a short vigil next to a treatment pool. John Worrell, a retired archaeologist from Massachusetts, read a statement he and Barbara, a screenwriter from California, had written for the delegation, declaring our opposition to the destruction that war brings to entire populations of innocent human beings and calling on all countries to settle differences nonviolently, "to heal past wounds through actions of forgiveness, generosity, and compassion toward all."

From there we branched out in two directions. The first group went to visit a farm at one of the former marsh areas that had been drained over the last twenty years. A large Iraqi population lived in houses built out of reeds on the marshes.

These houses were built on platforms over the water. Reeds were used because they were lighter than other building materials, such as bricks or concrete. The marshes provided plentiful fish for food. Our group was welcomed into a huge reed hall, 120 feet long and 30 feet wide, held up by bundles of reeds 3 feet thick, arching up over the 20-feet-high room. The roof and walls were made from plaited and woven reeds and grasses that were tight above and let airflow through for cooling near the ground. It was carpeted and lined with cushions for lounging.

We heard that the marshes were drained to get rid of the salt building up in the water, for developing the oil production in that area, and to eliminate places of hiding for those opposing Saddam Hussein. Environmental groups had been protesting the draining and the displacement of thousands of families from their traditional way of life, living off the resources of the land and water.

Four of us in the second group went with Kathy to visit families in the Jumarriyah neighborhood in Basra. This was probably the poorest neighborhood in Basra, with slum-like conditions, torn-up streets piled with trash and rubble, and pools of sewage. The homes were modest and in disrepair, but full of loving and welcoming people. Kathy had stayed in some of their homes for seven weeks two years ago and had kept in contact with them. As soon as we got out of the car, children swarmed around us, yelling, "Kathy! Kathy!" and, "*Sura! Sura!*" (asking us to take their pictures) and asking for money.

Iqbal, or Um Heider (meaning "mother of Heider"), one of the women living there, told us her story. She said that on January 25, 1999, after US planes flew over Basra, bombing their neighborhood, she found her sons, six-year-old Heider and four-year-old Moustafa, in pools of blood and covered with rubble. Heider was dead, but Moustafa was alive. Not able to carry both, she ran with Moustafa to the hospital. He had been hit on the head, legs, back, and hand. He lost two fingers and part of his liver, and had shrapnel lodged near his spine. He needed more surgery, and during the summer after the invasion, a group of Americans were finally successful in getting him into the US for surgery.

US officials had alleged that the damage was caused by Iraqi explosive materials hidden in private homes that somehow went off. Um Heider maintained, however, that when parts of the bombs were found, they were clearly marked "Made in the USA." We know this was possible. Although the US had earlier sold US bombs to Saddam, we also knew that the US had been bombing regularly in that area.

The last home we visited was that of Um Zanib, a mother of nine children. "Every time a plane flies over, my children cry in fear," she told us. I was impressed by these strong women, yet even they spoke of the possibility of war with visible fear. "Where could we run or hide? How can I protect my children?" Um Zanib cried out.

While we traveled around Basra, a very beautifully decorated mosque caught our attention. It turned out that this was one of the places we were scheduled to visit. It was Muinwi Mosque. We went between prayer times so we could have a tour and talk to Sheik Abdul Amir, an engineer.

Our driver took the women around the back of the mosque to go in a separate entrance, where a man gave us each an *abaya*, a long black robe to cover our heads and clothes down to our feet. He led us upstairs to the women's balcony and then down again to the large prayer hall to join the men. Abdul Amir informed us about the building and the prayer traditions, then took us upstairs to see a large, ornate hall with a huge, crystal chandelier hanging in the middle.

When it was time to go, the women went out the women's entrance, but were taken to the vans instead of to the place where we were to talk with the sheik. "Didn't he have time to meet with us?" we wondered. As we waited longer, we realized that the men were meeting with him without the women, as Muslims were accustomed to doing. Evidently they had a good talk, with the sheik expressing openness to a group of IPTers moving down to Basra in the event of war. But as women, we felt a bit frustrated, not only because we weren't included, but also because the men in our group hadn't spoken up on our behalf.

~ ~ ~

We visited the old ruins of Ur, the ancient city of Abraham in Iraq, November 2002.

The next morning, as we traveled north to the old ruins of the ancient city of Ur, we thought about Abraham and Sarah. Ur is often called "the city of origins," because Judaism, Christianity, and Islam all look to Abraham as an important ancestor in the origins of their faith. We walked around a reconstruction of what some believed was Abraham and Sarah's home and then walked to the top of the nearby ancient ziggurat, a four-sided pyramid-type tower temple with an outside staircase built by ancient Babylonians. This was believed to be a temple to the moon god, built about 2100 B.C. It had aged over the years but is deteriorating faster now because some US fighter pilots during the Gulf War used it for target practice. We could see the small pockmarks in the bricks.

At our brief vigil at the top of the ziggurat, we dedicated a campaign to mobilize people back in the US, to plan walks "in the footsteps of Abraham and Sarah." We decided on walking because it doesn't use oil, part of the reason the US threatened war with Iraq. Walking is a spiritual exercise that grounds our discipleship. It could take the shape of walks across the US and Canada to legislators' offices to urge them to visit Iraq, where they could see for themselves the possible victims of war.

All kinds of questions came up in our conversations on the way back to Baghdad about the future of our work in Iraq. The Iraq Foreign Ministry was putting pressure on Kathy to reduce IPT from about fifteen people to a core of eight people, with the possibility of some short-term delegations. Evidently, people in the government were getting nervous about so many US citizens staying on, thinking some might be spies. Would the Foreign Ministry allow more CPT delegations or long-term workers into the country? What would that mean for the presence of grandmas and grandpas in Iraq? Would our main work be to stop the war here in Iraq, or would we need to be active in organizing opposition in North America?

At this point we didn't even know whether the Foreign Ministry would give us an extension on our visas past the initial ten days. Would I need to leave soon? If so, would I go to Hebron and work with CPT there? Uncertainties abounded.

On Saturday morning, November 2, Kathy came to me and said it looked as though a small group of us who came here through CPT would be accepted to stay on, possibly Cliff, Kathleen, and me, in addition to the eight or nine VITW core group already approved. I felt relieved for the moment, but I would continue to deal with this kind of uncertainty about staying in the country throughout my pre-war stay in Iraq.

That evening five of us went to the Evangelical Presbyterian Church prayer service, all in Arabic. About forty Iraqi people were there. During the service we were asked to say something and offer a prayer.

Joe Heckle, a retired Presbyterian pastor from Pittsburgh, read from Galatians 6:2, about bearing each other's burdens. "There's a heavy burden on the Iraqi people," he said, "and we want to share that burden, even lift it if we can. I don't know if we can do that humanly, but I trust in God's power." I went up front and in a prayer thanked God for the opportunity to be there with our Christian brothers and sisters and asked that the children of Iraq would have a healthy and peaceful future. I prayed for US leaders to stop the rush toward war and that our countries could live in friendship and peace.

Afterward many people came and greeted us warmly. We talked more with those who spoke some English and gave our "magic sheet" to those who didn't. I felt God's presence in the warm, loving fellowship. I asked a woman who was studying theology if women could be pastors in Iraq. She said, "No, it's just the men. Women can only study and study." I admired her determination. Surely there was dissatisfaction with traditional limitations here, as there is in other societies. We would return to this congregation many times in future months.

In preparation for a press conference the next day, we had a short role-play session to practice being interviewed by reporters. We also spent time evaluating the delegation.

Sunday morning we traveled across the city to hold our first press conference in the courtyard at the ancient school, Al Mustansirya University, the oldest Arabic Islamic university, where math, philosophy, and astronomy have been studied since the thirteenth century. Associated Press, Al Jazeera, Agency France, and CNN covered the event.

In this ancient courtyard, our fifteen-member delegation announced our campaign, calling grandmothers and grandfathers to use their wisdom and moral authority to stop the war against Iraq. "It is the power of love between children and grandparents that can end war," stated Quinn Brisben, a retired history teacher from Chicago.

"I am here in Iraq to make sure my grandsons, or anyone else, never has to go to war," added Marian Solomon.

"CPT and the Iraq Peace Team have grandparents ready and willing to come and stand in solidarity with the Iraqi people in the face of war," another said. "There are no borders among grandparents!"

In the afternoon we refined our campaign proposal, "Walk for Iraq," which we sent back to the CPT office to put on the web page:

> People despair and say, "What can we do?" Folks have vig-
> iled, prayed, called, written, and demonstrated with little change.
> But we can do more. We can walk. We can put feet to our
> prayers. Walk, roll your wheelchairs, ride your bicycles to your
> legislators' offices and urge them to visit Iraq to see those who
> will die when the US war expands. Do it every week. Kneel in the
> doorway in a prayer of silent lament for the terror that is about
> to happen. Perhaps this prayer in the doorways must be continuous.

Even the judge, in Jesus' story, listened to the persistent widow, who kept hounding him until he gave in, just to get rid of her nagging. Put calluses on your prayer knees, wear out the leather on your shoes, retread the rubber on your wheelchair tires, fill the jails, and no longer pay the taxes that fuel this madness; make it clear to your grandchildren that this expanding war on the world is not in your name.

Later, the delegation met with Kathy to discuss what we could do when we got home. Any attack by the US could come later in the new year. Bush had been pushing a proposal in the UN Security Council that would restart UN inspections in Iraq and call for war if the Iraqi government didn't cooperate. It was still possible that Bush could do something before January, even if it was limited to bombing and not an invasion.

I went with others for a 5:30 p.m. Mass at Saint Raphael's Catholic Church, another place we would visit often in the months ahead. Afterward we met the four Catholic sisters of the Missionaries of Charity (Mother Teresa's order) who ran a small orphanage for handicapped children, called Dar al Mahabha Orphanage. They invited Anne and me to visit the home. There we walked among the twenty-two severely handi-capped children in their large crib-like beds and greeted each personally.

Later the whole team visited at the Beit Al Iraqi arts and crafts shop, in the home of Amahl Al Kedairy. We walked in awe through the three rooms full of paintings, woven rugs, traditional clothing, jewelry, and crafts. We sat around the courtyard garden, talking with Amahl and her friends, mostly foreign-schooled, professional Iraqis who spoke English. They talked very frankly to us as Americans about their criticisms of our government and the American people, pointing out the hypocrisy and problems in our society. "Don't come to Iraq!" Amahl told us forcefully. "Take care of things in your own country." She said that this was what all Iraqi people felt, but they hide it under the polite welcome they give us.

I didn't think it was the sentiment of most Iraqis, but it was important that we listen to their anger, pain, and concerns and not defend our country or ourselves. We said that we believed our coming there would help us work for peace back home. I

saw that just beneath the anger she expressed was a lot of pain
and fear. It was a gift to have her share in openness and honesty,
which allowed us to go deeper and grow and learn from her. This
is the only route toward healthier relationships across cultures.

~ ~ ~

One of the many gifts I received in my time in Iraq was to
see the biblical teachings and stories take on new life. The Bible
is indeed a living Word as it is read in the context of today's
struggles of greed and power, life and death.

One morning in our worship circle, Craig Spaulding, a delegate from Harrisonburg, Virginia, read the story of a woman
caught in adultery and brought before Jesus by the Pharisees.
This story is rich in meaning, with Jesus speaking to the men,
who were about to stone her, about their own sin and hypocrisy
and speaking compassionately to the woman to sin no more.
Craig pointed out, however, that the woman herself wasn't
important to the Pharisees; she was being used by the Pharisees
to get at Jesus, to test or trip him up.

"This story speaks to what is happening today as the US is
conjuring up all kinds of accusations against Iraq for its own purposes," said Craig. "So, in a similar way, the US administration
doesn't care about the Iraqi people. It is trying to get at, or get rid
of, their leader. And our government, through the US media, has
done a good job of leading the public to believe that we need to
bomb or invade Iraq to get rid of him. Can we speak to this today
as powerfully as Jesus spoke to the leaders of his day?"

~ ~ ~

One of the tasks I feel we are given as Americans in Iraq, and
as people of faith, is to speak the truth—to expose the lies that
we are being told. We are called to help the Iraqi voice be heard,
to make the Iraqi people visible—to help Americans simply see
them. They are here. They are the ones who suffer from the
power plays of governments. Our task is to point out and live
out the truth, to love, and thereby to transform "the enemy"
into our brother, our sister, our friend.

CHAPTER 3

Beginning Steps

"Don't give George Bush a blank check!" our banner read. It was Monday, November 4, 2002. We were standing in front of the United Nations headquarters in Baghdad and addressing our message to the countries in the UN. Other signs read, "Let's not attack Iraq," and "No to US War in Iraq!" For me, this action was more than a witness against war; it was also a form of prayer.

After this vigil at the UN, team-members fanned out to visit embassies from other countries, which were undecided or were challenging Bush concerning the proposal to the UN Security Council calling for a tougher weapons inspection. If Iraq did not comply with the proposed resolution, the US and UK could be given authorization to move ahead with military action against Iraq. So far, France and Russia have insisted that going to war wouldn't be automatic and that the UN Security Council would still need to decide if military action was, in fact, warranted and necessary.

Cynthia, Cathy, Cliff, and I went to the Russian and Chinese embassies to deliver letters urging the ambassadors to use whatever influence they had to withstand US pressure to vote for Bush's proposal to the Security Council. Even though representatives receiving our letters were not able to give any indication of what their diplomats would do, they expressed appreciation for what we were doing and saying.

The main CPT delegation had left Iraq that morning, and now the remaining CPT and Voices in the Wilderness workers were operating as one large team of IPT. We began to focus on:

1. Building the IPT as it kept growing, beginning regular planning meetings, dividing responsibilities, planning together for vigils and public witness
2. Planning and preparing for possible crises
3. Continuing to broaden and deepen our relationships with Iraqi people and our understanding of their current situation
4. Responding to Bush's move toward war through public witness in opposition to war. This includes speaking with representatives of international embassies and United Nations agencies, learning from them about the possible consequences of war, and urging them to take a firm stand for peace
5. Continuing to have a designated time and place each morning for those who chose to gather for a worship and reflection time

Three new people from the US joined the team, so we were now a larger group at our daily UN vigils. A busload of Italian peace musicians called "Help Them Live" interviewed us, took pictures, and played lively music. Many danced around with small peace signs. They invited us to go to their concert at the Palestine Hotel the next night. Many other people were curious about us and came up to find out who we were.

On Saturday, November 9, we got news that the UN Security Council had voted 15-0 to pass Resolution 1441. French and Russian diplomats said they felt good that the resolution mandated that if there was noncompliance, there would be a second Security Council deliberation about it, and the US and UK wouldn't automatically go to war. We were disturbed to hear and read that President Bush and Secretary of State Colin Powell said that if Iraq violated the resolution and the Security Council didn't choose to authorize war against Iraq, it "doesn't tie their hands." They could still go to war without the council's approval.

Iraq now had seven days to declare whether it planned to comply and thirty days to submit a comprehensive declaration of all its programs to develop chemical, biological, nuclear weapons, or long-range missiles, and to declare all its civilian petrochemical industries. We were afraid that no matter what the UN said about Iraq's compliance, the US would continue to make its own judgments based on its strategic interests.

In our team planning meeting, fourteen of us gathered to

build up our working relationships and organize ourselves better. We had an update on the latest news and discussed the implications of the UN's decision on our work. We assigned tasks for arranging information-gathering meetings with UN agency staff and planned for a workshop for us to practice speaking to the media.

Five of us went to the Food and Agriculture Organization (FAO), a UN agency. The Sudanese director, Dr. Amer Khalil, shared about impressive agricultural programs, but said that they weren't able to implement them well because they received few of the supplies they ordered through the Oil for Food Program (OFP) under the economic sanctions.

All the workers there (and in other UN agencies) agreed that the Iraqi monthly food rations program, carefully monitored by the OFP and funded from Iraq's oil revenues through the same program, is one of the best food-distribution systems in the world. Yet even its food contains lower than recommended protein levels.

Another day we visited with World Health Organization (WHO) Director Dr. Popal, who told us, "Any disruption of the food distribution system by war would have disastrous consequences. People will die. The most vulnerable are the mothers and children. Health is a human rights issue." He was also clear about the devastating affects of the previous war and years of sanctions on the health of Iraqis, due to widespread diseases and malnutrition. He and other UN agencies workers traveled to New York to appeal to the Security Council's 661 commission (in charge of the OFP) to allow more medical supplies in, but without success. He told us, "This has resulted in thousands of needless deaths of Iraqis."

Items not allowed in through the OFP included but were not limited to ambulances, medicines and medical equipment, antibiotics, water purification equipment, and infant vaccines. Popal said that ninety percent of people with appendicitis died within twenty-four hours, because hospitals couldn't provide them the surgery needed. "Our agencies are doing all they can," he said, "but our hands are tied by these policies."

Another UN organization representative we met with was the spokesperson, Mr. Humati, for the UN Office of the

Humanitarian Coordinator in Iraq. Two former coordinators had resigned in protest of the sanctions in the past four years. He said, "With sanctions you paralyze every single aspect of Iraqi society." The fact that infant mortality is extremely high and malnutrition continues to be a major problem is the fault of ongoing sanctions and the constant roadblocks the US places in the way of the flow of humanitarian supplies.

A small group of us went to a fire station in Baghdad to learn more about how they might prepare for the possibility of war. It was interesting seeing the very simple offices and sleeping area. There were two modern pump-and-ladder trucks, yet the firefighting uniforms were flimsy and the oxygen equipment dated back to 1978 and was starting to fall apart. They lacked nets, ropes, and other "standard" equipment. All these things were impossible to get because of the sanctions.

The firemen said that when the attacks on the Twin Towers happened on September 11, they were very sad and identified with the grief of the New York firefighters. But when team members asked about preparedness for the possibility of war, a government official quickly responded, "Our president can take care of that," and they didn't get any other information. This seemed like a "party line" answer given to cover up the lack of preparation by the government.

On Sunday evening, November 10, Cliff and I went to worship services at the Holy Family Chaldean Church, just off Sadoon Street. Men and women sat separately, so I went over to the women's section. A woman motioned for me to come and sit with her and her adult daughter, who had a congenital deformity. Her head and body were malformed, but she was accepted as part of the community. After a short homily, the Arabic Mass continued with the priests chanting and singing, similar in style to Islamic prayers, while the congregation responded with songs and recitation. Around me were the common people, a mixture of poor and middle class. Here and in many other situations, I thought of the possibility of these people being killed if there were a war. I prayed for them, for the soul of the US, and for God to give me love and compassion.

Afterward, I gave a "magic sheet" to the woman next to me and introduced myself. She looked at me in amazement to see someone from the US. When other women saw me give her the paper, they reached for one too, curious about this foreigner. Everywhere I was greeted with "Thank you" and "Welcome."

Out in the courtyard we met a young woman, Ghalia, who told us about the religious education school of about three hundred children, which met there for three hours every Friday morning. Ghalia took us to talk with the head priest, Noel Hannona and a dozen or more parishioners in his office. He was welcoming, but wasn't easy on us, asking us, "What good are you doing here?" He mentioned the thousands of Iraqi people living in America and that many of their relatives had been denied entry into the US to see them. "Why?" he asked. We sensed a lot of pain and anger underneath his and others' words to us there, but they were polite in expressing it.

"We are sorry for what our government has done to hurt the Iraqi people," we said. "We may not be able to do very much here in Iraq, but at least we want to let you know that American people care about you and don't want a war. We also want to tell American people about Iraqi people, so they can see you as real people and not as our enemies." Our conversation concluded with personal sharing with people there and an invitation to return on a Friday to their school.

The day's events picked me up emotionally, because I had more contact with Iraqi people. This helped me to focus on them, their concerns, and why I was in Iraq. It was a gift to have these personal connections on many levels: Christian to Christian, Christian to Muslim, woman to woman, and grandma to child. I was enlightened by my encounters with adults who didn't know how to relate to us but were polite, with business people or poor people who saw us as a possible source of money, and with government officials and media people who didn't quite know what to do with us, yet seemed to have a mixture of respect and condescension toward us. I hoped I could be here long enough to cultivate closer relationships with some of the wonderful people I was meeting.

A few days earlier, Thursday, November 7, I had been in touch with some underlying anxiety about being immersed in a whole new culture and team life. I realized that I had been keeping my distance emotionally from the Iraqi people, fearful, maybe, of carrying their pain more deeply. If I got close, they may expect me to give them material or monetary help, when I couldn't. I often felt uncertain how to help or how to relate with the cultural and language barriers. I prayed for grace to be able to open myself more, while knowing my limits.

Also contributing to my overall frame of mind were the allergy problems I had been having from the gas fumes and general pollution. Added to this was some worry that I might not get my visa extended and would have to leave Thursday or Friday. I didn't want to leave just as I was getting my feet on the ground and starting to build relationships. But I would need to accept it if I had to.

Back at the Al Fanar, Kathleen Namphy, who had stayed on when the delegation left, told us she was going to volunteer at the Sisters of Charity orphanage the next day. I expressed interest in going there too, so she said she would ask about others helping. By November 11, I had started going there on a regular basis.

As an American literature professor at Stanford University and expert on T. S. Elliot, Kathleen had already been spending time at Baghdad University classes, giving guest lectures and helping graduate students develop their poetry. Michael Birmingham, from Ireland, had been volunteering at the UN Development Program, coordinating efforts to bring medical texts into Iraq on compact disks. Kathy encouraged each of us to find ways to volunteer with humanitarian groups.

On Monday morning, November 11, many of our team went to the Baghdad School of Folk Music and Ballet, a primary and secondary school for three hundred students. We met and talked with the headmistress, who took us to visit small classrooms of grades one to five. When we entered each classroom, the children greeted us. Some of the classes sang songs or recited the Arabic or English alphabet or numbers. In one room was a child's drawing of a dove, which they told us was a peace bird. I told them that before coming, I had talked with many American school children who want peace and to be their friends.

In the first-grade class, surrounded by children, I thought of Tabitha, my oldest grandchild, almost their age. How hard it would be for her, or them, to have to live through war.

Siham and Samir at their Baghdad home, November 2002.

While walking back from the Businessman's Center that evening after making an international phone call, Kathy took me over to meet Siham, Abbas, and their four boys, living just a few blocks away from the Al Fanar Hotel. Theirs was one of several Iraqi families our minder had given us the okay to visit frequently. This was the beginning of an ongoing relationship. Tonight, while Kathy talked with Siham, I spent most of my time with sixteen-year-old Yasser, who practiced speaking English with me and showed me his English books. The three older boys taught me some Arabic words and told me about playing soccer.

~ ~ ~

Kathy came into the dining room with a longtime friend of the team, Waleed Al Jaborry, who drove a van for an Arab-Japanese tourist company. He shared about his sister, who had an operation for breast cancer and was prescribed a very expensive medication. Because they couldn't afford the medical expense, she told her family to just let her die.

Waleed said he was drafted during the Gulf War and was

positioned in a tank out in the desert. Twice he deserted and was caught, beaten, and put in jail. Eventually he finished his term. Several on our team shared about being conscientious objectors and resisters to war, something totally new to him. Kathy asked him how the ordinary Iraqi person was dealing with the possibility of war. He said the average Iraqi man was too busy working and caring for his family to listen to the news and worry about war. "They just have to go on with their lives. What else can they do?"

We asked many people about facing a possible war and got a variety of answers. They ranged from the national pride expressed by university students, trying to block it out of their thinking, like Waleed, to the mothers in Basra who were more open about their terror. Behind the strength and bravery of the Iraqi people, we saw a society already strained by twelve and a half years of war and sanctions and now becoming increasingly tense and fearful. Some told us about digging cisterns to collect rainwater, buying generators, and storing benzene, kerosene, and food. Others said their children felt the tension and were frightened by what they saw on TV and what they heard.

Artist, Amal Alwan, her husband, and their three children rented a small home near the Al Dar Hotel. She tried to keep her family out of debt by selling paintings at night after her children went to bed. She said that if an attack came, she would hire a taxi, pack what belongings she could, and flee to the north. There she would rent a home in the countryside. Many others spoke of trying to leave the city.

~ ~ ~

In our IPT meeting that evening we decided it would be good to divide the team into two groups when our current team was stronger and more stabilized. Even as new people came, there would be a core team that would keep some continuity, though we still didn't know how many the Foreign Ministry would allow to stay or how many more would be allowed to come. We got mixed messages.

We began meeting about four or five times a week as a larger team. In meetings we took time to share our fears and hesitations with each other and to reevaluate why we were there and what our role was. We each shared how we felt about staying on in a crisis. I didn't have clarity about this, but wanted to make responsible choices and remain open. I didn't want my decision to be controlled by fear.

One of the most fearsome scenarios was being in chemical or nuclear bombing, where there would be such extreme devastation that, if we survived, it would be difficult to help others. Another would be civil war, where Iraqi people would randomly target any foreigners. Even though our neighbors might know who we were, others wouldn't. It was impossible to guess what would happen, so we planned to explore ways we could be a positive presence in different situations. We needed to be careful that our presence didn't endanger the lives of people around us. Our list included helping in hospitals, staying in homes, staying at civilian sites, such as water plants, schools, or hospitals, setting up a peace tent encampment, and planning creative public actions.

After that meeting, we heard on the news that the Iraqi Parliament had voted to reject the UN Security Council Resolution 1441 and, therefore, not cooperate by submitting a list of all weapons and weapon sites. Much of their discussion centered on how the inspection process trampled on Iraqi sovereignty. We were aware, however, that this could just be a face-saving gesture to the people of Iraq and that their decision could still change by Friday, the deadline for an agreement.

Former chief weapons inspector Scott Ridder had been countering the US plan, saying that when he had finished his work in 1998, Iraq essentially had no weapons of mass destruction and no capability to replace them. Then Hans Blix, the new chief inspector, said he felt that the process didn't need a new resolution and should be wrapped up quickly.

~ ~ ~

Elias Amidon, and his wife Rabia Roberts, from Colorado and now in Iraq with IPT, were members of an international organization called Nonviolent Peaceforce. Elias led our worship on Tuesday, November 12, using parts of several Islamic prayers. Because this was the holy month of Ramadan, the Muslim month of fasting, spiritual renewal, and giving gifts of charity, it was good to affirm our common statements of praise to God in this way.

Some of our team planned to fast from food and drink during daylight hours as is the Ramadan custom. Others, who didn't, hoped to be mindful about not eating and drinking in public.

In our Wednesday, November 13, reflection time, Cliff read from Exodus 14:12-14 and talked about empires sowing the seeds of their own destruction and about how we are called to a different way of thinking and acting.

That morning a vanload of team members left with our minder, Zeid, a tall, thin, stern man, to travel two hours southwest of Baghdad to Najaf and Kerbala, places of holy shrines for Shi'a Muslims. We visited the shrines of Imam Ali and of his son, Hussein, both honored martyrs and founding leaders of the Shi'a branch of Islam. We were able to talk with Muslim leaders at each site. The women among us wore *abayas*. We saw the very elaborate ceilings and walls decorated with gold or facets of crystal. The shrine was full of people praying or trying to touch or kiss the barrier around Imam Ali's casket.

Most of the pilgrims who flocked there came from Iran, but others came from Turkey, Syria, or other Middle Eastern countries. Family members carried caskets of their dead loved one into the shrine to have the body given a special blessing before being taken to a nearby graveyard for burial.

We had some free time to walk along a market area across the street from the shrine in Kerbala, and some of us got into a conversation with a shopkeeper about why we were in Iraq. Our plan was to have time to visit another shrine, but team members started to scatter and Zeid became concerned about our security. He quickly rounded everybody up to go back to the van and then took us back to Baghdad without any more stops. Many of the team were frustrated that they did not have more freedom to roam on their own and take pictures. In spite of that, I considered the trip a valuable experience for understanding the Shi'a Muslims in Iraq.

Because we were back earlier than expected, Cathy, Cliff,

and I had time to go two blocks away from our hotel to a small fruit and vegetable market some of us had been going to for food. We explored further and discovered a bakery where we could buy fresh bread just out of the oven.

Just before going to bed, we heard that the Iraqi government had officially agreed to comply with the Resolution 1441 mandate, even if they saw it as humiliating and unjust. We felt relieved, because this put off any military intervention and gave more time for the possibility of a peaceful resolution.

~ ~ ~

It was another visa renewal day for Cathy, Cynthia, and me. With a bit of uncertainty we walked over to the Residence Office. We had gotten clearance for it from Wada, our primary minder. But sometimes his authorization doesn't get through to the office and it takes longer. This day there was no problem and our visas were extended another fifteen days.

The next day, Friday, November 15, in the morning worship time, I focused on the relationship between love and fear, reading from 1 John 4. We are more fearful and anxious when we focus on ourselves and less when we open ourselves to really loving others. In our time of sharing, Cliff took that to a corporate level and talked about the possibility of group actions of love, driving out the fear in situations of threat. We wanted to think more about how we could do that in crisis situations.

That morning six of us went with Zeid to visit the ruins of the ancient city of Babylon, where fragments of the walls of the ancient city still stand. On top of them, Iraqis had rebuilt the walls, trying to recapture what the city and temples might have looked like. Some of it was touristy, but still interesting to see. We went into two museums, one with information and relics relating to Hammurabi and the first written code of law, and another with artifacts found in the ruins. According to the manager, many of the ancient treasures from this site had been taken out of the country in the early 1990s by German and French archaeologists and put in European museums.

Zeid was more relaxed and not so hurried on this trip, and we were able to joke around with him. He took us off the path going into the ruins to a red date tree and showed us how to peel and eat the dates we picked up off the ground. This kind, one of over seven hundred varieties of dates grown in Iraq, was called "ladyfingers" and was mild and tasty.

On the way back, Cliff read to us from Revelation 18 about the fall of Babylon. We thought of the US being the "Babylon" in today's world and how it would someday also fall if it were not transformed. Cliff pointed out that today's "Babylon" might soon be coming over to destroy the ancient Babylon.

We got back in time to go to a traditional Iraqi *makam* music concert, which takes place every Friday evening. This is like an open stage for experienced vocalists singing with a band playing background music using traditional instruments. The hall was filled with laughter and friendly greetings. Men came around serving Numi Basra tea, a delicious traditional tea made with a small, black, dried lemon. We enjoyed this cultural immersion and a break from some of the heaviness we'd been experiencing.

~ ~ ~

What would it mean to stay on during a war? Vague images of war drifted through my mind, of houses crumbled and burning, of wounded people calling for help on the streets, and with it came a knot of fear in my stomach. I didn't know what to expect. I didn't know what I was called to do. Was my fear clouding my clarity, or was I not really called to stay? I felt two things: a desire to be there among the Iraqi people in their suffering during a war and to be a witness to it, and doubts about how my being there would help them. I didn't want to be separated from those I loved, or even die, but something kept me there, open to taking that risk.

~ ~ ~

On Sunday, November 17, three people came to join the team. Neville Watson, an Australian who had been in the Gulf Peace Team when the bombing started in 1991. Another new person was Charlie Liteky, from San Francisco, a former military chaplain during the Vietnam War. Later, while visiting El Salvador, he had a transformative experience and began working for peace and justice, mostly concerning Central America. The third was Bitta Mostofi, a young woman of Iranian descent raised in the US, who had been working in the Chicago VITW office. That expanded our team to thirteen, with four leaving in the coming week.

The first UN weapons inspectors were due to arrive in Iraq the next day. We had been thinking and talking a lot about WMD, and so I wrote an article to send back to my local paper called "Whose Weapons of Mass Destruction?" In it I wrote that the US had already used two horrible weapons on the Iraqi people. One was depleted uranium, used in bullets, bombs, and the coatings of tanks during the Gulf War, leaving more than 600,000 pounds of radioactive waste that will continue to contaminate the soil, water, and air in Iraq for billions of years. The second was economic sanctions, which UN agencies say have killed more than one million Iraqi people. Couldn't these be called weapons of mass destruction?

This picture looked terribly wrong: preparing to blow up a country to get rid of a brutal dictator. Bombing Iraqi people had been compared to bombing Washington, D.C., to get rid of snipers. Because Iraq had reason to fear the use of WMD by Israel and Iran, a disarmament process in the Middle East would only be successful if it were extended to those and other countries. Ideally, this would be followed by global WMD disarmament.

President Bush was right, but he didn't realize he was casting light on himself when he said on March 11, 2002, "Men with no respect for life must never be allowed to control the ultimate instruments of death."

On Monday evening, Wada and Zeid told us we could bring more delegations or longer-term workers to Iraq under IPT and that we could continue traveling to other cities such as Basra and Mosul. Immediately we sent word back to the CPT office in Chicago that they could plan for another delegation, possibly a smaller one of four or five, which might include people who would be able to stay longer.

In a team meeting we entertained some ideas for creative

actions, such as having international groups come and hold canoe races down the Tigris River to draw international attention to Iraq. And what about bringing well-known religious leaders such as the Pope, Desmond Tutu, and others to Iraq?

~ ~ ~

Each morning I, and often other IPT members, walked the mile to the Dar al Mahabha Orphanage in Baghdad. For two or more hours we played with and helped feed the children while the sisters got other tasks accomplished. As we came into the playroom, we greeted each child personally, and they responded with welcoming sounds and gestures. Several could talk a bit and respond to "Hello. How are you?" because the sisters spoke some English with them.

I found my way to the mat-covered half of the room, nestled in with the sprawling children, and started playing and talking with them. As the morning progressed we sang and clapped, sometimes with a drum, and played finger games. In the restless time before the 10:30 feeding, we blew soap bubbles, which they reached for in delight. I found several who could throw or at least push a ball a little, with encouragement. Soon we had many balls flying around the room.

As I learned to call more of them by name, I was rewarded with even more smiles and personal connection. Each day I discovered more things that certain ones could do. E'lias could stand up and "dance" with me to the music when I held her hands. Several could sing a bit, and about a third could crawl and sit up in a chair. Only three could walk.

"Hi, Dunia," I called to the girl sitting stiffly in a small infant chair. Her eyes lit up and a grin curled around her face as she looked up at me. We had connected at the sound of her name.

On the mat, Omar, Amil, Allah, and I sprawled around a picture book, pointing to pictures of animals and a clown mixing different colors. "Who's that? Amil? There's Omar! Where's Allah?" I said pointing at the figures in the book. It didn't matter what the figure was. It was the naming of names that was important, the recognition of the personhood of each child that fed their hunger to be known, to be unique, to be special.

The newest arrival at the orphanage was five-month-old Nurah. She needed constant care, because she was born with only stubs for arms and legs. Anyone's first thought would be "how sad," but after holding her and talking to her they would be rewarded by precious smiles. Nurah seemed to know her name.

I thought of other Iraqi children I knew. At the home of Siham, four-year-old Dhafer, with a dimpled grin, jumped around pretending he was a little monkey and delighted in the laughter of the American visitors, who cheered him on. Meanwhile sixteen-year-old Yasser had just completed a picture to send home with one of our team members. On it was written, over the shape of a heart, the message, "My name is Yasser. I love American children."

And adults on the streets of Baghdad often called out, "What's your name?" This became an open invitation to talk and share who I was and why I was there. Usually, suspicious and tense expressions relaxed when we shared our desire for peace, not war with Iraq. As we became vulnerable to each other, we became known as friend, rather than enemy.

～ ～ ～

One of our deepest desires is to be known by name, to be called out, to be loved for who we are. Isaiah 43:1-4 reports God as saying, "Do not fear, for I have redeemed you; I have called you by name, you are mine. When you pass through the waters, I will be with you; and through the rivers, they shall not overwhelm you. . . . For I am the Lord your God . . . because you are precious in my sight."

When we face fear, danger, confusion, and possible injury or death, our soul cries out for one who knows who we are, who loves us, who will be with us. We, just as the Iraqi people, want someone to know, to care, to remember us, to call us by name.

～ ～ ～

While the rest of the team went away on a trip to Basra, Cynthia, Cliff, and I walked over to the Al Dar Hotel, about ten blocks away from the Al Fanar and just two blocks from the orphanage, to look it over as a possible place for the first affinity group to stay. (An affinity group would be a small subgroup of team members and would have some difference in focus from the other groups.) We looked at rooms and the kitchen we could use, and decided it would work for us.

It took me a long time to get to sleep that night. I was wound up emotionally and thought a lot about the despair and humiliation Iraqi people had to live with, yet they still held on to hope and dignity. But I was thinking also about how hard it was to be an American seeing and knowing what the Iraqi people experienced every day. My anger found its way to the surface.

During my time in Iraq, I constantly experienced anger and grief when I saw the condition of those barely getting by or reduced to the humiliation of begging. They wanted so much to give their family enough food, medical care, or even some special treat at times of celebration. They watched helplessly as their child or spouse died from normally preventable diseases. They all felt fear and despair as they faced the possibility of attack.

Frankly, I hated this part of the situation. It was cruel, inhumane, and needed to stop. It was hard to be an American there.

Feeling this, I started to think that the world would be better if we didn't hold back, but would allow ourselves to become angrier about situations like this. I don't mean the petty, self-centered anger we usually struggle with. But it would be better if we all became more passionate about mass slaughter, malnutrition, economic and social injustice, preventable diseases, and the systematic, deliberate, and well-calculated policies made by those in power, which bring suffering in Iraq and many other countries.

We have been much too timid, too cautious, too wanting to be nice, proper or religiously correct, and, so, have been much too quiet. This has resulted in our standing by, giving consent by our silence or inaction.

Sure, it is important that we not get consumed or driven by our anger. Anger can lead to horrible violence and cruelty. Yes, we must constantly move beyond our anger to love and forgiveness. But to follow Jesus, to love the least of these, we need to allow ourselves to really see the pain that others are living with and become angry at what produces that pain. This means becoming passionate about seeking justice, as did Jesus and the Old Testament prophets. This means allowing anger to change us, to bring us to action, to lead us to give ourselves, stand against, stand for, support, or serve, and at times to put our bodies in the way.

Jesus didn't have any kind or comforting words for those who followed the law but didn't bear fruit or for those who cooperated and gained from the corrupt religious, political, and economic systems of his day.

We are certainly limited in our power and ability to change things. We face principalities and powers. But we have access to more power than we are ready to admit to ourselves. Yet we hold back.

For this we must not only cry out for God's mercy, but we must also cry out for God to give us strength to act boldly.

~ ~ ~

On Thursday, November 28, Thanksgiving Day, Neville presented some statements about the purposes of our team, and we adopted the following as our IPT charter:

A Declaration of the Iraq Peace Team
1. The Iraq Peace Team refuses to see the Iraqi people as enemy. It sees them as brothers and sisters.
2. The Iraqi people have suffered unjustly the past twelve years of sanctions.
3. Now they face the violence of war.
4. We intend to live alongside them should war occur.
5. We hope that our presence with them will indicate in a small way that war is not what we want for them. While political leaders call for war, ordinary people need not, must not, sever the ties that bind them together as human beings.
6. We see ourselves as part of a worldwide movement against war as a means of resolving conflict.

Later that day many of us went out to eat together. With us were May Ying, a reporter from California working with Deep Dish Broadcasting, and David Swann and Amir Khadir, two Canadian physicians studying Iraq's emergency preparedness and assessing the consequences of a war on the health systems of Iraq.

David and Amir had been attending meetings of an emergency preparedness committee organized by six UN agencies and two international NGOs (non-governmental organizations) in Iraq. This committee was working to devise and carry out a plan to prepare for the possibility of war. Plans were for stocking up on health and food supplies, making medical kits, and organizing and planning for workers to oversee the distribution of these emergency services. They gave us a copy of a large document describing this plan.

Archbishop Kassab from Basra came up to Baghdad, so some of us met with him and asked about his assessment of the situation in Iraq. He saw Basra as a place that would be targeted or invaded quickly in a war, because of the oil infrastructure in that area. He seemed open to an IPT affinity group staying there in the church complex in a time of crisis. He thought that, generally, people in Basra would treat American people who weren't "invaders" respectfully. But there were no guarantees if war broke out, especially if there was civil war among Iraqis. The next step, if we wanted to pursue it, would be to go again to Basra and talk to more people there, particularly those from the Islamic community.

CHAPTER 4

Staying On

November 23, 2002, I e-mailed:

Dear Art,
    I need to make a decision by next Thursday whether to change
my plane ticket and try to stay another two weeks or so (whatever
I can get a visa renewal for). Friday is when I would have to go in
to apply for a visa, or get ready to leave the country.
    Gene [Stoltzfus, director of CPT] called and told us that he
thought it more important for Cliff and me to stay here, even if
things are "quiet," if we can keep renewing our visas. Cliff also
urged me to stay longer, so I could be part of setting up an ongoing
CPT group here. He said, also, it would help to have someone stay
who has been here long enough to "know the ropes."
    I also want to stay on as long as I can without it being a burden
on you or others there. So I need to hear from you right away, if
you haven't already done so, about what you and others in the
community think, what are the needs there, etc.

Something had changed in me. Replacing the confusion and
doubts was a growing clarity that I should stay. I remember first
realizing this on November 20, when I wrote in my journal,

    This morning I feel more clarity. I know now that I would
    choose to stay on here and continue the work if it were not a
    hardship for Art and others back home. I don't know exactly
    what this means. The fears I have been dealing with have less-
    ened, and I have been given a deepening love for the people here
    and horror at the thought of their lives being shattered. I shared
    this with others on the team. I can't make this decision alone, and
    now need to hear from Art.

A few days later I called Art, and he said yes. He was very supportive of my staying on, but said I should keep discerning it with the IPT. It was good talking with him. I would have liked to talk longer, but it cost a dollar a minute.

On Saturday, November 30, Cliff shared a letter with our worship group that he had been crafting in his head and heart to his daughter, Miriam. It was a beautiful prayer of thanksgiving for her and for the ways God had broken into other hellish situations, intervened, brought life, and "gave the miracle." He prayed for God to "bring the miracle here to blow away the floodwaters and wash this land clean of violence."

It moved me, because I know and love Miriam, but also because I feel the same deep pain and longing for the people of Iraq. I too asked God to work miracles. It also triggered my love for my own family. I particularly thought of one of my sons who was not at all happy about me coming to Iraq. I wanted to say, "Please forgive me if something happens to me. Please forgive me for 'leaving' you, for also loving others here. It doesn't mean I don't love you deeply. I do . . . so very much that it hurts. But I have been given the grace to extend this love to others here as well."

～ ～ ～

As the team considered further the possibility of branching out into smaller affinity groups in different locations, we compared the positive and negative aspects of the idea. After some working it through, we decided that a smaller group would move to the Al Dar Hotel in the coming week to test it out before we came under the pressure of a crisis. We understood that this might lead to placing groups in other locations, such as Baghdad University, a hospital complex, or even Basra. The groups would be semi-autonomous and could have different projects, but would be linked through a representative council. When new people came, they would start with a time of orientation at the Al Fanar Hotel and then move out to one of the smaller groups.

At our next meeting the team decided that Cliff, Cathy Breen, and I would be the nucleus of the first affinity group and move to the Al Dar. We realized that this could just be temporary. We also discussed the idea of having an ongoing peace tent either at one location or moving from one location to another.

That morning, November 30, was my first of many visits to the Seventh-Day Adventist Church. People there were very friendly and helpful and made me feel welcome. During the worship service a man interpreted everything into English for me. There seemed to be many who spoke good English. Some had heard about Voices in the Wilderness and knew about Kathy and others staying with families in Basra.

It was raining lightly when I left, so a woman from the church offered to drive me to the Residence Office to try to renew my visa. Cynthia and Cathy were already there when I arrived. It didn't take long, and we were all given a fifteen-day extension. This gave me the go-ahead to get my plane ticket changed. The latest date to which I could extend it to was January 23.

December 1 was the day Cathy, Cliff, and I moved to the Al Dar Hotel. The Al Dar is a smaller, quieter hotel located in a poor and lower-middle-class, residential neighborhood in Karrada Dakhil (meaning the inside part of the Karrada peninsula that juts out into the winding Tigris River). We were still very close to the river, but about eight blocks south of the Al Fanar. Karrada Street, a block away, was busy with food markets and other shops. In the evenings it was alive with groups of young men hanging out and families strolling and shopping.

One of the first things we did was walk around the neighborhood, greeting people and giving out magic sheets, and finding the bakeries and the markets for our fruits and vegetables, eggs, milk products, and other staples. We wanted to get to know as many people as we could. We realized that in a future time of crisis, our security and ability to be a nonviolent, helpful presence would be tied to our relationships with the people.

As a kind of housewarming activity, we hosted the rest of the team for a meal and meeting in our new "home," something we would do often throughout the next months. We had access to the kitchen and would often take turns cooking a simple evening meal.

A couple of days later, David and Amir, the two Canadian physicians examining Iraq's NGO emergency planning, also moved to the Al Dar and planned to relate with our affinity group. Two weeks later, other team members also joined us: Irene Vandas and Jan Zieman, both from Vancouver, Charlie, and David Hilfiker, a physician who started and ran a health center for the homeless in Washington, D.C.

"What are our goals as individuals and as an affinity group now that we are here?" we asked each other in one of our first meetings around a supper of rice, lentils, and veggies. We already had our responsibilities with the larger team. I coordinated volunteer work at the orphanage and connected team members with the churches. Cliff and Cathy conducted orientation sessions for new members. Cliff was part of other committees working on emergency preparedness and planning actions. We would all visit and learn to know our neighbors, write, and be involved in symbolic public actions. Cathy would do more cooking and manage supplies for our subgroup. We started regular morning worship/reflection times, after which we would eat breakfast and talk about the day or the decisions we needed to make. Whenever possible we would eat evening meals together.

In one of our first worship times Cathy focused on "tent" as a symbol of vulnerability, simplicity, and being ready to move. It was also a symbol of stability and security in God, even when a people is uprooted or driven off their land.

When I went to the Internet center at the Palestine Hotel to read the news, I met other new team members who had just arrived: Dean Jefferies, another Australian who had been in Iraq in 1991 as part of the Gulf Peace Team. Peter Thompson, a lawyer from Minneapolis who had worked in efforts to abolish the School of the Americas (SOA); Steve Clemens, also from Minneapolis; and John Evans from Santa Fe, who had worked for Habitat for Humanity. We also met some of a large Italian delegation that had just arrived that evening.

~ ~ ~

Some people back home have called activists like us who seek peaceful alternatives to war in Iraq "dupes." Are they right? Were we being deceived by Iraqi propaganda? Were we hearing only one side?

While we did face limitations on our movements and speech, it was actually surprising how much freedom we were allowed in Iraq. A minder usually accompanied us when we visited institutions (hospitals, schools, or public service facilities) or when we traveled to other parts of the country. Yet we often visited families, daily walked the streets of Baghdad, visited shops and met people at random, and met with UN agency representatives on our own. Our group initiated most of our contacts and appointments. We felt we got a fair view of the living conditions and varying perspectives of the Iraqi people.

The more I think about it, it seems there are many ways in which American people are "duped" by power structures in our society. We are daily fed lies and half-truths, one-sided and distorted facts. Fair and balanced stories that challenge our administration's positions rarely make it in our mainline media. Do we take the trouble to find alternative news sources? How many Americans have understood how the sanctions have been a weapon of mass destruction? We have been programmed into identifying with the wealthy and the powerful, and into excusing or downplaying the crass sin, injustice, power plays, mass murder, and exploitation our government and corporate elite are engaged in. We are taught to be suspicious of or even to hate certain groups of people. Is this not being duped?

Yes, those of us who come to Iraq cannot know for certain that our efforts won't be distorted or used by others, that we won't be slandered or thrown into prison by the Iraqi or the US government, but that is a risk we are willing to take. We have a choice between taking the risk of seeking to do what is right or holding back out of fear of making mistakes or being taken advantage of. Maybe that is why, whenever we step out in faith, it is important to also seek humility, humor, childlike faith and vision, openness, and the ability not to take ourselves too seriously. And, most of all, it is important to be grounded in a faith that God is caring for us, is ultimately in charge, and is the one bringing about change.

~ ~ ~

Wednesday, December 4, was the last day of Ramadan, the Islamic month of fasting, which meant that the next three days were Eid, holy feast days and holidays during which government offices and most shops would be closed. Many of our team got up early the following morning to go to the large, beautiful mosque on Firdos Square for the special Eid prayers.

While the men went in the front door, we women put on scarves and black *abayas* and went in a side door to the women's area. We followed other women up a narrow, winding stairway to the balcony. We could look out over the main hall below, where the men gathered to pray. There were about thirty other women with children who prayed together and listened to the "sermon."

With "Salam Alekum," (Peace be with you) and "*Eid Mubarak!* (Blessed Eid!)" we greeted many people there, on the streets, and in the two homes we visited near the Al Dar that afternoon. Both families were ones Kathy had known from visits in previous years when VITW members had stayed at the Al Dar, and ones we had permission from our minders to visit frequently. Because it was Eid, we took gifts of cookies and sweets.

First was the home of Amal Alwan, the artist, her husband, Safah, and their three children, Abeer, ten, Omar, eight, and Ali, four. We would go to Siham and Abbas' home the next day. Then, just around the corner was the home of Kreema and her nine children. Kreema spoke little English, but our visit gave the children an opportunity to teach us bits of Arabic. I spent most of the time with her eleven-year-old twins, Duah and Hebe, who drew us pictures and braided my hair. Kreema's husband, a taxi driver, had been killed about four years earlier in a traffic accident. She and her children eked out a subsistence living by selling spices or baked goods on the streets. She had just received an eviction notice that her family would have to leave their run-down dwelling within a month, so the owner could remodel it. "I don't know where we will go, or what we can do now," she lamented to us.

~ ~ ~

"For me? Oh good!" I'd finally gotten an e-mail message from home, from my close friend. It had been so long since I had heard anything from home, and I had been feeling more and more cut off from people and happenings. Home felt like a far-off world. I found out that the server had been down. They hadn't gotten all my e-mail messages, and I hadn't received ones they had sent. I was glad to be in Iraq, but a wave of loneliness also rushed in. I realize how very much I missed my friends and family.

~ ~ ~

"An Iraqi child asks, 'Will I die today?'"
"No War, Cherish Life, not Oil!"
"Don't Nix Blix!"
These were some of the signs we held the day of our vigil at the UN Development Program (UNDP) offices. For two and a half hours we stood, also talking to international reporters. We wanted to give a message of support for the UN's work at resolving the issues concerning Iraq through other means than war. We were also aware that this was the day the Iraqi government was supposed to submit the declaration of their weapons programs to the Security Council.

David Swann, David Hilfiker, and I holding signs at a vigil in front of the United Nations Development Program offices in Baghdad, December 9, 2002.

Now that Eid was over, we could proceed with some of the public actions we had been planning. The tent action idea had been tossed around in our meetings a lot. Earlier thoughts had been to set up a stationary "Peace Tent" or "Peace Embassy" near the UN headquarters, which would be a drop-in center for journalists or people from international delegations. We could have workshops and press conferences there. Different members of the team would rotate in and out, keeping a continual presence there. The other idea was to have a traveling tent we would take with us as we made a peace pilgrimage around the city, setting it up at facilities like water treatment plants, hospitals, schools, and bridges. Neither of these fully materialized, but different actions evolved from the theme.

After one of our planning meetings, Wada gave us general approval for some of our action ideas, such as having vigils across the street from the UN headquarters when the inspectors would leave in the morning for an assignment and having a press conference at a water treatment plant. The conversation soon moved to a discussion about the political situation. He was pessimistic and believed the US government was set on war. He thought what we should do to help was to bring to Iraq well-known politicians and people like Jimmy Carter. We brought up the possibility of Iraq using nonviolent resistance, as Gandhi had led Indians to do. Wada listened politely, but obviously didn't see any value in that. He did, however, agree to the list of new people we wanted to get visas soon and for the next CPT delegation to come in after December 28.

On December 10, Tariq Aziz, foreign minister of Iraq, unexpectedly invited some of our group to talk to him. I missed the visit because I was at the orphanage at the time. Evidently, he had been impressed by the media reports of our vigil the day before. He encouraged us to continue our protest work. Different team members took turns sharing about why we were there and what other things we would like to do. Team members felt good about the exchange and were hopeful that it would mean we would be given more freedom to do creative actions.

~ ~ ~

"It's up to the American mothers to say, 'That's enough! No more war!'" one woman told us in a gathering of Iraqis at Beit Al Iraqi gift shop on the evening of December 10.

"We are real human beings, not monsters!" said another.

A physician added, "With all the money the US spent on bombing Iraq, we could have found three or four cures for cancer." They shared their criticisms of the US democratic process, which allows the media to distort the truth and one man to wage wars around the world.

Amahl, the shop owner, said that her son was accepted for a master's program at the University of Toronto, but couldn't get a visa because he was Iraqi. He wanted to study physics, but felt compelled to change his field of study to computer science.

"Let's think and talk about what we could all do," she said. "Is it possible to stop the war?" One suggestion made was for Iraqis to be interviewed by foreign media. Amahl said they had done this in the past, but reporters twisted and took their comments out of context. But still, she thought maybe they should try it again.

Before leaving, we all sang "Happy Birthday" to Kathy. Amahl gave her a gift. Several people from our team gave her silly gifts and Cathy read a funny poem she wrote about Kathy, a fun way to complete another busy day.

On Thursday, December 12, some of our group went to the UN headquarters and followed the inspectors out to one of the inspection sites, an antibiotics plant operated jointly by several Arab nations. We went to talk with media and to voice our affirmation of inspections as a way to deal with the unanswered question, "Does Iraq have dangerous biological, nuclear, or chemical weapons and the missiles to deliver them in an attack against others?"

Around this time we developed a friendship with Amar, a twenty-four-year-old worker at the Al Dar Hotel. He asked us if we had been at the Amariyah Shelter yet. Then he proceeded to tell his story:

Amar grew up next door to the shelter and was eleven years old in 1991 when it was bombed. His face became almost ashen as he shared about seeing the dead bodies of some of his friends carried out of the shelter. At first we could only listen. Then we were able to say how sorry we were and that we wanted to work so that such a thing would not happen again. What do you say to someone who has experienced this horror and now fears there will be another war?

~ ~ ~

Zeid came to us one day and asked if we would like to go visit his extended family's fruit farm in the Diala area, northeast of Baghdad. Nine of us went with him on this all-day excursion. We found five families living on and managing this forty-five-acre farm, with some hired help. The orchards produce a variety of fruit, all kinds of citrus, pears, pomegranates, grapes, peaches, figs, apples, apricots, macadamia nuts, and dates. The date palms grew among all the other trees and provided a canopy, which kept the shorter trees warmer in the winter. I enjoyed being out in the trees and grass.

At first, we women were taken in to be with the women and children of the household and enjoyed being with them as they prepared the meal and, sitting or squatting on the floor, washed clothes by hand in a big tub. But we also wanted to get the tour of the trees with the men, so one of the women, who couldn't speak much English, showed us around a little. Later, before we ate the meal with the women, we joined the men visiting in a long sitting room and were part of the conversation.

I asked what kind of message they would like us to take back to the American government. "All people come from the same mother," responded one of the older brothers. "We are all one people and should live in peace, share the world's resources, and take care of each other. There is no reason for war." At the end of the talk, this brother said that they appreciated the ways their president had cared for them and other Iraqi people. (When we hear such statements we always wonder whether they are made for obligatory "political correctness.")

~ ~ ~

"This water plant was damaged by bombs in the first Gulf War, and because of the sanctions, it has never been completely repaired. Even today, it runs at only half capacity," the director of the Al Wathba water treatment plant just north of Central Baghdad told the crowd that came to our press conference there on December 14. Drs. David Swann and David Hilfiker spoke about the health problems this had caused in Iraq and the greater disaster that would result from another war. Peter Thompson spoke as a lawyer, pointing out that bombing such a facility is a war crime under international law. Rabia Roberts also spoke and monitored the discussion.

We had originally thought our presence would only be a vigil, but it became a much bigger event; there was a large crowd. We set up a tent for the occasion and served refreshments. But press and other visitors didn't come only to learn about the water plant. They also came to see Sean Penn, the US movie actor who had come to Baghdad. While there, he consulted with our team, and we helped him make some contacts for visiting a hospital, school, families, and UNICEF.

He and Norman Solomon, director of an organization called Public Accuracy in the Media, stayed in the background as observers and did not want to speak publicly, so as not to draw attention away from our event. Penn expressed respect for the work of our team, even though he was not exactly at the same place in his critique of the threat of war.

The following evening at his own press conference, Penn said, "I needed to come here and see a smile, see a street, talk to people, and take it home with me. . . . I didn't come to criticize any government, but I need to ask 'why, if our government has the evidence it claims to have against Saddam Hussein's government, doesn't it reveal the evidence.'" When asked by the *New York Times* reporter why actors would speak out on political issues, he responded, "We face the prospects of an apocalyptic war. We all have a responsibility to oppose such a danger, whatever we do for a living."

Meanwhile, with more people on the team and more on their way, the larger team planned to divide into at least three affinity groups. A nuts-and-bolts meeting to make large-group decisions would be made up of representatives from each affinity group. Cliff and I started making plans for the next CPT delegation to come on December 28 or 29.

Those of us who were planning to stay longer started meeting to share our thoughts and feelings and to talk about logistics. From time to time during those weeks, as I continued to get my visa renewed, I dealt with ups and downs in myself. At times it was the heaviness and weight of the tension I was feeling among the Iraqi people. Other times it was a mixture of anger and grief about Bush's determination to go to war and the consequences for the people. And then, even though I continued to reaffirm my decision to stay on with the team in Iraq, I still had to battle occasional doubts, fears, and feelings of loneliness that plagued me.

To get through these times, I had to face squarely what I was experiencing and to ask God for new strength and hope. Our group's worship and sharing gatherings were helpful for me; they provided safe places to share weakness, fear, or confusion with each other and give each other support and encouragement.

I still wondered if I would stay through wartime or leave before it really came. The reason to stay on wasn't entirely clear to me. Were we called to just try to prevent war and witness to this pre-war preparation, or would our presence in the midst of it also be important? Or would being at home and working for peace there be more important? Would we even have a choice if war happened suddenly? I was getting wonderful, supportive messages from family and friends back home, calling me courageous, but I didn't feel any more courageous than anyone else. I was afraid, but I chose to face my fear and walk ahead in it. I kept coming back to the commitment that I had made to be willing to give up my life "for my friends." But that's hard. I kept praying for the strength to face and do what I needed to do in all this.

One morning, David Hilfiker read Scriptures depicting struggle with despair and finding hope and faith that is not dependent on things turning out all right. One person spoke about finding hope when we take action. We gave thanks for those back home also working hard for peace, harmony, and justice. "It's in seemingly impossible situations," Cliff said, "that hope can take root, flourish, and be real and alive."

~ ~ ~

"What surprised me the most," said a Czech reporter who had been in Iraq for five days, "is that even though Iraqis expect bombing to start any time, life seems to go on in a normal way." He had expected to see empty streets, closed shops, and massing of troops. I too didn't know what to expect when I came and had been impressed with the "business as usual" appearance on the bustling streets of Baghdad.

Each morning when I walked to the orphanage to help with the children, I was greeted by a crew of seven or eight men rebuilding a house, throwing bricks up by hand to the one above, or pulling up materials by a rope. Gutted buildings and vacant lots filled with rubble were common, some from bombing, but more from normal deterioration. Twelve years of sanctions slowed restoration, but in the past two years some improvement in the economy had made occasional repairing or building possible.

On a small side street, I passed a metal workshop where the work spilled out onto the sidewalk. They were soldering, welding, and remolding broken bed frames and metal gates. In other shops, workers repaired and reupholstered broken-down furniture. A man came along with his donkey-pulled wagon, picking through trash to find recyclable materials. With the scarcity of new products and materials, recycling and reusing was a way of life.

Along Karrada, a busier street, I passed tiny shops with olives and a variety of pickles, and I was drawn to the bakeries, where men were taking fresh, hot Iraqi flat bread out of ovens. Here and there stood fruit and vegetable stands with mounds of tomatoes, peppers, onions, garlic, cucumbers, potatoes, beets, eggplants, zucchini, and cauliflower, as well as oranges, grapefruit, lemons, apples, pomegranates, persimmons, and bananas. Unfortunately, less than half of the people could afford to buy them. Every family received the government-provided monthly food basket, which included rice, flour, oil, some milk powder, and beans, but it didn't provide any fruits or vegetables or the full daily requirement of protein. At least sixty percent of the population depended on this handout for survival.

Other shops, selling clothing, shoes, household goods, hardware, and musical instruments, dotted the street, but had few customers. I was accustomed to seeing men milling around the shops, sitting or standing in doorways, most of them unemployed. Fewer women were outside. Surprisingly, there was little military presence or build-up around Baghdad or even in other areas of Iraq that I'd seen.

Walking across streets was usually a defensive sport, with lots of fast-moving cars and only occasional traffic lights. I saw some shiny new Mercedes and BMWs belonging to the small wealthy class. The average car was older and badly needing bodywork or a paint job. Among the cars was an occasional donkey pulling a wagon full of kerosene tanks, or men pulling carts with fish floating in shallow water.

Happy playing noises let me know I was passing a school, where children milled in crowded, walled play yards. Many children did not stay in school past primary grades, so they could work in the home or help their families make money. Since 1991, the literacy rate had been steadily decreasing. Fewer girls had gone on into upper grades, and very few youth were able to afford to go to the university, which was free before the Gulf War.

One evening, our peace team attended a rehearsal of the Iraqi National Symphony in Baghdad. About fifty musicians continued the work of what used to be a large, thriving institution. Economic sanctions had made it difficult for the musicians to maintain their instruments and impossible to travel abroad. Some had left Iraq; most had to take other jobs to make an income. But despite the difficulties, they played with gusto.

We were part of a press conference at which four Canadian members of our team presented the symphony with gifts of musical supplies donated by musicians in Vancouver. These included strings, reeds, rosin, bows, and musical scores, all not available to them because of sanctions.

The next morning Tuesday, December 17, we heard a rumor that bombing would start in ten days, and people were visibly afraid. This sent the value of the Iraqi dinar on a downturn. The week before, a retired professional woman had took me aside after a church service to describe the difficulty she was having making ends meet because inflation had made her fixed pension almost worthless. She said that poverty was pervasive, but mostly hidden. "This should not be, in one of the richest countries in the world," she said.

The longer I was in Iraq, the more I saw behind the outward picture of normalcy and the more I felt the heaviness the people carried as they went through the day. But I also saw a very strong spirit and determination to survive, to rise above the moments of despair, even if it was only for the sake of the children. There were still times of celebration and joy. Families joked and teased each other. Children were playful and mischievous. The streets of Baghdad still bustled with work and activity. New buildings rose out of the rubble. Musicians continued to make music that brought them life. As much as possible, even in the face of war, life went on—because it had to.

~ ~ ~

Again our team of twenty-seven people gathered to speak out publicly at a press conference. It was a cold, windy evening, December 19, at the Al Taji power plant on the northern edge of Baghdad. Men and women from two Japanese delegations joined with us. Holding our candles based in sand inside empty water bottles, we were the backdrop for Iraqi speakers.

As she held her son Ali in her arms, Amal Alwan spoke

Vigil at the Al Wathba water treatment plant in Baghdad, December 19, 2002.

about how she, as a young mother about to give birth, had been traumatized during the Gulf War when a nearby power plant was bombed and the bombing of another home in her neighborhood caused the cellar in her home to collapse. She urged world powers to prevent a new war and spoke about how hard it is to protect children when war breaks out.

The plant director told of how the plant had been bombed and partly destroyed in 1991, at the beginning of the Gulf War. Over the next six years they had gradually built it back up. Then during the 1998 "Desert Fox" bombing, the plant was damaged again. During a tour of the facility, the director showed us the generators, many twenty-six years old, which had been damaged and rebuilt. Six months earlier they had paid six million dollars for each of six new generators from the UK. Economic sanctions prevented the British company that sold them to deliver crucial supportive items such as needed computer software and the installation manual, or to come and give Iraqi engineers training.

The next day we experienced our first dust storm, or *shargi*. The wind blew a fine, sandy dust in our noses, and eyes. It was difficult to be outside, so we stayed mostly indoors. But that night was the Christmas music program at the Adventist Church, and I wanted to go. Cynthia, Cliff, and I ventured out and were glad we had. Children from age six or seven to teenagers sang out with joy and spirit. It lifted us beyond the heaviness we felt.

Afterward, I talked with nineteen-year-old Mona, who was engaged to Haitham. They hoped to get married next summer after she finished secondary school. Mona's father, a leader in the church drove us back to the Al Dar.

On Sunday evening, December 22, I didn't go to the worship service at Saint Raphael's or the symphony orchestra concert, because I was coughing, feeling tired, and needing rest. The next day, after our "nuts-and-bolts" meeting, I began to feel worse, developed a high temperature, and was getting sick. I just had to rest. But this was hard for me. There was so much to do, to be a part of, but I was also afraid that if I got worse, I would have to go home. I wanted to get well so I could stay and continue with our work in Iraq.

The next day, I didn't take part in any group activities, but stayed in bed. I thought of Art as he traveled that day to the West Bank for two months of work with CPT and prayed for God to guide him. I was sorry to miss the Christmas Eve gathering at Beit Al Iraqi and the candlelight vigil at Saint Raphael's, during which the group dropped a banner saying, "Peace on Earth." That was followed by a play presented by twelve young children acting out the story of Jesus' birth. But in the middle of the angels, shepherds, magi, and holy family, the children also enacted the story of the parable of the good Samaritan. This was unusual, but also somehow appropriate.

Christmas morning, fellow team members brought breakfast to me on a tray. There, on a napkin was a tiny ceramic baby Jesus surrounded with six white origami stars, a special gift from Cathy. In the afternoon they brought in a cup with six roses that the group at the Al Fanar had sent for me, so I felt surrounded by love and care. I found out that three others in the team were also sick.

The main disruption on Christmas Day was my sudden move to another room in the hotel. Others had been smelling oil in my room, and we found oil or grease dripping down the outside of a pipe in the bathroom, along with water. I had been so congested that I couldn't even smell it. But it was very likely that this was aggravating my allergies and contributed to me getting sick. The air in the new room did seem fresher and easier to breathe. Being forced to rest, I had time to read, but also to catch up with myself and clear my spirit of the pain and anger that had been building up.

I thought, "All these years our country caused so much damage and suffering to this society and people I care about. Even now we torment them with the threat of war. Rich, arrogant, and power-hungry people must not be allowed to kill these beautiful children, women, and men. God, please don't let this happen!"

Saturday, December 28, we heard that the CPT delegation had arrived in Amman and had just gotten their visas to come into Iraq. By Sunday, December 29, I was better and went with others to the residence office and received a visa extension, to January 15. Because Zeid said we couldn't house the new delegation at the Al Dar, we arranged for rooms in the Andalus Apartments, next to the Al Fanar. Cliff and I were to lead the delegation, so we moved there and were ready to greet them at ten when they arrived.

CHAPTER 5

Unexpected Death

The New Year came in with energized hope for the possibilities of peace. The new fifteen-member delegation swelled our ranks to thirty-seven and brought new energy. A group of about thirty IPT members gathered in front of the UN headquarters in Baghdad, shivering in the early morning air.

Micah Keller Shristi held a frightened dove in his hands. "We release this dove with our prayers for peace for Iraq and for the people of the world," he declared as he gave the bird its freedom. Ellen Barfield lifted and freed a second one. Quickly they soared into the sky, separated, and then circled back and around the UN buildings in a surge of freedom and majesty.

New Year's Day Vigil in front of UN Headquarters in Baghdad.

Camera crews from around the world recorded this moment.

It was New Year's Day 2003. We had come there with our world flag and our large banner that said, "New Year's Resolution: Peace, No Attack on Iraq." We had also been there the night before with candles, sparklers, group singing, and a festive Iraqi "wedding band" playing to celebrate that so many people and countries around the world wanted a peaceful solution in Iraq.

As the UN inspectors drove past us that morning on their way to an inspection site, they smiled and waved at us. Their work must be hard and thankless, as they carried the weight of an impending war on their shoulders, we thought. Our prayers for the New Year included them.

~ ~ ~

One of our first January activities with the new delegation was an outing to Zeid's fruit farm. Both Wada and Zeid came along. Once we got there, we divided into two groups and went into two different households, where I met new families.

It was a beautiful, sunny, and cool day, and it was wonderful to be outside in the fresh air, especially with my lingering respiratory problems.

This time, women and men were together on the tour of the farm. Oranges, tangerines, and grapefruit were ripe and plentiful, and our hosts kept picking and peeling them and passing around the fruit for us to eat. At one point, an eighteen-year-old worker climbed up a date palm tree. A wide belt around his waist held him to the tree as he walked up the trunk with his bare feet.

With a machete-like tool, curved at the end, he trimmed off dead leaves. When he was done, we joked among ourselves about some of us trying it and turned to Cliff, the most likely. So he took the challenge, removed his shoes, arranged the belt, and inched his way up the tree.

The family showed us a large warehouse in which were piled huge bags of dried dates, ready for sale. Before the sanctions, Iraq had been one of the world's leading exporters of dates. Now they can't be exported outside the country and the Iraqi markets are full of them. Crops like this, all over Iraq, may rot in storage sheds when it gets hot next summer, we were told. The picture of these dates would remain in our memory and would be the inspiration for a possible action.

Men and women visitors together ate the feast they had prepared for us at a large table, the women at one end and the men at the other. Wissam, Zeid's wife, sat next to me and shared about her life. Wissam graduated from Baghdad University in English language studies and had intended to work as a teacher or translator. Then her family arranged with Zeid's family for their marriage, and their son was born. She told me she had some regrets that, after going through all that training, she had not been able to use it in some kind of work.

She also said that most Iraqis were fearful of the rumored bombing to come. Their family had a private shelter on their property in Baghdad, built during the Iran-Iraq war. They had it stocked with fuel and supplies and felt more prepared than most families.

The next morning, Saturday, January 4, 2003, the new delegation began a trip destined for Basra and to Al Safwan, just north of the Kuwait border. Once in Basra, we made some usual kinds of visits. Zeid was our primary minder, but other minders from Basra also joined some of our excursions.

A controversy came up about our desire to go to Al Safwan, a town south of Basra where much damage was done in the Gulf War. Many Iraqis had suffered illness from the radioactive wastes of depleted uranium (DU) or had been killed or wounded by the sporadic bombing in this no-fly-zone during the past twelve years. However, Zeid told us that even though other delegations had gone there, we should not. "The high radio-activity there is too dangerous," he told us. "Our going will endanger the drivers and minders." He did not want to go and would stay in Basra if we did. He thought we could see Al Safwan children getting treatment in the hospital there. Most of us still wanted to go and visit the people in their homes, but under pressure from Zeid, we decided to let that trip go.

Zeid's alternative plan for us was to drive down a road along the Shatt Al Arab River to the southernmost seaport, the city of Faw, where the river empties into the Persian Gulf. He promised that as we drove along that road we would at times be able to see across the river to the shores of southern Iran. We drove through long stretches of desert wasteland, where a few families still lived. Farming villages used to occupy this land, but it was devastated during the Iran-Iraq War in the eighties and again in the 1991 Gulf War. We could see trenches left from the fighting, the tops of date palm trees bombed off, and some wreckage of tanks along the road.

The city of Faw, 120 kilometers from Kuwait, was an ancient Muslim city. It was destroyed by Iran in the eighties, rebuilt in 1989, destroyed again in 1991 by the US and UK, and rebuilt again in 1993.

This town had a special, personal meaning for me, because my maiden name is Faw, I wrote home a silly message to my family telling them that I'd found a city started by a branch of our ancestors who had gotten lost in the desert and homesteaded here. I told them this wing of our family seemed to produce trucks and double-decker buses, because there are such vehicles all around Baghdad with the letters FAW, an acronym for Federal Automotive Works, printed on the backs. (They are actually made in China and imported into Iraq.)

We walked along the harbor, which was filled with fishing boats. While we milled around and talked with some of the people there, our minders stayed close, worried about our safety as Americans and Canadians, and maybe their own as well in this off–the-beaten-track city. They didn't want anything to happen to us that could be a pretext for the US to intervene more quickly militarily. People seemed very curious about us, and Zeid told us he thought we were the first international delegation to come to this part of Iraq.

The old mosque in Faw had been damaged in the Gulf War and near the remains stood a new one. We toured the new mosque and talked to one of the imams. Some of us ventured up a steep, winding staircase of the minaret and had a great view of the city.

On the way back to Basra, we asked to stop at one of the Iran-Iraq War memorial markers at the side of the road. Deciding that this place, where there had been heavy combat and bombing, was a good place to pray for peace, we gathered in a circle on the muddy ground. Michelle Narr, a medical pathologist from Duluth, Minnesota, talked about prayers for the healing of the earth. Sue Gray, a commercial decorator from Colorado, burned some sage, a Native American symbol of healing that she had brought from the US. Someone read Isaiah 35:5-7: "Then shall the eyes of the blind shall be opened, and the ears of the deaf unstopped; then the lame shall leap like a deer, and the tongue of the speechless sing for joy. For the waters shall break forth in the wilderness, and streams in the desert . . . and the thirsty ground springs of water." We shared our prayers aloud and sang "O Healing River," while the smoke of the sage blew up around us. "Please, God, hear the prayers of the men in the mosques today, and hear ours." I silently prayed: "Grant peace to this people, to this land." As we walked back to the vans, our minders and drivers, who had stood around in the background, thanked us and seemed moved by what we had done.

Back in Basra, we were able to visit with Gilbert Andraas, pastor of the Evangelical Presbyterian Church, and one of his parishioners. We asked him about a group of us coming to stay in Basra. With Zeid there, however, he didn't respond freely but deferred to Zeid, who proceeded to share all his reservations about it.

∼ ∼ ∼

The next morning, January 6, we woke early and set off on our trip to Baghdad, hoping to stop at Ur. Little did we know that this would be a tragic journey.

After about forty-five minutes of driving, the left rear tire on the GMC van in the middle of our caravan suddenly blew. As the car swerved, the driver frantically tried to regain control, but it went off the road and flipped. It was upside down when it stopped. As soon as Sattar, our driver, saw it through his rearview mirror, he gasped and stopped our van. We ran back as quickly as possible, feeling very anxious. We didn't know what we would find, but held on to hope that it wasn't anything too bad.

Le Anne was the first to arrive on the scene and see George lying on the ground; she had the presence of mind to cover his head with his coat. George Weber, 72, of Chesley, Ontario, had been thrown out of the vehicle and was killed instantly after sustaining massive head injuries. Others in the car—Michelle; Jim Loney, a writer and member of a Catholic worker community in Ontario; Larry Kehler, a Mennonite editor and pastor from Winnipeg; and Pat Basler, a special education teacher from Wisconsin—crawled out with some facial cuts and minor injuries, and were shaken by their experience and the discovery of George's death.

Charlie Jackson, a software consultant from San Antonio, Texas, was in shock and had pain in his neck and back. Later we found out he had compression fractures in three vertebrae, as well as bruised ribs and muscles. Michelle had a broken nose and whiplash. Both ended up staying in Baghdad, receiving treatment, and participating in team activities until January 26.

Raza', the driver of the overturned van and brother of Sattar, was not physically injured but was wracked with emotional pain. At the scene, he leaned over the wrecked vehicle and cried. Sattar and the other driver were upset and shaken. The vehicles were fairly new and in excellent condition, and the US-made tires were just a week old. We cried and held each other, but also took care of the injured, and made plans for dealing with the tragedy.

We helped our injured into the remaining two vans as carefully and comfortably as possible and drove back to Basra very slowly. Our drivers took those in the wrecked van to the hospital for examination and treatment and the rest of us to the hotel we had just left that morning. Anne stayed most of the day at the hospital with Charlie.

Immediately Cliff was on the telephone, having a hard time making calls out of Basra. He was trying to call back to the Chicago and Toronto CPT offices, so they could notify families. Zeid made arrangements for an ambulance and made plane reservations for us to fly back to Baghdad. Delegate Robert Leonetti from Colorado went along to bring George's body back to Basra. Six of us gathered in a circle in the hotel dining room to share and pray. We were all shaken, but people at the hotel were calm and caring toward us.

It's ironic that we dealt with the possibility of team members being hurt or dying in a war or insurrection, but didn't expect the first CPTer to die in an auto accident. (Actually, statistically the most dangerous thing CPTers have done on any project was ride in automobiles.) We couldn't help but speculate that because of the sanctions, Iraq had very little control on goods coming into the country and was sold defective tires. (In the weeks that followed, CPT staff in the US investigated the serial numbers of the tires, but did not find any evidence that they had been recalled.)

We were concerned for Raza', the driver of the wrecked vehicle. Because a death occurred, he was charged with reck-lessness and was in jail. As a team, we drafted a statement saying that we did not see him as careless or personally responsible and did not want to make any claims against him. Those who were in the car wrote a report of what they remembered about the accident. Iraqi police came and questioned those in the accident, and later a judge came and held "court" in the dining room, questioning them again.

After a difficult night, the next day was full, making arrangements and taking care of each other. Tom Finger, a seminary professor from Evanston, Illinois, led us that morning in our own memorial service for George. We shared about George and his life and our experiences with him. We sang and prayed. It was a healing time.

"On this day, Christians celebrate Epiphany, when strangers brought gifts from the east," said Mary Ellen McDonagh, a Catholic Sister from Chicago. "Our delegation came from the west. George Weber brought the gift of life." Weber was a retired history teacher and trained CPT reservist. He had served in 2001 and 2002 with the CPT team in Hebron. There he took a particular interest in accompanying Palestinian school children to classes under curfew in the occupied city. When Weber first applied to CPT in 1999, he wrote, "I think that most of the calamities that befall ordinary folk could be alleviated if it were not for the selfishness and greed that motivate the power struc-tures which are in place throughout the world. But there are also many people of goodwill, who wish to treat everyone fairly and with charity. I try to be among this group."

Around five that afternoon we flew on Iraq Airlines to

Baghdad, with Charlie and others on board. There to greet us at the airport were other team members, Wada, and a lot of media personnel, interviewing us and taking our pictures. Delegation members went back to our hotel, only to have to pack and prepare to leave the next morning to drive out of Iraq to Amman, Jordan, to catch their flights returning home.

Those two days seemed like weeks. I was thankful for my life and to be back in Baghdad again. It felt like coming home.

A week later, Raza' was released after George's wife, Lena, and Kathy wrote statements saying they would not press charges against him.

As CPT started the process of transferring George's body back to Canada, we found out it wasn't so easy. When the Iraq Foreign Ministry started making arrangements with Jordan and Canada we found out that the UN sanctions committee would need to approve the shipment. Any transfer in or out of Iraq needed their clearance. Fortunately, that approval came quickly, and George's body was flown out on January 10. George's last act was to break the sanctions!

~ ~ ~

January was a time for more international delegations in Iraq. A three-member CPT delegation came to Baghdad on January 11-25 to join thirty-five US professors in a three-day symposium for peace. This was hosted and held at the University of Baghdad, where fifty percent (about seven hundred) of the senior faculty had received their doctorates in the US and spoke English.

Their days were filled with lectures, discussions, and day trips. One session was devoted to research on the affects of DU. Medical school faculty from American universities agreed that the research was high quality and that the epidemiological studies were convincing. They agreed that the increase of leukemia and similar cancers in children under five and malformations of infants should be addressed in the US as a human rights violation.

During the rest of their time in Iraq, the three delegates participated in other IPT activities. They were there when thirteen leaders of mainstream American churches came on a delegation through the National Council of Churches (the same week as the university symposium) and issued a statement declaring that an attack on Iraq would be both immoral and unjustifiable.

Another group coming to Baghdad was the Peaceful Tomorrows delegation: Colleen Kelly, Terry Rockefeller, Kristina Olsen, and Kathleen Tinley, all family members of September 11 victims. In their statement of intent, they said,

> We are four . . . who have lost children, brothers, and sisters in the violence of September 11. We have come to your country at a time when our country is threatening war against the people of Iraq. We, who have the lost members of our families to violence, want to be with Iraqi families who have suffered such loss because of war and sanctions and continued bombings of Iraq. We want to honor the memory of the dead by finding ways that the world's conflicts can be resolved without killing, without violence. We want to break the cycle of violence so that no more families in Iraq or anywhere will suffer the losses we have suffered.

On January 15, for the commemoration of Martin Luther King Jr.'s birthday, our team held a press conference along the Tigris River. The group took turns reading King's April 4, 1967, "Riverside Speech," concerning the war in Vietnam. King's words in America thirty-five years earlier seemed very relevant to the situation we were facing.

"A time comes when silence is betrayal." This is how King began his speech, which articulated his clear opposition to the terror and destruction of the Vietnam War. King's agony about it was evident as he continued: "Many persons have questioned me about the wisdom of my path. They say, 'Why are you joining the voices of dissent? Peace and civil rights don't mix.'" To this he responded, "When I hear them, though I often understand the source of their concerns, I am nevertheless greatly saddened, for such questions mean the inquirers have not really known me, my commitment, or my calling. Indeed, the questions suggest that they do not know the world in which they live."

King's speech went on to describe the horrendous effects of war on the people of Vietnam. "The world demands that we admit that we have been wrong from the beginning. . . . The situation is one in which we must be ready to turn sharply from our present ways. . . . This calls for a worldwide fellowship, that lifts neighborly concerns beyond one's tribe, race, class, and nation."

~ ~ ~

On January 25, President Bush said to expect war soon. Iraqi people heard this, and their tension increased. We also heard voices of leaders of the world community urging restraint, to give the inspection process a chance. On January 27, we listened carefully to the news about the weapons inspectors' reports to the UN Security Council. Hans Blix, chief UN weapons inspector, said that Iraq's cooperation had been a "mixed bag." He criticized Iraq for blocking U2 aerial photography flights and for failing to prove it eliminated illegal weapons. But he still said the inspections team was making progress and should be given more time to deal with these problems.

To us it seemed clear that Iraq was not a threat to the US. UN inspectors had not found evidence of nuclear, chemical, or biological weapons, or delivery systems for them. The CIA had said there was no terrorist threat from Iraq. Connections between Al Qaeda and the Iraqi government seemed unlikely. Furthermore, Iraq was no match for the US militarily and could never win a war against it. It was no match during the 1991 Gulf War, and during twelve and a half years of sanctions the Iraqi military capacity had deteriorated. On the ground, we saw little evidence of military preparation.

The Bush administration made it clear that the US was willing to go to war in a pre-emptive action without UN approval. This would further weaken the power and reputation of the UN. War would result in many other serious consequences, such as the horrible loss of life, damage to Iraqi infrastructure and society, increasing worldwide anger against the US and UK. We held on to hope that it could still be stopped.

~ ~ ~

"How can a Christian consider killing innocent people, even babies and children?" asked Sister Bushra, director of a Dominican maternity hospital. "I'm embarrassed to tell people that I'm a Christian." She had just given the new thirteen-member CPT delegation a tour of the hospital and had responded to someone's comment that her name sounded similar to President Bush's.

Allan Slater, a dairy farmer from Ontario, had brought along a tiny pocket cross with a poem attached, saying that "Jesus is your constant companion." He offered it to Sister Bushra. At first she took it, but then quickly handed it back to him. "Please give it to President Bush," she said. "He needs it more than I do."

Cliff and I traveled north to Mosul with the delegation representing the US, Canada, the Netherlands, and the UK. Our plan to visit a Kurdish refugee camp didn't materialize, but the group was able to visit a hospital, an old Armenian church, the ancient ruins of Nineveh, and a place said to be Jonah's tomb. At the church, Father Karikem Hopsepien introduced us to the three-day Bauuta, a yearly period of fasting and praying for repentance, inspired by the repentance Nineveh experienced in response to Jonah's warnings. Later some of our team members observed this fast.

Back in Baghdad, about thirty gathered at the Al Wathba water treatment plant, where the CPT delegation planted a young date palm tree as a symbolic "tree of life." Also present were Iraqi friends of the team, an engineer working at the plant, Chaldean Bishop Shilimoon Warduni, several members of the press, as well as other team members. Three of Siham's sons, Yasser, Samir, and Maher, came with me and helped hold some of our picture posters of Iraqi people.

The ceremony focused on the conditions of the treatment plant and the horrible consequences of another war. It was a celebration of the promise of life and of God's creation even in the threat of war. As delegates planted the young tree, Heather Angus, a technical writer from Urbana, Ohio, read the verse from Revelation, "On either side of the river, the tree of life with its twelve kinds of fruit . . . and the leaves were for the healing of the nations." We prayed for this healing.

CHAPTER 6

Emergency Preparedness

"We are not 'human shields,'" we told reporters. There had been reports in the media about hundreds of people from countries around the world converging on Iraq to be human shields. They were dedicated volunteers who cared deeply about the Iraqi people and wanted to do what they could to prevent war. By the third week in February an estimated 170 were already in Iraq. They were choosing to be present at civilian sensitive sites, such as water plants, electrical facilities, hospitals, oil refineries, and food storage sites in hopes that their presence would be a deterrent to US attacks on these locations. We objected to the Bush administration's attempt to discredit this bold and effective peacemaking effort.

We chose not to call ourselves "human shields" for several reasons. The concept of human shields was associated with innocent people in the West Bank last spring being forced at gunpoint to enter dangerous situations ahead of Israeli troops. Also we did not want to be under the same restraints as the people with "human shield" stamped on their visas. They were under obligations to go where government officials told them. We had the advantage of having more freedoms to determine our work and locations.

We realized that we could not shield anyone from the devastation of war. We wanted to think that our presence would provide some safety to the people threatened by violence and influence our government not to go to war, but our role was also to live among the people and "accompany" them in this threatening situation. We wanted to tell their stories to people around the world, to unmask the lies and violence of our government, and to advocate for peaceful solutions to the conflict.

In Bush's State of the Union speech on January 28, he called Iraq a serious threat that needed to be disarmed. He said he would seek the support of the world in this effort, but "would not wait." A couple of days later Bush warned Iraq that it only had "weeks, not months" to disarm or face invasion. On February 5, Secretary of State Colin Powell presented satellite photographs of what he claimed were chemical and biological facilities in Iraq and recordings of conversations of Iraqi military officers alluding to hidden weapons-producing labs. He called for the UN to support war. The next day Bush began a drive for a new UN Security Council resolution authorizing military action against Iraq.

As the talk of war heated up again among the Bush administration in February, speaking out against war seemed more urgent. Some of the mixed messages we received from the US suggested that the Joint Chiefs of Staff disagreed about timing. NATO was divided. Many UN Security Council members voiced strong opposition to war, and various international polls showed massive opposition to it. US opinion polls showed growing questions among the people.

Bush and Powell said Iraq was in "material breach" of the Resolution 1441 and that war could start soon. In contrast to this, Hans Blix, and Muhammad El Baradi, head of the International Atomic Energy Agency, reported on February 14 that they did not find Iraq in material breach. They refuted Bush's accusations step by step. The UN called for restraint, and France and other nations insisted on giving the inspectors more time. Yet we knew that all this might not stop Bush from going to war.

The weapons inspectors cited measures Iraq had taken that were evidence of its increased cooperation and judged that they were making progress. These included Iraq allowing surveillance flights, providing new documents and open investigations of past arms, and proceeding on March 1 to destroy forbidden missiles and other weapons. The inspectors disputed the satellite images and much of the other "evidence" Powell had presented earlier.

In the middle of this, our team stepped up our symbolic public actions and was meeting for "emergency preparedness." During the week of February 10-15, team members visited a local electrical power plant, a water treatment facility, a children's hospital, and a school, and at these places hung banners that read, "To Bomb This Site Is a War Crime," (under Geneva Convention Article 54). In the 1991 Gulf War, US and UK forces bombed most of these facilities, resulting in an increase of disease and death over the past twelve years. During this week leading up to big anti-war rallies around the world on February 15-16, the team invited people around the world to join in similar actions in their communities. We wanted to remind people of these likely targets if Bush's plans were to be carried out.

During that week we also put up a large tent across the street from the UN headquarters in Baghdad, with one large banner reading "Inspections, Yes; Invasion, No," and several smaller banners. Each morning many team members went out early to be there when the UN weapons inspectors drove out in their white vans to go on assignment. One morning one of the inspectors got out of a van and took a picture of our vigil. Another day, a different inspector walked across the busy street and thanked us, saying that they appreciated our presence and that it boosted their morale.

On Sunday, February 6, we joined other international peace groups and Iraqis to "plant" a peace pole in the courtyard of the UN Development Program (UNDP). The pole was brought to Iraq by the Mid-Hudson Peace Brigade in New York as a gift to the Iraqi people. The next day we were encouraged to hear the news about huge rallies and marches around the world to protest war in Iraq, with at least 400,000 people gathering in New York City and millions more in cities across the globe. It was called the "largest day of protest in world history." The *New York Times* dubbed its participants "the other superpower." When this and other worldwide protests occurred, many Iraqi people told us they appreciated it; they felt supported and not forgotten. Later in the summer we heard that thirty-seven million people around the world had protested.

At a visit to the Holy Family religious education school, the junior-high children's class went to the front of the sanctuary and knelt down to pray for peace. I felt close to Ghalia, teacher of the teen's class, as she talked about her fears of the war coming. "As Christians, we are more scared about the possibility of an uprising, in which Muslims might target Christians, than of bombings or invasion by Americans," she said. "It would almost be better to get the war over than to have it hanging over our own heads like this." If she could, she would have taken her mother and family out of the country.

On Saturday, February 22, the preacher at the Adventist Church announced a special prayer services for peace that evening. We found out that this was a special day of prayer and fasting for peace for Christians all over Baghdad.

On my way home that Saturday morning, a man sitting in front of a shop called out to me, thanking me for being in Iraq. I stopped, and we were soon in a very animated discussion about why our group was in Iraq, about the US government, and about the possibility of war. He spoke loudly and passionately and at times seemed on the verge of tears. Soon a small crowd of people gathered to watch and listen. I was a lone woman surrounded by a crowd of men, but I was treated respectfully and felt very safe. At one point the man who had initiated this conversation said that the "Christian prophet" called for peace on earth, giving Christians and Muslims a common unity. He kept thanking me. I felt awed by this experience. I was reminded why I was there and I knew that I should be.

~ ~ ~

Woven through all the events, actions, and times of planning were the strands of my own decision making. At key times during those months, I was faced with whether to go home or stay on.

When I extended my original plane ticket, I was scheduled to return home on January 23. But when that time came near I felt drawn to continue on. I tested this with Art, my community back home, and the CPT staff. CPT Director Gene Stoltzfus encouraged me to stay, assuring me that CPT would provide a new return ticket for me. Art said he had a "slight preference" for me to come home then, because it was also important to bring my experience to the peace movement in America, but he didn't have any clarity. He said I should take the discernment of the CPT community seriously and that he supported my staying, if that was what I decided. Our common vision and experiencing the struggles and rewards of such work had helped us in times of tough decision making. I wrestled with feelings of responsibility to family and friends and a desire to go home and work for peace there. I gave this much prayer and thought, but still decided to stay longer, but not knowing how much longer.

I wrote the following to family and friends back home:

> There are "head" or rational reasons why I feel led to do this such as (1) to continue to work with this experiment of nonviolently resisting the US attempts at military control or war with Iraq, (2) to be an eyewitness on the ground and share what I see to folks back home, and (3) to speak with my presence as well as actions and words. But beyond these reasons, I feel on a "heart" level something that has been harder to put into words, but I will try.
>
> In my time in Iraq, I have experienced something greater than the power of the military might of the US. I've experienced the power of love between the people of two countries on the brink of war, to break down of the label "enemy" imposed on us. This power of love cannot be taken away from us or conquered even if there is war. I have experienced this as these imperfect people (with their problems, just like us) open their hearts to us, to receive us. Everywhere we go, we have immediately known that we aren't enemies and have experienced a natural human bond that transcends the power of our governments. And this simple experience is seen as radical, threatening, and even subversive to our governments who try to prevent us from coming together.
>
> Iraqi people have told us that our presence helps encourage them and keep their hope alive. In turn, it has fed me with hope and encouragement on a deeper level. So, one of the more difficult experiences of my life has also been one of the richest. It is not that we are doing it, but has been a gift of God that I have had the privilege to be a part of.
>
> Yes, I want to see this through, because my heart is here. God has given me a deep love and desire for peace and wholeness for the people and the land. And this has also increased and enriched my love for each of you and for all the people back home. If I can be one tiny part of what God wants to do here, I want to be part of it. War may break out, and the people may be crushed, and I would feel a deep pain, disappointment, and grief. But it would

never negate the gifts that have been given in the work that has been done here and in local communities around the world. Acting and not giving into despair or helplessness, gives all of us hope.

At this point, what I do next is not clear. When I do come home, my prayer is that I come back with the hope and love I have received and the images of people I have come to know and love, and share them with each of you!

As the various delegations came and left the country, I still at times wondered if my mission in Iraq had been accomplished and if I should also leave. Our minders wanted to pare down the numbers on the IPT and were encouraging those who considered leaving before war started to leave soon.

A couple of my close friends at home pushed me to test this carefully and be clear that staying was what I was called to do. On February 15, I wrote home in response to these messages:

> At this point, I can say that, at least for now, if a war starts I will stay here as long as we are able to discern that our presence is positive for the Iraqi people. If at any time it looks like we would be a burden or that we see no reason to be here, I will come home. It is also a good possibility that we will have no choice, but be forced to leave by officials here.
>
> But if I follow my heart, I would stay on and see this through. I care very deeply for the Iraqi people and the people of the world who would be affected by such a war. . . . I also feel deeply concerned about each of you and grieve at the thought that this could be something that could separate me from you. This has always made my decision to stay on more difficult. I love you all very deeply and have treasured your prayers and notes of support.

Of course, fears and uncertainties continually came up, and I had times of doubt. There were certain times of worship that spoke to and strengthened me in a powerful way or during which I renewed my commitment to follow Jesus wherever that led.

One such time was in late February at Saint Raphael's. Father Vincent read from Isaiah 43:1-2: "Do not fear, for I have redeemed you; I have called you by name, you are mine. When you pass through the waters, I will be with you; and through the rivers, they shall not overwhelm you; when you walk through fire you shall not be burned." The power of love had also pushed me to go beyond my own fears I felt God's presence and knew that even if I lost my life in Iraq, it would be okay because God had called me there and was with me in this.

∼ ∼ ∼

I was one of many who liked the idea of a date-boat action. The plan was to haul one ton of Iraqi dates down the Shatt Al Arab River into the Persian Gulf for shipment to international markets. It would be an invitation to all nations to open trade with Iraq by ending the sanctions. We could take the dates on one of the routes invading forces could take. Others thought that now that war was threatening, it was too late for something like this. We had not received permission from our minders to do it, so we put it off as a possibility for a smaller part of the team to do later. However, our alternative plan, to go down to the Kuwaiti border for a time of prayer, fasting, and protest, was approved. Plans finally came together for us to do this on Monday, February 24.

Early that morning we flew on Iraq Airlines to Basra and drove down to the Kuwaiti border just south of Al Safwan. We passed through the demilitarized zone to one of two crossing

Iraq Peace Team group holding a banner at the Iraqi-Kuwaiti border for a time of prayer, fasting, and protest, February 2003.

points on the entire 150-mile Iraq/Kuwait border. On both sides of the border was a no-man's land marked by long mounds of sand and protected by UN guards. From this side we could see the checkpoint and buildings with the Kuwaiti flag on the other side.

We had a large tent open at one end, with rugs covering the ground and chairs lining the inside walls of the tent. This was pitched about sixty yards north of the Iraqi edge of that no-man's land. Journalists came down with us and took pictures of us holding a banner reading, "Take a Risk, Sit Down for Peace." We were there through a rainstorm, a day of *shargi* (dust storms), and a day of bright, sunny weather.

Our days were full of quiet, prayerful times, a mixture of serious and playful moments. We walked along the road leading to the border, carrying our large pictures of Iraqi people, holding a banner, draping paper cranes around signs, or reading letters from US school children about peace. We felt connected to God, to each other, to the earth, and to the soldiers on the other side of the border. For many of us this time at the border was like a retreat that gave us an opportunity to reflect, pray, and share. It was a spiritual and emotional preparation for more difficult times ahead.

Our group sent a letter to the commanding officer of the US troops massing on the other side and to the soldiers. Charlie, one of the veterans among us, had received a medal of honor for bravery during the Vietnam War, but later turned it in because he saw the effects of foreign policy on the people of Central America. He climbed up on a tall metal structure and read aloud our statement to the military and made his own comments about war. Our message to the troops was not one of condemnation, but a prayer that they would be able to return quickly to their homes safely and without having to participate in actions they would regret.

One evening, while we were in Basra, we heard an air-raid siren and a loud boom. A chill went through us as we realized that this was a bomb being dropped, probably on the edge of Basra.

When we got back to Baghdad, we sent out a call for "pre-emptive nonviolent civil disobedience actions" to "use our collective resourcefulness to find ways to throw sand in the gears of the war machine." Pre-emptive nonviolence would mean sit-ins, blockades, and a national moratorium on March 5 to call for "no business as usual," knowing the destruction and suffering that war could bring.

~ ~ ~

We got back to Baghdad in time to receive another CPT delegation of ten people. I didn't have direct responsibility for this one, but took part in some of their meetings and activities, taking them to visit families and to volunteer at the orphanage. One Saturday, a delegation member and I left the orphanage and found a taxi to take us to the Adventist church service. Very quickly we were in a meaningful conversation with our warm and friendly taxi driver. He thanked us when we said why we were in Iraq, and then he told some of his own story.

He was forty-three and had married when he was forty. He and his wife were uncertain about whether they should have children, because of the dangers from depleted uranium and diseases Iraqi children had been plagued with since the last war. Or if they did, they thought they should wait until there was peace. "So many people are poor and hungry here," he continued. "Many die because they are too ashamed to beg for the money they need for food or medicine." He also asked, "How could Bush be a Christian and do what he is doing?" We responded that Jesus asks us to love everyone and not to kill, so Bush isn't acting now as a Christian.

When we arrived at our destination, Tom took out an extra large amount of money to pay our driver. He refused to take anything, however, saying, "It means so much to the Iraqi people to have you here."

We heard in the news that US Special Forces soldiers were infiltrating into the western border of Iraq. Lisa Ndejuru, a Canadian of Rwandan origins, and Cliff came up with the idea of a small group of team members going to the western border to document and report on where these forces were located and also try to talk to them. There was disagreement among the team, with some thinking the plan was too dangerous. But the group decided that the five of us who were interested in pursuing it would be free to do so. Later, however, Zeid told us that it was unlikely that the Foreign Ministry would approve the project. He said that the western border areas were heavily guarded by security, and they wouldn't want us there.

In March, the news continued to go back and forth between strong statements by US administration that war was imminent and times when it seemed it would be postponed by international pressures, giving us hope that it still might not happen. We continued with a sprinkling of actions.

~ ~ ~

"Another delegation . . . when war could be coming so soon?" Many of the whole team questioned the wisdom of bringing in the next CPT delegation planned for March 18. Many doubted they would even get into the country, but the main concern was the lack of time for them to really get oriented and build trusting relationships with other team members, important for working together in the midst of war. The current team had already been through a lot together and had connected in many ways.

The circle of CPTers in Iraq had discussed this, saw the potential problems, but also saw a lot of value in bringing many people over to Iraq for the witness, but also because it would mean more people going back to share their experiences. There were many seasoned peacemakers on this delegation, and one of the members, Jim Douglass, a writer and peace activist from Birmingham, Alabama, was going to Rome on his way to Iraq to try to convince the Pope to join the delegation. We decided to err on the side of hope in the war not coming immediately and in being able to more quickly orient a small group of experienced people. We recommended to the larger (IPT) group that we accept the delegation's coming, thinking that if the war started, they would not be able to come in. But if it didn't, we would have time to integrate them into the team. We agreed to take responsibility for the delegation if a crisis did arise. With much hesitation, IPT went along with this plan.

~ ~ ~

Throughout the month and a half before the war started, the Iraq Peace Team (IPT) continued to discuss, and sometimes debate, how we could prepare ourselves for war. Our "emergency preparedness" focused on three issues: (1) team structure and decision-making process, (2) material preparations, and (3) locations and activities during crisis.

Some of our earliest work back in November and December had entailed gathering and organizing material necessities for a time of crisis, including bottled water, dried foods, a couple of bicycles for transportation, buckets, shovels, and a stock of first-aid equipment to be divided among the affinity groups. There were designated "bomb shelters" in the basements of the Al Fanar and the Andalus Apartments, and a first-floor room at the Al Dar, fortified to be more protective.

Thinking they might stay on, team members began preparing what was called a "crash kit," a small carrying case in which we would pack personal items we thought necessary to keep us going for at least a week in case we were separated. This we would keep next to our bed, where we could grab and carry it with us in an emergency.

We each studied and answered for ourselves questions on an "intentions sheet," which challenged us to consider whether we were prepared to be there during a war and what choices we would make if we were. It included questions such as what we would want done with our body if we were killed (if there was a choice). This wasn't pleasant to do, but we weren't ready to stay if we were not able to face the possibility of death. Our hope and love would have to carry us along, even through the hell of war.

Decisions had been made to break up into affinity groups living in several locations with the possibility of some difference in their focus or projects, but to keep larger group identity and activities. Larger group decisions would take place through "spokes" meetings made up of representatives from each of the affinity groups. As the time moved on, team members began to discuss within their affinity groups possible locations and activities for small groups during a crisis.

We each filled out an emergency information sheet, which we would carry both with us and in our crash kit. And as a team we wrote the following statement, which many of us signed:

> We are international members of the Iraq Peace Team
> presently living in Iraq. We recognize that we could be injured or
> killed in our line of peacemaking work, but we have chosen
> voluntarily to come. We understand that Iraqis are much more at
> risk while the threat of war by the United States looms on the
> horizon. Our commitment to nonviolence as a better way to
> resolve conflict leads us to this statement which we ask all parties
> in the setting to understand.
>
> We ask that armed action not be used to protect us or extract
> us from this setting if our lives are in danger. If there are those
> who feel led to intervene, we ask that it be with prayers for the
> safety and security of all people in this volatile region, and with
> valiant efforts to remove the weapons of war from all countries
> of the earth.

As the possibility of war seemed closer in February and
March, several shifts began to take place in team-thinking about
how we would structure and operate as a team during a war.
Several people on the team believed that our consensus decision-
making model was fine for our current pre-war situation, but
during a crisis it might be necessary to switch to give the
"spokes" representatives the power to make quick decisions for
the entire team without consulting others in the affinity groups.
If that wasn't possible, there would be a designated person, such
as Kathy, who would be given the authority to make immediate
emergency decisions that would be binding for the whole group.
Or, if possible, the "primary decision maker," in consultation
with two or three "designated consultants," could make quick
decisions. If something happened to that person, there would be
a designated order in which one of these consultants would take
over that responsibility.

Some supporting this "chain of command" emergency
decision making had been a part of the 1990-91 Gulf Peace
Team, during which they remembered that too many "free spirits"
among them had made decision making very difficult. When
crisis occurred, it was impossible to reach consensus as a group.

Our affinity group discussed these issues. While we respected
the experience of others, we still came to a different conclusion.

We thought that with the kind of trusting relationships we had developed in our group, we could come to consensus or defer to others' wisdom to direct us in an emergency and that a command structure wasn't necessary. We also wanted to keep space in any situation for God's Spirit to speak through any of us or to us as a group. Because the entire group never came to complete agreement, this issue was never completely settled when the war came.

The other shift and source of tension came concerning where we would be located and what activities we would aspire to be involved in during a time of war. Most of us wanted to be as engaged and as mobile as possible in such a time, and we came up with a list of many possible scenarios.

The CPT circle sent out an "Iraq Urgent Action Alert" on March 6 over CPTnet, calling on people in the US to write to their representatives about where the team here was planning to be if a war started. We listed various goals and criteria for staying on, such as being a help or encouragement to Iraqi people or NGOs trying to alleviate the suffering, not wanting to be a burden on Iraqi people or their system, being able to witness and report what happened in a way that mainline media might not, and if possible, respond proactively with nonviolent actions. The statement listed many sites, including our hotels, Basra, CARE International, University of Baghdad, Saint Raphael's Church or hospital, the orphanage, Al Mansour Children's Hospital, the water and electrical plants, and others. On the CPT web page was posted a map of Baghdad with some of these places marked.

Our affinity group began visiting several of these sites to check out the feasibility of being located there. It seemed our most likely choice was to stay at the Al Dar with the orphanage complex and Saint Raphael's Church and hospital all within two blocks of each other. Charlie and I asked the sisters at the orphanage, who said we would be welcome to come and help during the day, but not to live there or stay overnight. Saint Raphael's and the Syrian Catholic churches had similar positions. They had difficulty seeing how our presence with them in a war would be helpful to them and did not share our vision for nonviolent public symbolic action during such a time. We also pursued contacts with the Al Wathba water treatment plant and confirmed that we would be welcomed there. CARE was open to our working with them, but any persons staying there would be far away from the rest of the larger group and could possibly lose contact with the others.

One difference came up as some other team members came to the conclusion that during a war we could be stuck in our hotels and not able to move around Baghdad or be able to help out at any institutions or do public actions. Also, one person calculated that in a war we had about a 15- to 20-percent chance of survival. If this were true, we should not spend too much energy thinking about actions, but should make decisions based on what would increase our chances of survival so we could be witnesses and help after the war.

Another expressed that we would have a greater chance of survival if we were close together and not spread out. That meant it would be better for those at the Al Dar to move over to either the Al Fanar Hotel or Andalus Apartments.

During one of our meetings, Wada came and said he believed there was more danger for those living at the Al Dar, because next door was a telephone communications billing office, which could be a target in a war. Other team members began to put a lot of pressure on the Al Dar affinity group to move. One person even told us that it was "suicidal" for us to stay at the Al Dar, and another, that it could jeopardize the whole team.

Our Al Dar affinity group gave this serious consideration, but resisted leaving for three reasons: (1) We had no way of knowing what would happen and whether the Al Dar was actually more dangerous than any other location; (2) we found safety in relationships among the people living in our neighborhood, so felt safer at the Al Dar in the possibility of a civil or guerrilla war situation; and (3) we saw more possibility of mobility and being able to work and act more boldly and independently from "minder-control" there. We also suspected that our minders were telling us this because leaving Al Dar would make it easier for them to watch over the whole team.

The other team members never told us we had to move, until the very end, when some of us were being expelled from the country. As it turned out, the building next door was not hit, and the team later discovered that the Al Fanar, located near a building connected with the Iraqi military, was in greater danger.

We also decided that we did not want to operate and base our decision making on a worst-case scenario. We cared about our survival and didn't want to act carelessly, but we wanted to discern where our presence would allow us to be the most helpful or to have a violence-reducing affect. We saw more possibilities in a residential neighborhood such as the Karrada district, where we currently lived, or in the neighborhood of the water treatment plant and hospital complex.

It would have been easy to let my imagination run wild and get engulfed in fearful thinking, but I resisted this. Yes, we all had our fears. Being there at all was a big risk. No place was guaranteed safe. Life isn't safe anywhere. There was no way of knowing what places would or wouldn't be hit, although government and military sites were more likely. It was better to focus on these other criteria. We helped each other in these decisions, but when it came down to it, each of us had to struggle through decisions for ourselves and were given the freedom to do that.

Several of our affinity group eventually did move to the Andalus or Al Fanar, just before or after the bombing started. Although tensions over some of these issues persisted, team members were able to continue to relate together in a respectful way and to act as a unified team when war did come.

~ ~ ~

On March 10 we heard from a friend that there was more bombing in Basra and near the Kuwaiti border, where US troops were making entry points across the border, preparing for an invasion. We didn't know if this was the beginning or just preparations, but it sounded serious.

Over the past week, many embassy and UN agency staff members had already started to evacuate Iraq, after Bush declared that Iraq had failed to disarm and that the US would proceed to get the Security Council vote on a resolution to go to war. France, Russia, and China dismissed the proposal, and Blix bluntly contradicted some of the Bush administration's assertions about Iraq's violations. We got up early on March 12 and went out to the UN headquarters for a vigil. "Who will protect the children of Iraq, if the UN leaves?" read the large banner we held.

We went that evening to Amal and Safah's home to say good-bye. About midnight they planned to leave for Syria and would try to make it to the Syrian border before it closed to Iraqis fleeing their country. We hoped they would make it, find a good place to stay, and be able to return safely when there was peace. We remembered them in times of gathered prayer.

The next day, ten of us went to the Al Wathba water plant, where we had a short worship service with reading, singing, and praying for peace. We took turns pouring water on the small "tree of life" the delegation had planted there. Plant workers took us around the grounds and showed us where the other gates were, from which we could walk to the Al Mansour Children's Hospital. Three days later we came back to the grounds for a picnic.

Many of us also went to the Amariyah Shelter to join in a

CPT members joined a pre-war vigil sponsored by a Spanish delegation at the Ameriyha Shelter in Baghdad, March 2003.

vigil sponsored by a Spanish delegation. They had written a statement calling on the people of the world to unite against the war. It was read in English, Spanish, Portuguese, French, German, and Arabic. We were part of a large group of people standing and sitting behind the speakers, holding large banners and pictures of Iraqi people.

On Wednesday, March 12, our minders told us that our request to go down to Basra and stay there during the war was denied, because they considered it too dangerous for us. "We are here to go into dangerous places!" Cliff responded.

We had been able to do many meaningful and powerful symbolic actions throughout our time in Iraq, but we were frustrated. Creative ideas, such as the date boat project, the plan to go to the western border to camp and try to talk to US troops infiltrating there in late February, and the earlier plan for a peace walk around Iraq using tents had been squelched, either by members of our group or by the Foreign Ministry and minders who felt responsible for us and were nervous about high-profile actions that they thought could be dangerous for us. We thought, however, that highly visible, symbolic actions had the potential to reach the conscience of people in the US and around the world, possibly interrupting the movement toward war.

On Friday, March 14, the news was more hopeful. More and more countries declared that they were not going along with the resolution the US was trying to get passed, authorizing war with Iraq. But two days later, Bush called for war. He announced that by Monday, March 17, diplomatic efforts would end and he would make a decision about war, even if the UN Security Council couldn't come to agreement.

~ ~ ~

"It just isn't right! It just must not happen!" I cried out to God one day when grief and anger overcame me. I just couldn't imagine the terror of it all—what people will suffer. "God, you must step in and do something to stop it! It is the innocent, the helpless, who will suffer, not the ones who are greedy and ruthless and uncaring, not the ones who are orchestrating this war." But, I wondered, what good would it do for me to die here with them? Does that help them? No, except that we share in their suffering. We must not give up, lose hope, stop praying, walking, writing, visiting, and putting our bodies on the line. What I really wanted to do was stop this horrible thing from happening.

I was afraid. I didn't want to die. But I was willing to take the risk if my presence could help prevent thousands of people from dying and suffering war here or elsewhere, in the next countries on Bush's agenda.

I believe that it is important for thousands of us to be willing to die, not because dying is important, but so that we can say no to war so strongly that governments lose the support for these wars and there are no people left to fight them.

It is especially important that people of conscience and faith act strongly and boldly to declare a gospel of peace, or we lose our very soul. Christianity loses its soul if it loses its witness of the one who laid down his life for his friends, who gave us the ministry of reconciliation, of peace, of nonviolent, suffering love.

~ ~ ~

In the increasing tension, Siham told me that neighbors were asking her if her family had government permission to have these Americans coming to their house so often. She and her husband expressed fear that this could result in some kind of reprisal from the local Ba'ath Party. She asked if we could get our minders to sign a statement saying that we had approval from the Iraqi government to visit them or that a minder go and talk to their Ba'ath Party representative in their neighborhood.

This took us aback, because all this time there had been no problem. But we didn't want their family to be harmed in any way. We thought of just not going to their house, but our relationship had been important to me through these months, and I didn't want to cut it off suddenly. So I talked with Wada about it and he said he would try to take care of it. Kathy recommended that the next time we go accompanied by Muhammad, one of our taxi drivers, who would function as a representative of our minders.

~ ~ ~

On Saturday morning, March 15, three of us went to the Seventh-Day Adventist morning worship. The preacher said that in prayer, God will strengthen us and give us courage. The music lifted my spirits. At the end of the service, the children started walking up to the front of the sanctuary. Then the adults followed. More than one hundred people knelt down there and prayed for peace. It was a powerful moment. God was with us. "Please, God answer these prayers!"

On Sunday evening, March 16, several of us went to the Evangelical Presbyterian Church. I appreciated the spirited singing. During the service the pastor greeted us personally and read parts of our magic sheet out loud. The pastor spoke about how God can move us through troubled waters and meets us with miracles. A young woman named Luma translated for us and expressed her faith and hope.

We got back to the Al Dar just in time for the IPT party. In the midst of the heaviness and seriousness, it was good to put it aside and just have fun together. Kathy Kelly and Jerry Zawada, a Franciscan priest from Indiana, did a spoof interview of Fox News with "Ronald Dumbsfield," using a musical version of a recent Donald Rumsfeld's speech. Cliff told a story of peace-making in Gaza. Shane juggled, did a back flip, and walked on his hands. Charlie did some comic ad-libbing. Jerry gave humorous tips about how peace activists could get along in prison, several of us did a silly rendition of the "Saga of Little Nell," and we had refreshments. We needed that!

That evening, all over the world, there was a wave of candlelight vigils following the dusk westward around the world. This involved an estimated one million people in more than six thousand gatherings in 130 countries and in every US state.

The next day, some of us attended a four-hour time of prayer for peace at the Evangelical Presbyterian Church. Luma was there again and translated as different ones fervently asked for God to stop this war, to be very present with the Iraqi people, and for strength and courage. "God of grace and God of glory, on thy people pour thy power." The words of the old hymn ran through my mind. "Cure thy children's warring madness, bend our pride to thy control. . . . Grant us wisdom, grant us courage, for the facing of this hour."

~ ~ ~

In the midst of the doom and gloom we were hearing daily and the increased tension and fear permeating Iraqi society, we continued to relate as much as possible to the Iraqi people. In these contacts, I experienced joyful, loving moments that helped to keep me from getting completely weighed down by the fear and dread of war.

I had an especially joyful morning with the children at the orphanage. Amil and Quar-Quar, two of the children, began playing a game with me. They would roll over and over away from me, saying, "Bye-bye, Peggy," and then roll back saying, "Hi, Peggy!" For a long time we greeted each other that way, expressing our delight in being together. At that moment this experience was more important to us than any fear of war.

On another day, I took a turn going with the team's group of volunteers to take arts and crafts materials to the cancer ward of the Al Mansour Children's Hospital. Others in IPT had set this up and had been going there regularly, but I had not gone yet because of my work at the orphanage.

An interpreter went with us to help us talk with the mothers of the sick children, but I ended up in a different room and needed to rely on the little bit of Arabic I knew. We spent time with the six to eight children in the wards, giving them paper and crayons for coloring, cutting out paper doll chains, helping them cut and glue paper chains together, or whatever they wanted to do with the materials we had brought along.

At one point that morning, an Albanian TV reporter came in and started taking pictures of the children and their mothers and interviewed me for five minutes. The mothers were shocked to hear that we planned to stay in Iraq even during a war. "Aren't you afraid?" the reporter asked. "Yes, I am especially afraid for the Iraqi people," I responded.

~ ~ ~

At a team meeting on Monday, March 17, while we began to discuss human rights monitoring forms we might use during wartime to report abuses, we got the word that Bush was about to declare war. He gave Saddam a forty-eight-hour ultimatum: resign and leave the country with his sons or the coalition would come in and begin the war. UN inspectors were told to leave the country.

This raised a lot of fears in us and the Iraqi people. Everywhere we went, people were tense. After a team session on emergency first aid, a group of us (Neville; Lisa Martens, a full time CPTer from Winnipeg who came to Iraq in early February; our driver, Muhammad; and I) visited Siham's family. Siham served us a special meal, but the joy of being together was coupled with an underlying sense of heaviness.

Fifteen-year-old Samir asked if we were going home. I said, "No, not now, at least." He told Lisa, Neville, and me that he thought we should go home because it would be dangerous here, and he didn't want anything bad happening to us. But Lisa responded that it isn't any more dangerous for us than for them. Yet we were touched by his concern for our safety. I thought it might be our last time to eat with them.

Meal at Siham's before the bombing started in Baghdad.

The day's events stirred up my fears and uncertainties again, and I shared this with Betty Scholten, a CPTer from Maryland who stayed on after the last CPT delegation, and Cliff. Cliff reminded us that worst-case scenarios are usually given before a war to scare the people, and he urged us not to make decisions under pressure. We talked about the possible roles we might play, such as being eyewitnesses and helping and comforting people, or confronting the military powers nonviolently somehow.

I sent off a letter to the editor of the *Athens Messenger* back home (though it was not printed):

> I write this from Baghdad, a city of five million people, as it braces itself to be leveled by massive carpet-bombing. I hear our President say once more that he intends to go ahead with war no matter what the UN or people of the world think or do.
>
> I have not lost faith in the American people, who, if they had the same opportunity to walk the streets of Baghdad and personally meet the people, as I have had the privilege to do, and really understood the situation here, would be repulsed by such an attack. I wish every American could have experienced, as I have, the graciousness and openness of the people, how much they are just like us, and how they have suffered and will suffer if Bush proceeds with his plans. They would not begin to tolerate this war.
>
> So what do I have to say on the eve of a possible massacre? My first call continues to be to do all we can to prevent this disaster from happening. But there is more.
>
> I want the American people to not give in to the propaganda war that Bush has been waging, and to realize that there is no actual evidence, at this point, that Iraq even has weapons of mass destruction (WMD). Even if they were discovered tomorrow, there has been no evidence that Iraq is capable of using them or has any intention to use them. Since the summer of 1990, Iraq has not threatened or demonstrated any threat toward its immediate neighbors, Israel or other Middle Eastern countries, or the United States. We are talking about the most powerful country in the world, with huge stocks of WMD, who has not only threatened to use it, but has in the past, now bullying and threatening to destroy a country that is almost defenseless.
>
> Bush talks about "liberating" the people of Iraq. It's not hard to make a case that there is repression or a lack of freedom here. But there is no way that killing and maiming thousands of people, destroying the infrastructure and the very society they live in,

polluting the land with tons of depleted uranium, as in the last war, which will last for billions of years and continue to produce epidemics of malignancies and birth defects in the generations to come, provoking civil unrest and chaos, will bring liberation. After all the destruction we have caused in Afghanistan, there is no evidence of liberation there.

We liberate by building up, not tearing down, giving people the opportunity to live normal healthy lives, to treat them with dignity, not humiliation, to offer them opportunities for education, meaningful employment, by giving them hope, not a legacy of despair and desire for revenge.

Preventing this war is also crucial for the whole world. This is just the first step for the Bush administration to proceed with military intervention and economic control with other countries, which do not capitulate to its demands. This means not only more suffering and oppression for these peoples, but also the loss of the greatness and soul of our nation.

I am grateful that so many of you have courageously spoken and acted for peace. The time has come now for more than ordinary action, but for all caring Americans to put ourselves to blocking the way of this war effort, to stop "business as usual," to make our voice heard. The lives and future of billions of people around the world depend on it.

~ ~ ~

Tuesday, March 18, was harder. I got a call from my son, Dale, and his wife, Debbie. It was wonderful and encouraging to talk with them, but it also brought up a lot of grief and fears about possible separation from them, and I cried. In our worship time, Lisa read from Hebrews about faith being about what we don't see, and from Romans 8, about nothing separating us from the love of God. That was helpful, but all day I was on a roller coaster of feelings.

I went to the orphanage to help feed the children, and I gave pictures I had previously taken to the bakery and construction crew near the Al Dar. Everywhere people seemed depressed, worried, and tense, and they all talked about the war starting.

The whole team was called over to the Al Fanar Hotel for a meeting with Wada and Zeid. Wada told us that our team needed to pare down and some go home. Kathy did a good job of defending the value of having more of us here. After they left, she told the group to let it ride unless anyone had doubts; if they did, however, they should consider leaving right then. She emphasized how important it was that we not feel it is any dishonor to leave, that it is just as important to be back home working for peace from that end. Two team members decided to leave and made immediate travel arrangements.

When many of us returned to the Al Dar that evening, we gathered in Cliff and Scott's room. Needing a little reinforcement of my earlier decision, I asked others to share why they felt it was important to stay. The deep conversation we had was very encouraging to me. Once more I felt clarity that I should stay.

After that, Randy Ludlow, a newspaper reporter from the *Columbus* (Ohio) *Dispatch*, called and interviewed me. I also had a phone interview with a woman at the *Cincinnati Enquirer*. I talked about my plans, about my feelings at that time, and about how the Iraqi people were facing war.

I woke up Wednesday morning feeling a lot of grief, plagued with doubts, mostly worrying about what my family back home might be feeling about me staying, and wanting to be with them. It helped to talk with others in our group.

Later I called Art and talked with him on the phone. It helped so much to talk about it with him and hear him voice his love and concern for me, as well as his support for whatever I decided to do. We were both crying as we said what might be our final good-bye—just in case. But after that talk, I felt stronger, more peaceful, and committed to staying on.

We then heard that Saddam Hussein had rejected Bush's ultimatum ordering him to leave the country or face war by 4:30 Thursday morning. Our whole team met, and then went out and had a vigil around the new "flying carpet" sculpture near the Palestine Hotel. Some of the street children and shoeshine boys we knew joined us.

About eight of us made plans to go out to the children's hospital, pitch two tents, and sleep in them during the nights of bombing. If it let up during the day, we would try to help where we could, walk around the neighborhood, and check in on families and the water plant. Our new minder, Moussa, assigned to those at the Al Dar because of our distance from the Al Fanar, helped us work it out.

We got all our gear together to move out to set up our tent encampment that afternoon, when Wada and Zeid told us that we couldn't sleep on the hospital grounds, but could at the Al Wathba water plant. And we couldn't go today, but the next morning. So we returned to the Al Dar, hoping for a peaceful night.

CHAPTER 7

Bombing

If you stand before the power of hell, and death is at your side,
know that I am with you through it all. Be not afraid, I go before
you always.

—Bob Dufford

"The bombing could start tonight! There are US war planes in the sky over Baghdad!" called Cliff as he knocked on our door at 2:30 a.m., Thursday, March 20, and woke us up. We had dreaded to hear these words, but now it was really happening.

With heavy hearts we began carrying our bedding and crash kits down to the two shelter rooms on the first floor, made our beds using mats stacked in a corner, and tried to go back to sleep.

We had already planned earlier that evening to get up at 4:00 a.m. for our group prayers, knowing the possibility of war starting that morning or in the coming day. So at four, after a half-hour of sleep, I was awakened again. Jerry, realizing that bombs could start falling at any time, led our small group of six in a time of worship. We vocally reaffirmed our commitment to follow Jesus and to give our lives out of love for our brothers and sisters, even if that meant our own death.

Once again we straggled to our mats to try to sleep.

The first bomb blast came at 5:35 a.m., followed by many more. They sounded farther away, not close to our hotel. But then closer by, we heard what sounded like rapid shooting or fireworks. Later we found out that was the shooting of Iraqi anti-aircraft missiles aimed at US warplanes.

Lying in bed, in the darkness, hearing the booming sounds, I wept. Tears of grief and dread that had been building up in me in those months leading up to that night came pouring out. Images of Baghdad and other cities in Iraq burning or being leveled, of the mothers wailing uncontrollably as they see their children engulfed in collapsed buildings, of depleted uranium, invisible, but deadly over time, showered on population centers—all swirled before my mind's eye.

We had spent months there, saying the very obvious truths about the horror of war and about the people of Iraq and their right to live, and trying to expose the lies our government had been telling to justify this horrible act of aggression. I wished that people in the US could have seen beyond the smoke screen of fear fanned by Bush so he could continue his acts of aggression around the world in the guise of "the war on terror." At a time like this, all the right, religiously correct answers fall away, and for a time, you feel only the helplessness, anguish, and pain. Is God still here in this darkness?

The war was here now. I couldn't hold it back. What would happen now? What would we do in the midst of it? What kind of hope could we have as we tried to do it? There's not much I could do but to claim and rest in God's love, knowing God *was* there. In fact, this was exactly where a God who cares for all who suffer war *would* be.

The bombing came in three waves, stopping at about 7:00 a.m. It was scary, but my dominant feeling was grief, thinking of all the people of Iraq who could be killed or maimed. How much more suffering must they go through? I couldn't believe my country would actually do this.

Later in the morning we heard that the main targets were Iraqi military command centers and places the US military believed Saddam Hussein to be. But we knew Saddam had not been killed when he appeared on Iraqi TV, announcing that Iraq would stand up against the US air strikes.

On the streets we were thankful not to see any damage around our area, but we knew there would be more to come. My grief became heavier throughout the day, as the reality settled in.

Phone calls started to come in from the US and Canada, from CPT support persons, but also from the media. We heard that all over the US and Canada thousands of people were out on the streets protesting this war, many doing civil disobedience to make a strong statement. In my hometown, thirty-nine were arrested in such an action, including Art and many of my friends.

In a quick meeting, we decided that Lisa and Scott, full-time CPTer from Downers Grove, Illinois, who had come in early February, would stay at the Al Dar and respond to phone calls, while Betty, Cliff, and I would go with the other IPTers to the Al Wathba water plant in northeast Baghdad, near the Saddam Hospital complex, to set up our tent camp.

While Cliff and the others gathered equipment and prepared for going to the plant, Betty and I took the chance to go to the orphanage and check how they had fared the night. The streets were deserted, except for a couple of men and a group of school boys who had ventured out to play soccer. At the orphanage none of the usual Iraqi volunteers had come to help, so we spent the next hour and half playing with the handicapped children on a large mat in the crib room.

Cliff and Moussa, the minder newly assigned to those living at the Al Dar, picked us up in a taxi and took us to the water

Peace Tent Encampment at the Al Wathba water treatment plant in Baghdad, March 20, 2003.

plant. Seven team members put up two tents, the larger for the men and the smaller, three-person one for the women. In the grassy space between the tents and near the "tree of life," we strung a rope where we hung our large, plastic-coated pictures of Iraqi people and the large Iraq Peace Team banner. Nearby was the "To Bomb This Site Is a War Crime" banner, put up a month earlier. This became our Peace Tent Encampment.

We camped out for several reasons. First, it was a symbolic statement about the vulnerability of the Iraqi people. Out there we were in not much more danger than the Iraqis in their homes. We were also there to accompany this neighborhood, which included the water plant, the twelve hospitals in the medical complex next to it directly serviced by this plant, and the families who lived around us.

It was a full afternoon. Our time was first spent talking with plant workers and small groups of other IPTers who came out to visit us. We walked around the neighborhood and visited families living nearby. We went to the Al Mansour children's hospital and talked with Director Murtada Hassan, who told us there were very few children in the hospital anymore. After the morning's bombing, mothers who had been staying with their sick children took the children home, wanting to be with all of their children and family during the war. He predicted that most of those children taken home would soon die.

It seemed all the more tragic that, after all the people had gone through and suffered over the past years of the first Gulf War and economic sanctions, we would bomb them again. Kathy said yesterday, "We kept the sanctions going so we didn't need to bomb them. Now we bomb them to end the sanctions."

That evening, the workers at the plant brought a TV set to the small, block shelter building near our tents. On an Al Jazeera news broadcast we saw pictures of the sky over Baghdad, showing the flashes of lights of the jet bombers releasing bombs. It was horrible to watch and to think about. Was this the "shock and awe" Bush had promised? We didn't know what would happen that night.

We spent some time in worship, asking God to bless our camp and work there. Shane Claiborn, from Philadelphia, paraphrased several verses from Psalm 37:

Trust in Yahweh and do what is good. Make your home in the land and live in peace . . . not worrying about men who make their fortunes, about men who scheme to bring the poor and needy down. . . .

A little longer, and the wicked will be no more, but the humble shall have a land for their own to enjoy untroubled peace.

And from Exodus 13, we read about God leading the children of Israel through the wilderness with a cloud by day and a pillar of fire by night. Truly, God will be with the Iraqi people. We read from Isaiah about the vision of a new kingdom of peace. We prayed for God to block and end this war, for the Iraqi people and those protesting back home, and for God to lead us.

Before settling in for our first night, we signed up for two-hour shifts of being on "watch" through the night. The person on watch would wake the others if it looked like the bombing was getting close. People would then have the option of going inside the block building nearby. Some decided to put ear plugs in their ears to protect their eardrums in case of very loud blasts.

At 8:45 p.m., the first air-raid siren went off, and we soon saw white and red flashes in the sky (Iraqi anti-aircraft missiles exploding). We stood by our tents, watching, while we heard bombs exploding in the distance. Eun Ha Yoo from South Korea, Betty, and I crawled under our blankets in the women's tent and tried to sleep. Until 11:30 there were two more sirens, followed by bombing attacks. I woke up a lot, but I was thankful it was quiet the rest of the night. Meanwhile Scott, Lisa, and Stewart Vriesinga, another full-time CPTer from Ontario, who had come in late February, were at the Al Dar and other IPTers were at the Al Fanar and Andalus taking shifts answering the phone and responding to interviews.

The following day, Friday, March 21, several of our group went by taxi through semi-deserted streets into central Baghdad to see other IPTers at the three hotels. Team members told us there had been a huge explosion that night across the Tigris River, probably at one of Saddam's palaces, which shook the buildings and was frightening for the people in the whole area. Throughout this and other days of bombing, we would hear occasional blasts during daylight hours.

News reports indicated that at least thirty-seven Iraqis and forty Americans were killed in Baghdad on the first day of bombing. We also heard that US and British soldiers, coming in from Kuwait, were close to Basra and would soon be progressing northward toward Baghdad. Articles we read from the US media on the Internet said that so far the bombing was just a small beginning, hoping to prompt Saddam to give up or the Iraqi people to rise against him, and that if neither happened, the bombing would be more massive.

Over the past two months we had heard reports about different US battle plans ranging from using nuclear or chemical weapons to bombing Baghdad "flat." We didn't know what "shock and awe" would be if and when it would come. And we didn't know how Iraqis would respond, whether there would be an uprising against Saddam, civil war, or a long and hard siege of Baghdad, with bloody battles. We could only pray for the strength to be given to deal with whatever came.

Betty, Jerry, and I went back to the orphanage and helped for an hour. They helped feed the children, while I helped the sisters with the laundry, all washed and rinsed by hand in large sinks. After rinsing and wringing the clothes, we carried them onto the roof and hung them out on long lines. Before we left, I spent time greeting each child personally, never knowing when or if I would see them again. Their smiles and expressions of love were precious gifts in that precarious time.

Other IPTers, who had stayed at the water plant while we were gone, walked over to the nearby Hadeed Bridge, where they prayed and talked to Iraqi soldiers stationed there. When we returned, we took another walk. This time we were invited into a neighbor's home and then into the Lebanese embassy a block away, where remaining staff offered their help if we needed it.

Walking on to the hospital complex, we went to the Specialties and Surgery Hospital and talked with the director and staff, asking if we could be of help. They had just dismissed all the patients who weren't in critical condition, so they still had a floor of patients they had moved down to the ground level. They had plenty of staff and weren't expecting the wounded from the war to be brought there.

During our evening meeting we discussed who would stay

on at the camp. A few of us said we would stay during the bombing, but when the invasion came we wanted to be back at the Al Dar to relate to neighbors and possibly be a nonviolent presence on the streets. We didn't know when US troops would reach Baghdad.

At about 8:20 p.m., bombing interrupted a first-aid briefing being made by Martin Edwards, a newer member of IPT from California. We could see the sky light up from explosions, mostly south and west of us. One blast was louder, and we figured it might be a half-mile away. Then for about fifteen minutes it seemed that planes were flying over us and Iraqi inter-aircraft missiles were shooting, so we moved to the side of the building under the overhang of the roof and away from the windows in case any shrapnel would fall from the sky.

One amazing gift that night and during bombings in the days ahead was that soon after each bombing started, we would hear Muslim leaders chanting, *"Allah Akbar!"* translated literally, "God is greater" or "God is greatest," and the words of the call to prayer from mosques all over the city. They were calling people to trust and praise God even in these circumstances, defying the fear and horror of what was going on.

When the bombing quieted, we gathered in the shelter building and sang. As we finished, we got a call from Kathy saying that everyone at the three hotels was okay, though those at the Al Fanar saw fire across the river from their windows.

Once the others had settled in the tents for the night, I was on the first shift of the watch. I drank in the quiet, the calm, and gathered strength for the night.

As I crawled into bed at the end of my watch, the air-raid siren went off and sent a wave of adrenalin through my body, a mixture of fear and dread, so I had a hard time going to sleep. Just as I would relax, another siren or wave of bombs would come. Sleep finally came at about one in the morning, with loud interruptions stopping around seven. "How were the millions of Iraqis dealing with this?" I wondered.

I got up feeling very tired and heavy with grief. In our time of worship, I realized I was carrying a load of grief and anger. I shared this with the others and let the tears flow. This was helpful.

Driving into central Baghdad on the morning of Saturday,

March 22, we saw increased Iraqi military presence on the streets. There were soldiers, groups of militia, and sandbagged forts on street corners, preparing for an invasion. We saw several bombed-out and burning buildings along the way. Throughout the day there were clouds of black smoke all over the city, from the buildings burning but also from oil fires set in trenches around the city to make it hard for US aircraft to operate.

The larger IPT group met in the hallway of the Al Fanar, sharing and discussing plans. Later at the Al Dar, our affinity group met and decided Stewart and I would return to the Al Wathba peace encampment that night, while Betty and Cliff stayed at the Al Dar. We also heard that the CPT delegation was in Amman, trying to get visas to come into Iraq. We were concerned about the dangers of trying to travel by car from Jordan to Iraq during the bombing, knowing that there had been vehicles bombed along the roads in the past few days. But we also thought it was unlikely that they would even get in. We decided to welcome them, if they, knowing the dangers, still decided to try, so we asked Wada to do what he could to get the visas approved. That was the last time we saw him until after the invasion.

Three new team members came to our camp that night, increasing the number to nine. We ate and sang together, and visited with Iraqi workers before settling in. Off and on throughout the night there was bombing, with one very loud blast fairly close by.

On Sunday morning, March 23, after our time of worship, some of our group went to the Al Fanar for a meeting with Zeid, now our primary minder, who told us that we would be able to continue with our activities, with the same freedom of choice, but that the higher-ups in the Foreign Ministry will be considering us "human shields." We wouldn't need to call or consider ourselves that, he said, but they needed to do this in order to justify keeping us internationals, mostly Americans, in wartime. If we didn't agree, we would need to leave.

To us this meant the possibility of more restrictions on our movement and being told where to go in our work. We were disturbed by this, and many said they wouldn't be able to stay under the new circumstances. Others thought they could live with it if it didn't really change who we were and what we did. We left the meeting with some feelings of turmoil.

Most of our IPT group went with two of our minders to the Al Yarmouk Hospital, where about two hundred of the injured from the bombing had been taken. We were able to mill around the wards and talk with the patients, when possible, and their families. In some cases the doctor accompanying us gave us a description of their injuries and the situation of the attack. A couple of team members took pictures, trying to be careful not to be too intrusive. Later, after our visits to hospitals or bombed sites, we pooled our information and wrote careful reports, which we sent back to our organizational offices to send as listservs and to send to North American and international media services.

What we saw was heart-wrenching: men, women, and children severely injured from shrapnel, requiring surgery. Twelve-year-old Sa'ad Hassan had a hole in his abdomen about the size of a grapefruit, through which we could see his intestines. Twelve members of his household were in that hospital because a bomb had exploded in front of their house. A five-year-old girl with injury to her spinal column was likely paralyzed. Seeing them made the effects of the bombings more real and horrible.

On one of our visits to the hospital, an eighteen-year-old wounded man expressed what we believed to be the dominant sentiment of the Iraqi people: "What kind of liberation is this that kills our people? This is not liberation; this is aggression! If this is democracy, we don't want it."

Our affinity group at the Al Dar met and agreed that we would try to work at particular locations in small groups, but never alone. I said that I was willing to come back and stay at the Al Dar but preferred being out at the tent camp. There were three reasons. First, in central Baghdad, around the hotels, there was heavier air pollution from burning oil, causing me more allergy problems. Second, as strange as it might seem to others, I felt safer outdoors (with the possibility of the shelter building nearby), than being in a three-story hotel building, which could cave in during bombing. And, third, at the water plant we were out among the grass, trees, and birds, which fed my spirit.

On our way back to the camp, we saw more buildings bombed and burning. Our taxi driver told us a US plane had gone down in the Tigris River not far from us. We drove to the place, saw a crowd of people, but could no longer see the plane.

That night I slept better, going back to sleep after the waves of bombing. I got up at six the next morning, Monday, March 24, to be on the last "watch" of the night. We had planned to have our group worship at eight and meeting at half past, so we could leave at nine. But when the time came, no one came, so I had extra time alone.

Quickly, I realized how frustrated I was becoming with the insensitivity and poor group participation of one person in the peace camp group. It was extremely difficult trying to talk through issues and make decisions. This was harder because we were all under a lot of stress. I had to spend the rest of the time praying about and dealing with my own negative spirit. Later I talked to the person and apologized to the whole group for the way I had expressed my frustrations.

At our IPT meeting at the Al Fanar, Zeid asked us to sign up for what our main activities during that stage of the war would be: (1) maintaining the peace camp, (2) visiting the trauma hospital, and (3) going out to document and report on civilian bombing sites. He okayed a few of us continuing to go and volunteer at the orphanage. He clarified that the Foreign Ministry didn't consider us human shields and we wouldn't be treated as such. It seemed as if they were backing down on what he had told us the day before. Many of our group still went away feeling concerned, because he said he wanted us to go around Baghdad only when accompanied by a minder.

When Betty and I went to the orphanage, a new minder, Omar, took us there in a taxi and waited outside to take us back to the Al Dar when we were done. This felt uncomfortable. Omar, a soft-spoken, friendly man, said the Iraqis would be afraid for our safety if we walked alone on the streets. Later, Cliff, Scott, and Lisa talked with him about this, and he seemed more open to giving us more freedom around our own neighborhood.

In our affinity group we shared together how we were feeling and discussed how far we would be willing to be restricted, or "minded." Was there a time we would refuse to cooperate?

As we talked about the peace camp, it became clear to me that with the current dynamics among the group there, I didn't feel the emotional energy to stay and work in that situation. I was feeling drained and was not getting spiritually fed and supported there. And in order to make decisions in a future difficult situation, I would want more unity. So I decided to stay at the Al Dar for this kind of support, which was more important to me than my location. Stewart decided to return to the peace encampment that night, and Lisa and Scott decided to move to the Al Fanar, leaving only Betty, Cliff, and me at the Al Dar.

That day was the anniversary of Archbishop Oscar Romero's murder in El Salvador in 1980 for defending justice for the poor. Betty led us in our time of worship that evening, during which we took turns reading some of Romero's words. Our time of singing and prayer was interrupted by international media interview phone calls, but it was renewing for me to worship again with a more unified team. I felt increasingly more peaceful and re-centered. We each took another interview call or two before settling in the sheltered area for the night.

Between 11:00 and 12:30 in the night, there was about an hour of heavy and loud bombing, the longest, most intense bombing I had experienced so far. I slept better the rest of the night, which was more peaceful.

No minder showed up the next morning, Tuesday, March 25, so we walked over to the Andalus for an early-morning IPT meeting. It was good to be out on the streets of the Karrada neighborhood, greeting people and not being "minded."

Betty and I went to the orphanage, where the Papal Nuncio (ambassador to Iraq from the Vatican), the Chaldean archbishop, and another bishop came to briefly check on the sisters and the children. We helped feed the children and spent time talking with the sisters about what we had been seeing and experiencing in the days of bombing.

Walking back to the Al Dar by way of Karrada Street, we greeted people we knew and stopped and bought fruit and vegetables at the small market. About ninety-five percent of the shops were closed, but we were surprised to see more cars and people on the streets. It seemed people were getting used to the bombings and feeling more comfortable going out in the daytime.

During the rest of the day a *shargi* was building up, so it was nice to stay indoors. At about 4:30 p.m. we were amazed to find that the CPT delegation of nine had arrived at the Al Dar. We really hadn't thought they would make it, so we were very thankful for their safe arrival. Betty and I made a big pot of soup for supper.

That evening the delegation shared the story of their harrowing experience. They had arrived in Amman on Wednesday, March 19, still hoping war would be adverted. But the next morning they woke to scenes on Al Jazeera and CNN TV of Baghdad burning. After consulting with others and praying together, the group decided to stay and keep trying to get visas. If that continued to be blocked, they would go to Hebron instead. Finally, four days later, they were given visas, and at about 2:30 the next morning they left Amman in two vans and headed for Iraq.

Along the way they saw a number of burnt-out vehicles and a couple of bombed overpass bridges. At 2:00 p.m., west of Ramadi, the delegation saw a burning car ahead on the right shoulder of the road. After the smoke cleared, they saw four Iraqi soldiers in the road with their guns on the ground and their hands in the air. A unit of US troops was on the hill about twenty yards above the road. Their machine guns and the barrels of their armored personnel carriers were pointed at the delegation's vehicles. The troops motioned for the team to stop. Then the troops hastily waved them to move on. Delegates in the rear van looked back to see that the Iraqi soldiers were running toward them, trying to jump onto their vehicle. They were within a few feet when the driver realized what was happening and sped away. They had no more problems as they drove into Baghdad.

Now that they were in Iraq, they would join the team as it visited bombed sites and the trauma hospitals.

That night there were about two waves of bombing, but nothing close. I slept through the four or five o'clock bombing that others heard.

After an IPT meeting on the morning of Wednesday, March 26, I waited to go with a group to see bombed sites, but ended up dropping out when too many wanted to go. So I went with Charlie to the orphanage, arriving in time to help feed the children. Then back at the hotel, some of us met to discuss what we might do during a time of invasion.

By this time another *shargi* was well underway. But this time the color of the air went back and forth all afternoon between a bright orange to an eerie red. Many Iraqis told us this was very rare. Others said they had never seen anything like it. To us it seemed like an act of God. It was as though God was expressing outrage at the bombing and trying to clog up the war machine. It did not stop the war, but it slowed down ground troop operations and movement for the second day in a row.

At 4:00 it was time to take the delegates over to the Andalus to meet the larger IPT group, but it started raining, and it was raining mud! It took longer than usual to get taxi drivers willing to come to take everyone over.

After supper all the CPTers met together, had a check-in time to see how each person was doing, and then talked about possible activities. Then I met with a subgroup to plan for actions in which we would go to sites where civilians had died from the bombing and hold a simple service of mourning.

It was my turn to talk with Doug Pritchard, CPT staff

Bombed and burned buildngs at the Al Shaab commercial district in Baghdad, March 27, 2003.

person from the Toronto office, when he made his nightly call since the bombing started. He shared news and greetings. I felt encouraged by that as I went to bed. I ended up sleeping down in the sheltered area again, because loud bombing started just as I was going to bed.

The next morning, Thursday, March 27, after our time of worship, team members went to the IPT meeting with Zeid. Others there liked our suggestion of memorial services for bombing victims. Zeid said it would be okay if it were not an extra trip requiring a minder, but done at the same time as a documenting visit to a bombed site.

After the meeting most of the team divided up and went to visit hospitals or bombed sites. The group I was in visited the Al Shaab commercial and residential district in North Baghdad, where the day before two missiles had exploded, one on each side of the four-lane divided street. We saw the two craters, about three feet deep and six feet in diameter. The missiles exploded out horizontally, damaging at least fifteen cars in the street and buildings for a block-long stretch on both sides of the street. Thirty-five were killed and fifty were injured, all civilians. We saw twisted metal in destroyed storefronts, mangled cars along the street, and burned-out residential houses.

Sala Myeed, a civil engineer living in the neighborhood who was present at the time of the blasts, told us of a pregnant woman who was burned to death in her second-floor apartment. Marwan Nasweer, a medical student living in the next block along that street, told of two men who were killed while working in an electrical shop. Abu Hassan, forty-five, and father of five; Manikit Hamoud, seventeen; and Saliah Nouri, twenty-eight, were killed as they were working in a restaurant. Also mentioned were thirty-six-year-old Sarif Albari and his eleven-year-old son, Safe, killed in a car repair shop, and three killed in a car: seventeen-year-old Safah Issan, twelve-year-old Marwan, and their father, who was driving.

Some of the men in the crowd around the site began to express a lot of anger toward America and Britain to us. One man pointed to his shoe and pretended to stomp on George Bush. They never directed their anger at us personally as Americans. I have been constantly amazed at the genuine graciousness and goodwill that lies under any anger Iraqis have, which allows them to welcome and be respectful to us and to see us as their friends, even in the midst of war.

Our minders took us to the home of the Abdulla Hamad Hassarri family in the Al Tujjaar district, also in northern Baghdad. We could see damage to windows of the Balquis Secondary School for girls next door as well as bomb damage to this home. The father, Moneed, twenty-five, his wife, Sahar, twenty-three, and their six-year-old son, Quiser Muhweb, were injured while sitting on a floor mat watching TV. We saw the bloodstained mat. After our visit, one of our team went to the Al Nooman Hospital and found the injured. Moneed's leg injuries were very serious and the doctors thought amputation might be required. Both mother and son had broken bones.

In examining the damage to the walls of the first and second floor of the house, we concluded that a fragmentation bomb had exploded about eight feet above the roof patio, sprayed uniform, cubed metal pellets into the walls (which we picked out), and propelled shrapnel and broken glass that hit the family. This was evidence of anti-personnel weapons, whose purpose is to maim civilians, a war crime. Later, when we talked to a doctor in one of the trauma hospitals, he showed us X-rays of a girl who had scores of these kinds of pellets throughout her body. He had already treated about forty such cases.

After the visits, several of our team shared our notes and I wrote a report of each of the situations we had seen. Team members April Hurley, a physician, and Doug Johnson, a postal worker from Louisville, Kentucky, spent several nights in the Al Kindi Hospital, helping in the emergency room as the wounded were brought in; they also wrote reports about what they saw. Our offices in Chicago sent these reports out widely to the media, but very few used them.

I still had some time before supper, so I found Muhammad, one of our designated taxi drivers, and had him take me over to see Siham, Abbas, and their four boys. It was so good to see them after more than a week. I talked at length with fifteen-year-old Samir, who went into a short speech about the war. At one point he asked, "Why does Bush want to kill us?" While we talked we heard several bombs explode in the distance.

When the boys were in the room, they expressed a macho attitude and said how strong Iraqi people are, but when Siham and I were alone, she shared that when awakened in the night by the bombs, the boys sometimes ran to their parents, crying. She shared some of her fears and grief, and we cried together.

Siham questioned me about my family and whether I should stay on during the war. Before I left, the family expressed their fear for me and others on our team. They were concerned not only about the dangers of the bombs, but that Iraqi people might take out their anger against the US on us.

Back at the Al Dar that evening, we were a smaller group, because Zeid required all but three of the delegation to move to the Al Fanar. As soon as other rooms opened there, he wanted the rest to move too.

The next day was a beautiful, sunny, cool day, but the Iraqis set off petroleum fires around the city again, so there was more black smoke.

It was 11:20 p.m. when a series of loud explosions shook the building. The eighth night of bombing had begun. Feeling an initial surge of fear, we woke from our sleep. Most of us grabbed our crash kits and wandered down to the sheltered area. Others stayed upstairs and tried to go back to sleep in their rooms. Like the Iraqi people, we were becoming accustomed to the reality of war.

CHAPTER 8

Kicked Out

Suddenly, at seven in the morning there was a loud boom that shook our hotel. We felt shaken as well! We knew that this bomb had hit close by.

Soon we heard from Iraqi friends that the telecommunications building on Sadoon Street about four blocks away from the Al Dar had been hit.

After breakfast we had an IPT meeting to go to at the Al Fanar. Six of us from CPT waited for our designated taxi drivers to take us there, but they didn't come. We couldn't call the Al Fanar and ask for a taxi to come, because now the phone lines were dead, so we decided to walk. We were joined by two Japanese journalists also staying at our hotel, Takashi Morigumi, who had produced a book about the victims of depleted uranium (DU) called *Children of the Gulf War*, and Kohsuke Shirai.

As we were getting ready to leave, we decided to walk near the bombed site on our way. It wasn't far off our path, and we wanted to take a quick look. In the past few days our minders had not been strict about us walking around our home areas without official accompaniment. Two days earlier, two IPTers had been detained, reprimanded for being out unaccompanied at a party, and told they would need to leave the country, but that had been in the evening. Also we thought it would be okay to keep pushing the limits, as CPT does in many other projects. We didn't want to get ourselves locked into too many restrictions on our movement and be confined to our hotels.

We walked down Karrada Street to the Karamana Square, where we saw some police. We gave them a magic sheet, and

133

asked if it was okay for us to walk over to look at the bombed building. They confirmed where it was and waved us on. We took a sharp right turn and walked about two blocks. When we were about a half-block away, we could see the damaged building on the opposite side of the street. Its outer walls were still mostly standing and the communications tower was still up, but the roof and the interior were completely destroyed.

We also noticed that the blast had broken and blown out many windows, some of them stained glass, of a nearby hotel-restaurant. The manager, standing in the door, was upset and urged us to come in to see what had happened. Once inside, Cliff videotaped some of the damage, and others took pictures. As we were leaving, the manager wanted Cliff to also film the damage on the outside of the building.

As we were saying good-bye, a police car stopped and an officer questioned us. We showed them our magic sheet and explained what we were doing. It seemed that we were going to be allowed to go, when another police car arrived with an officer of higher rank. He told us we had to go with them to the police station. There they took our names and passport numbers three times and looked at the video footage Cliff took. They suspected that we had filmed the destroyed communications building, but we had only taken pictures of the restaurant.

The officers were friendly and gave us water and dates, and we talked with them in our broken Arabic and their broken English as we waited. We couldn't call our team or Zeid because phones weren't working, but we asked the officers to contact them. To pass the time and not get bogged down in anxiety or frustration, our detained group of eight sang, told stories, and checked in on how each of us was doing.

A police officer came into the room one time and searched our packs once more. He took a map of Baghdad out of Kohsuke's case and said it was a crime to have it. Another time they called Cliff out of the room and suggested to him that we could leave in three minutes if we gave them some money. Cliff didn't, but we realized that many of these accusations and stalling procedures were part of an effort to be bribed.

After almost four hours, Farouk, one of our taxi drivers, came in with Omar, our minder, and then Zeid came. He seemed very angry with us and scolded us for walking over to see this site without a minder. Even though we explained that we didn't go close to the building or take pictures of the site itself, he took everyone's cameras and all the journalists' film. He said we would each have to pay a fifty-dollar fine, took our passports and visas, and said we would all have to leave the country by four o'clock that afternoon. We protested, reminding him how dangerous it would be to travel on the highway to Jordan, especially at night. We had heard the story about sixteen Syrians killed on a bus driving to Baghdad a few days before, by US bombing.

The men drove us back to the Al Fanar, where the rest of the team greeted us with relief. Some had feared we had been kidnapped or something worse. Some expressed frustration with us for what we had done.

Kathy spoke to Zeid on our behalf and managed to persuade him to postpone our departure until the next morning. Later we found out that Zeid's home had been damaged in the bombing the night before, with his wife and son there. We heard also that, in the morning meeting we missed, Zeid had told the team that no one would now be allowed to go anywhere without a minder. We knew he was under a lot of pressure from other officials to be tough with any lack of compliance by these internationals in their midst and that he was under pressure to reduce the numbers on our team.

This was a real blow to me. I felt a mixture of grief and regret. I wasn't ready to leave. And I felt anxious about traveling in such a dangerous situation. I was also disappointed that I wouldn't be able to do many of the things I had planned: work on the writing I wanted to do, go to the Chaldean religious education school that day and give them the pictures and the rest of the supplies, and many other things. And I had prepared myself to stay on during the rest of the war. It was helpful to share and talk about this with others on the team.

After I calmed down, I talked to Zeid and told him I was sorry for what had happened to his home and also for causing him grief because of our actions. His stern manner softened, and he was personable once again.

Later he came around and told us that because Shane, and Kara Spelt, a longtime peace and justice activist from Oakland,

California, had independently decided to leave Iraq and travel out with our group, we could do a trade. Two of the other CPTers, Weldon Nisly, pastor of Seattle Mennonite Church, and possibly Betty, who had just been deported, could stay and take their place, but not Cliff or me. Zeid mainly held Cliff responsible for our actions but included me, because I had also been there longer and should have known better. He also told us it was too late to change our exit visas, but that if we wanted to wait in Amman a week and come back in, he would see that we got visas. We didn't know, however, if he really did have the ability to do that or if it would even be possible or wise. Zeid said for one thousand dollars they would return all the cameras to us. We collected that amount and paid it, though we didn't get all of the cameras back.

Omar accompanied us as we went back to the Al Dar and quickly gathered our belongings and took them to the Al Fanar, where we were supposed to sleep that night.

By the time of our larger team meeting that evening, I was packed and ready to go. It was still a little hard for me to believe what was happening. I was sad, but accepted it and realized that it might be actually the best for us.

In talking with other CPTers, we realized that some were feeling angry with us for doing something that would get us kicked out of the country without talking it through with them first and allowing them to be part of the decision-making. I spent time talking this through and tried to resolve some of the tension between us before we left.

During the larger team meeting, I spoke on behalf of those who were being forced to leave, sharing a brief version of what had happened and apologizing for the grief it had caused them and for any negative consequences it might have.

What a day it had been!

As our CPT affinity group gathered for worship the following morning, Saturday, March 29, we heard several bomb blasts. Jim Douglass read a prayer by Thomas Merton, and we prayed together for our trip and the group remaining behind.

Breakfast time was full of hugs and good-byes and last greetings to many Iraqi people as well as to people on the larger team. It was hard leaving the place and the people I had learned to love and with whom I had gone through so much in the past five months. Zeid and our other minders wished us well as we said good-bye.

~ ~ ~

At about nine we left in three cars. I was in a GMC van with Betty, Leah and Jonathan Wilson-Hartgrove, living and working with the poor in Durham, North Carolina, Kara, Michael Birmingham, a human rights advocate from Dublin, Ireland, and our Iraqi driver. Cliff, Weldon, Shane, Bae Sang Hyun, a longtime peace activist from South Korea, and their driver were in another. Takashi and Kohsuke and their driver were in the third. During some of our quiet moments of driving, I spent time silently saying good-bye to Iraq and the Iraqi people and feeling the pain of leaving.

The first part of the trip was peaceful. There were several checkpoints along the way, evidence of bombing at one of the rest areas, at two overpass bridges, and places where parts of the four- or six-lane highway had been damaged. Every so often burned or bombed vehicles appeared, and shrapnel littered the pavement.

Our driver stopped twice for gas, but both times found the stations closed. At the third stop, all three vehicles were on empty, but without electricity the gas pumps wouldn't work. A van full of creative Somali men, who had been studying in Iraq and were returning home, took the battery out of their van and hooked it to the pump. Every car there was able to fill its tank. If they had not done this we might have been stranded there for some time.

Just beyond the turn-off for the city of Al Rutba, we saw clouds of smoke rise from bombs exploding first on the left side of the road and a few minutes later on the right. Because our drivers were extremely nervous, they drove very fast, and our car, in the lead, sped ahead of the others.

About forty-five minutes later, we realized that the other two vehicles were not in sight. It took us a while to convince our driver to stop and wait for them to catch up. Only the second car in our caravan came, so we were worried. Soon the car of Somalis, who had helped us get gas, drove up, recognized us, and stopped. They said they had seen the yellow taxi, wrecked near the Rutba turn-off, stopped to look, but found no people, so they assumed they were taken to a hospital in Rutba. "Oh no! Not again!" I was afraid, but I held myself back from assuming the worst. We also felt bad that our two cars had gone so far ahead without knowing anything wrong had happened.

Our driver wanted to keep going to the border, because he was afraid of being bombed. We insisted, however, and refused to get back in the cars or go any further until we found our team members. Finally he agreed to turn around and head back. We heard jets overhead, but they didn't bomb us.

We found the wrecked taxi on its right side, stopped just before a steep drop off the side of the road. We looked in and around the car, saw that no one was there, but saw blood around the open driver's window, where we figured they had climbed out.

Our drivers took us to Rutba, where we saw several buildings that had been bombed, but no Iraqi military presence or evidence of military installations. People from the town directed us to the hospital. When we got there, we saw that it had been bombed, and the insides of the buildings had been demolished. People nearby told us this was a children's hospital that was bombed three days earlier.

So where were our men? After inquiring further, we were directed to a small medical clinic a few blocks away. Our two journalists lingered to take pictures, but we were too eager to find our team-members, so we went ahead.

When we drove up, Shane was outside watching for us, with his arm in a sling. "I knew you would come back for us!" he greeted us with enthusiasm. Quickly he told us that no one was killed or critically injured. We were so thankful to see them alive!

Inside a room with four beds, we found Cliff with his head bandaged. He had ten stitches in his scalp. Most of the blood on the car, we heard, came from him, but his injury was not critical. Sang Hyun had a small cut on his cheek and bruises. Shane had either a dislocated shoulder or a fractured upper arm. The taxi driver had some small facial cuts and an injury to his leg. Weldon had sustained back, rib, and shoulder injuries and a few stitches in a cut on his head. He seemed to be in the most pain.

Those stitched up had been given a shot of antibiotics, but the stitching was done without any anesthesia, because the clinic, as many others like it, didn't have any.

Later the men told us that the left-rear tire had blown, causing the car to swerve. The driver had lost control of the car, and it had flipped over on its side. The driver insisted that the tire had been hit by a missile and exploded. We didn't believe that was true, because there was no damage to the body of the car around the tire. We thought the tire had blown out after rolling over a piece of shrapnel. They all managed to climb out of the driver's side window, and before long an Iraqi man in a station wagon had picked them up and driven them to Rutba, even though they heard and saw jets flying overhead.

While others were helping the men get ready to leave, I talked with the doctor. He began expressing his anger and grief about the men, women, and children dying, suffering, and being terrorized by the bombs. As I listened to him, it triggered my own grief, and tears came to my eyes. He looked at me and stopped. He said, "But you are all good people."

We offered to pay for the medical care they gave, but the doctor refused it and said, "Christians, Muslims, Jews, Iraqis, or Americans . . . you are all our brothers and sisters, and we will take care of you." And this, in the midst of their town being bombed by our government.

Weldon was helped to lie down on the middle seat of the van, Cliff in the front passenger seat, and the rest of us squeezed in where we could. Betty sat on my lap in the back seat. The driver of the wrecked taxi stayed there with the agreement that our driver would pick him up on his way back from the Jordanian border. Before we left, both the taxi driver and the doctor reached down in the van and kissed Weldon on his forehead.

We stopped at the wrecked car and got all their belongings out of the car and trunk. Then we drove to the Jordanian border, another two-hour drive.

Going through the procedures to exit Iraq went smoothly. Our driver had agreed only to take us that far, but because we had injured men aboard, Iraqi authorities allowed him special permission to go further and drop us off on the Jordanian side, before turning around and heading back east.

As we asked people there about finding vehicles to drive us to Amman, a man from the International Organization of Migration (IOM) came up to us and offered to help. IOM is an organization that helps refugees or people crossing borders during wartime. He offered to take us to their camp and then get a bus to drive us to Amman.

We weren't sure what to do, but it soon was clear that we didn't have any choice. While we were waiting to go through immigration, Weldon fainted, and we laid him on the floor with his feet propped up. Border officials brought in a doctor, who quickly checked his pulse and blood pressure, which was low, and right there gave him an intravenous solution. We accepted the offer of the IOM representative to take Weldon to their camp, where a doctor would examine him and see if he needed to go to a hospital near there or be taken to Amman. We used his cell phone to call the Al Monzer Hotel in Amman to tell them we were on our way there and hoped to be there tonight.

When our border work was completed, we all got on a bus that took us to the IOM camp, a tent village where many refugee families were living temporarily. Workers there filled out data and registration forms for each of us, gave us each a sack lunch, and put us on a bus at about half past nine to go to Amman.

The doctor decided that Weldon was strong enough to withstand the drive to Amman in an IOM-provided ambulance. Jonathan went in the ambulance with Weldon to help him on the trip. Twice Weldon was transferred to a different ambulance because the first blew its engine, and the second, a tire. It was a long, painful ride for him over the bumpy roads. Once in Amman they took him to the Al Arabi Hospital, where he stayed four days.

On the bus I had a talk with Cliff, who was doing amazingly well for what he had gone through. We talked about being deported from Iraq, the accident, the team, and briefly about the past five months. Then it was helpful to rest after a long, difficult day.

We arrived at the Al Monzer Hotel at about two o'clock Sunday morning, March 30. Cliff immediately called the VITW office in Chicago, and they said they would call CPT staff to tell them we had arrived safely. Later in the morning, after a few hours of sleep, Cliff called the CPT office. We found out that different rumors had circulated around about us: our vehicles had been bombed or shot, we were all killed, seven of us had been wounded, but not killed. They had been extremely worried about us, but thankfully, had not called our families to give this information until they had something confirmed.

Rick McDowell of American Friends Service Committee (AFSC) in Amman told us that an IPT person had sent him a message through a journalist staying at the Palestine Hotel, across the street from the Al Fanar in Baghdad, that we had left Baghdad the morning before. When he heard some had been injured he called and arranged for staff of a hospital near the border to get us and take us to the hospital for care. Later he called back and didn't find us there.

We also found out that when CPT staff heard we were on our way out of Iraq, they notified the US State Department to express concern that we be allowed safe passage through battle lines. The State Department then followed the situation and maintained contact with CPT staff.

That morning, when we saw the CNN coverage of the war in Iraq on the TV in our hotel lobby, we were aghast. Everything was from the US military perspective, celebrating every successful maneuver. There was no mention of the victims of all the strikes or images of their casualties. It seemed to me like the reporting of a football game rather than war coverage, as if CNN were just keeping track of the score.

Our traveling group, minus Weldon and our Japanese and Korean friends, ate together and had a time of worship before media interviews took over our time. There were NBC, ABC, a French reporter, and others. Cliff and Shane went to the hospital to have their injuries checked and to see Weldon. Cliff had a few more stitches and his bandages looked more like a turban. Shane's X-rays indicated that his problem was a dislocated shoulder, but he still needed to wear his arm in the sling for some time. Weldon had a cracked rib and sternum and a broken thumb, and was still in a lot of pain.

I had a short respite from interviews by going to the Internet center, where I was able to send messages home and send an article for a newsletter. The rest of the day was filled with more interviews and sharing with the team over supper.

~ ~ ~

Early the next morning (Monday, March 31) CPT staff person Mark Frey called to ask how we were doing emotionally after all our recent experiences and urged us to be supporting each other and talking about what we were feeling.

At the end of our time of worship, we went around the circle and described how we were doing and what needs we were bringing into the new day. What could I say? How does one unwind from all the stress of that long and dangerous ride and near tragedy? How do I begin to put into words the jumbled mixture of extreme gratefulness, anger, and pain? You hear the bombs exploding all around you and then suddenly you are supposed to feel safe. It felt like being thrust out of a tornado.

The VITW office in Chicago called and informed us that twenty IPTers were leaving Baghdad the next morning to come to Amman. We didn't know the reasons or who was coming. They would all be in our prayers as they traveled the same dangerous road we had.

Leah, Jonathan, Kara, Shane, and Cliff were able to get a partial refund on their airline tickets with Jordanian Airlines and planned to leave the next morning. Betty and I found that the cheapest flights for us were with British Airlines, but we needed to wait until Thursday. This gave me more time to adjust to the sudden changes and to prepare for returning to the US. It would also give me time to see those who planned to come out of Iraq on Tuesday, if their trip wasn't delayed or beset with problems.

I missed the group interview with CNN, but was invited to go to their studio for an interview for their live broadcast. It lasted only three minutes, so there wasn't much time to say all I wanted to say. They were going to record a second, longer interview for later, but someone higher up canceled it.

Rick McDowell, Mary Trotochaud, and Doug Hostetter of AFSC invited our entire group to their house for a meal, along with Menno and Debra Wiebe of Mennonite Central

Committee in Amman. In the course of our conversations, Mary talked about the importance of getting help, if needed, for dealing with any trauma we must be carrying.

Before Leah, Jonathan, Cliff, Kara, and Shane left the next morning, Tuesday, April 1, for the airport, our group had a time of worship and ate breakfast together. It was sad to see them leave. During our worship, Betty read from John 15 about the vine and branches. As we had worked in Iraq together we had felt connected and empowered by God. I saw that any fruit coming from our work would be God's doing. And as we dispersed, we would still be connected by God's Spirit.

Most of the day was spent with more media interviews. I spoke on the phone for an hour with Radio China, with a Brazilian Christian news service, and in person with reporters from Croatia, Japan, and France, telling them about our experiences and what we has seen happening in Iraq.

We were disturbed to hear a rumor, reported to have originated by the Ministry of Information in Baghdad, that a group of human shields were hit by an American bomb while traveling from Baghdad to Amman. Another version of the rumor was that a group of Americans were bombed and injured near Rutba. That sounded like a twisted version of our travel story.

Mazen Jibreel, the manager of the Al Monzer Hotel, got an e-mail message for us, giving a list of fourteen who were on their way and the twelve who remained in Baghdad. All of the CPTers were on the list of those coming out of Iraq. We were relieved later when the group called from the Jordanian border, saying they were okay and were on their way to Amman.

About midnight the group of fourteen, including Jerry and Sis Levin, CPTers who have worked in Palestine and were part of this last delegation, arrived, and we went downstairs to meet them. They said they had no problems along the way; in fact, they had not even heard about our accident and adventures until they got to the Jordanian border.

They told us that in the days since we had left Baghdad, control on their movements and activities had continued to get tighter. They couldn't go anywhere without a minder, and the hospital and bombed-site visits were more restricted. They were almost confined to their hotels. Those camping at the water treatment plant couldn't walk around outside the grounds. Kathy felt the need to drastically reduce the number of the team, because they were running out of money and they didn't know if there would be a long siege of Baghdad. She suggested in a meeting that she and about six others stay and the rest leave. This was a hard and tense time for everyone.

On the morning of Wednesday, April 2, all the IPTers in Amman had a meeting together to think about different possibilities for going back into Iraq after an invasion of Baghdad. Some were considering staying and trying to do that. Others were making plans to return to the States or Canada.

Afterward all the CPTers went to the AFSC house, where Weldon was staying after being released from the hospital. After Weldon led our worship, the two different traveling-out groups told each other about their journeys.

We then moved on to more difficult ground and expressed our feelings about the incident that led to our expulsion. I invited others to communicate remaining thoughts and feelings to Betty and me, now that Cliff was gone. People were frank with their criticisms and concerns. Two people said they still felt hurt by what had happened. Betty and I listened once more and said we were sorry for how our actions affected them.

Back at the hotel, I was interviewed by a Japanese reporter, and by phone by Randy Ludlow from the *Columbus Dispatch*, a woman from National Public Radio (NPR), and Ryan Warner from a Dayton, Ohio, NPR radio station. Finally I had a chance to finish packing and say good-bye to people there.

It was late, but before we went to bed, Gene Stoltzfus, director of CPT, called to see how we were doing and asked me to consider staying in Amman with the others and trying to go back into Iraq. This was only a few hours before I was to get up to leave for the airport to catch my flight home. Yes, part of me would have wanted to return and continue my work, but I didn't feel like waiting around in Amman for another two to four weeks not knowing if we could even get back in. Now that I was out, it seemed right for me to go home. I also realized that I needed a break and that it would be good for me to report on my experiences in the US.

~ ~ ~

All kinds of feelings rushed through me. It was Thursday morning, April 3, and Betty and I were in a plane headed toward London. I had been reading newspaper articles describing the exploits of the war. I felt so horrible. How could this tragedy be reported so glibly? How could I be flying away from Iraq when all this was still happening?

It felt so wrong to leave and go back into a society that had the arrogance to go and invade another country, gloss over the destruction and killing, and pretend that it was liberating that country. I didn't want to be in this world of sham—in acquiescence to this lie. Those five months of seeing and experiencing had been too real!

But I couldn't turn the plane around and go back. I had to face what it meant to go home. Many people there were working to help our country break out of the destructive path it was taking.

At that moment I had to struggle with my own anger and grief and prepare myself to meet what might be the hardest part of the whole adventure.

In London's Heathrow airport, Betty and I talked before we got on our separate flights. We felt a similar pain about leaving Iraq, leaving our support community there and in Amman, and going back to the US. We had felt very close during the past two months in Iraq.

Going through immigration in the Boston airport was no problem. I told the officials that I had been in Iraq and answered their question truthfully about what I had been doing there. They seemed surprised, but waved me through. I could have faced serious consequences for violating the sanctions by having gone to Iraq.

The TV, with CNN covering of the war, dominated the lobby. "It is hard! It is so hard to be here now," I yelled silently, "to hear the justification for this folly, this horrible act!" No one going through what I had could defend it. It was hard to come back and hear the petty complaints, the expressions of hatred, and to see the willingness to go along with our government to sacrifice a country, a people, for our political purposes. I felt so alienated from my own society.

At the Columbus airport, Art and Trisha and several newspaper and TV reporters stood in the middle of the airport hallway, cheering for me when I came. First it was time to greet Art after five months apart, and Trisha, who had given me so much support. Then the reporters surrounded me and fired one question after another. Other people, walking by, stared as they wondered what was going on and who this was. It was overwhelming.

During the drive to Athens, I could hardly believe the beauty all around me. It was another world! It was spring in southern Ohio, with flowering trees, redbud on the hillsides, and so much green. I saw forsythia and daffodils in full bloom.

We stopped in Athens and went straight to the WOUB-TV studio for an interview. From there we went to a vigil in front of O'Blenes Hospital, where I helped hold a banner that read, "To Bomb This Site Is a War Crime." It was wonderful to see my friends working hard to counter the war mania. It was what I needed to soften my grief and my readjustment pain.

The next day, at the farmers market, I was overwhelmed by the love I felt from people greeting me and welcoming me home. I soaked up the beauty of this different world. I prepared to do my first talk on Sunday at the Friends Meeting and then a public talk in Athens the next week. In the coming week I was interviewed for part of an eighteen-minute segment on NPR's "Talk of the Nation." In the weeks ahead, I would find healing in the garden and woods, with family and friends, and in speaking about my experience.

It felt strange, but good, to be home again. I felt so grateful to be back safe with the people here that I love.

PART 2

Repairing the Breach

June 7, 2003–September 3, 2003

And you shall be like a watered garden,
like a spring of water, whose waters fail not.
And your ancient ruins shall be rebuilt;
you shall raise up the foundations of many generations;
you shall be called the repairer of the breach,
the restorer of streets to dwell in.
—Isaiah 58:11-12, RSV

CHAPTER 9

The Aftermath of War

I had been home from Iraq only about two weeks when the phone rang. It was Gene Stoltzfus giving a friendly call to see how I was doing since my trip. But there was more. "It may seem a little soon to ask you this, and I know the summer is your farming season, but I wonder if you would go back to Iraq and work with the team this summer. The team is very small and we really need more people there. It would be helpful to have someone with your experience."

"Already?" I blurted out, surprised at the question. "I don't know if I'll be ready by then. I know I'm not ready now. And that is during our busy growing season. I'll have to think more about it and talk to Art," I managed to say.

Art wasn't very positive about the idea. We had just had a short time together after five months apart. I needed time to unwind from the stress I had carried home, time to heal, to work in the garden, walk in the woods, and be with friends and family. And I was already spending much time speaking locally and around the country. I had mixed feelings. But part of me wanted to return and reconnect with the people I knew before the war and see for myself what conditions were like in Iraq. We let the issue rest, but I didn't forget it. And Gene called a few more times to see if I had decided.

Later, in May, after time at home, many speaking trips, including one to San Francisco arranged by my son and daughter-in-law, Dale and Debbie, Art and I discussed it once more. This time it was different. Art sensed that the time was right for me to go and that this post-invasion work was important for CPT and for me. In spite of my hesitation, I felt a real pull toward returning to Iraq. I had been able to talk about it with others in the small Christian community we lived with and family and close friends. I felt a lot of love from Art and others in their willingness to sacrifice to let me go.

~ ~ ~

On Sunday, June 8, two months after leaving Iraq, I was in Amman and on my way back. The other nine people in the CPT delegation I would be leading had started arriving on different flights. The team in Baghdad had arranged for Sattar, the man who had driven for us regularly last winter, to take us in. I was excited.

Early in the morning on June 10 we were on our way. For the first stretch of the trip through the more barren part of northeastern Jordan, I talked with Sattar. He began to describe the conditions in Iraq since the invasion. "We now have freedom of speech and political freedom, and that's good, but otherwise things are getting worse. Very few people have work, enough food, and medicines for their families. There is still widespread looting and robbery. People are afraid to go places."

He went on to tell how many people heard the promises of the US and expected that their country would quickly rebuild its infrastructure and economy and that life would soon be better. So they welcomed the US troops as they came in. "Whole units of Iraqi soldiers did not resist, because they were promised jobs of high rank in the post-war military. But now they are disillusioned and angry. No one believes that the US came to liberate them. People think they are here for the oil." What Sattar told me didn't represent all Iraqis, but I came to see that his views were fairly typical.

As we got close to the border, Sattar became increasingly tense. I was feeling a mixture of excitement and uncertainty. What would it be like in Iraq after the bombing and under the occupation?

At the border, I could see a big change. Where Iraqi guards had previously been stationed, American forces had taken control. "This is not right," I thought, as the reality of the invasion hit me. I resented their presence. I could tell that underneath the forced politeness in answering the questions of the US soldiers,

Sattar was holding in his anger. He stiffened and his jaw was tight, but he kept his feelings under control. The soldiers searched one of our vans, but otherwise the crossing was simple. There were no visas, and little questioning of who we were or why we were going in.

Along the long stretch of road from the border to the population centers around Ramadi, near the Euphrates River, the mostly sandy desert seemed to stretch out endlessly. Along the road were signs of the war. We rode under an overpass with slabs of concrete hanging down. Occasionally, there were carcasses of burned or exploded buses, cars, or trucks. At one place, much of the six-lane pavement was broken up by explosions, leaving only one lane where our vans could pass. Closer to the Euphrates River we saw many destroyed electrical towers, as well as smashed guard rails, where it looked like heavy military vehicles had wielded their way.

Near Ramadi, about sixty miles west of Baghdad, where we knew the road was more dangerous, we saw a man driving toward us on our side of the road. He warned everyone that there were robbers ahead. We knew that many cars had been ambushed recently. Drivers in our and other vehicles made quick U-turns in the road and went back the other direction, until we met three US military vehicles coming toward us. They motioned for all the cars to turn around once more and follow them until we were past Falluja. Then the soldiers pulled off the road and we went on our own. Sattar told us that this was part of the military's routine, but we still felt uncomfortable about it. CPT as an organization had an understanding that in our various projects we did not want to be escorted or protected by any armed persons or groups.

We passed US military bases and saw destroyed Iraqi tanks and other vehicles where there had been battles. Coming into Baghdad, I began to see more signs of the war, more bombed and burned-out buildings than when I had left two months ago. This was a clear reminder of the times of attack and invasion in March and April. So much had happened with our team since I had been forced to leave on the tenth day of the bombing of Baghdad, March 29.

~ ~ ~

Shortly after my return from Iraq to the US in April, I had received reports from the small group of IPTers who had stayed on in Baghdad through the rest of the bombing and the fall of the Iraqi government. On the morning of April 9, US troops in tanks, Armored Personnel Carriers and other military vehicles arrived at the Al Fanar Hotel. The team dropped a banner from one of the second-floor balconies that read, "Courage for Peace, Not War." Some of the team went down and started talking with soldiers, giving them water and dates. Others were unable to do this because of their conflicting emotions: a mixture of anger, grief, and weariness. Some team members spent time sitting or kneeling in prayer on a large canvas painting brought by the Korean Peace Team, which they spread out near a US tank. There they listened to soldiers sharing their fear and pain from being a part of this war and experiencing some very bad things.

As team members ventured out that day and walked around the city, they saw burned cars, bombed and burning buildings (often the results of looting), roads blocked, and most stores and shops closed. They heard about schools, universities, and hospitals being looted and no longer functional. The sick and dying were being turned away. There was no electricity. A person working in a relief office in the same hotel saw five dead bodies along a street and another team member saw nurses digging graves for babies in front of the children's hospital, because they couldn't get them to the cemetery. Amahl's Beit Al Iraqi craft shop, where we'd had conversations with groups of Iraqis before the war, was also looted.

Cathy Breen wrote the following on April 10:

> The mood had definitely shifted from one of relief to one of resignation and deep sadness. It is written in the faces of almost everyone I see. The regime has fallen and for that they are grateful, also that the bombing has, for the most part, stopped. But the reality that their beloved country is now an occupied one is set-tling over them like a gray, ominous cloud. Massive looting is taking place throughout the city; even government hospitals are not spared. There is still bitter fighting in some areas, and there have been numerous accounts of suicide bombs, one last night which took the lives of the perpetrator and three US Marines. Many areas of the city are unsafe. There is no police force

whatsoever, and as the occupying troops have orders not to police, they are left standing around to watch.

Team members found out that Amar, our friend who worked at the Al Dar Hotel, and his wife had their baby during the bombing, just before the invasion. She had given birth at home because no hospital would take them. Cathy found a blanket made by US children for Iraqi families and gave it to them for the baby. Amar was very grateful, saying that this was the first gift they had received to welcome their new child.

Within two weeks, April 16, around the time the last IPTers were leaving, five CPTers came back into Iraq from Amman (Lisa Martens, Scott Kerr, Stewart Vreisinga, and Sis and Jerry Levin). So many things in the society had changed. Very quickly they found an apartment to rent on Sadoon Street, about six blocks from the Al Fanar, and found work to do. In a mission statement, the team later listed the tasks of CPT there: (1) accompany the Iraqi people in this continued crisis, (2) accompany Iraqis who claim to be victims of human rights violations by the occupying authority, as they seek information and resolve, (3) support and encourage local nonviolent efforts to rebuild community and deal with the problems they face, (4) intervene nonviolently in volatile situations and where appropriate, challenge unnecessary or provocative military presence or orders, and (5) pray for peace and carry out public actions for peace.

During the next weeks the team visited hospitals that were operating at about 20 percent of capacity with few medicines and dealing with an increase in waterborne diseases from impure water. They talked to teachers who were cleaning up schools that had been occupied by US soldiers or looted, trying to start classes without receiving their pay until late June. Religious leaders told about isolated incidents of Muslim-Christian violence, but more about how people of the two faiths were cooperating to give material aid to others. International aid organizations shared about their warehouses being broken into and their vehicles stopped at gunpoint and stolen.

General living conditions were also difficult. Team members found that a limited amount of fresh fruits and vegetables, dairy products, meat, and eggs were available in the market, but at four times the pre-war prices, allowing fewer Iraqi families to buy them.

There was more than just violence and chaos on the streets, however. Every day hundreds of Iraqi people were out on the streets taking part in peaceful protests, using their new freedom of speech. As the weeks went by, with little improvement in the conditions of their lives, they became more disillusioned and bitter. One person expressed it this way: "What is the use of freedom of speech if no one is listening to our concerns?"

One day team members were walking near a US military checkpoint near the Al Fanar and intervened when they saw two soldiers pressing the face of an Iraqi man against the sidewalk and handcuffing him. They took photographs and questioned the soldiers and detained man. He had been trying to go through the checkpoint to seek out a job possibility. Team members stood nearby and watched, and after being detained for a while, the Iraqi man was let go.

In late April, team members brought to the attention of a US military colonel the problems of unexploded munitions (mortars, small rockets, mines, and missiles) left exposed around Baghdad. They had documented twenty-five such sites. A number of times they pressed authorities and asked them to at least cordon off the sites, they were told that this was not a high priority, that they didn't have enough personnel, or even that they didn't have colored tape.

Team members visited four-year-old Ali at a hospital, who had been blinded and brain damaged after picking up a bright-yellow cluster bomblet on April 10. They had heard about many Iraqi children and adults who had been killed or maimed this way. Later UNICEF released a report that more than one thousand children had been killed or wounded by these weapons. The team sent out an action request to CPTnet, asking people in the US and Canada to send brightly colored tape in the mail to US and British legislators and embassy staff for cordoning off these sites.

On May 21, in Baghdad's Firdos Square, two team members staged a "Live Cartoon" to bring attention to the disparity of wages and the lack of wages for teachers. One dressed up as a

US soldier, the other as an Iraqi school teacher with signs in Arabic and English reading,

US Soldier:	Iraqi Teacher:
Job: Guarding Oil Ministry	Job: Forming Young Minds and Future Leaders
Pay: $4,000 / month	Pay: $0.00-$20.00 / month

In late May, team members tried to visit the Detention Center at the Baghdad airport to speak with US soldiers and observe how Iraqi prisoners there were being treated. Despite several attempts, they were denied access. But while they were waiting, they met several Iraqi families who had come there to find loved ones who had recently disappeared or been arrested. They too were being denied access and information, so they asked the team to help them.

Army Lieutenant Colonel Stewart Gordon told the team that, while the military was coordinating with the Red Cross regarding prisoners of war, no system existed for locating the prisoners arrested or for granting them a trial. Later CPT found out there was a computer list at the Iraqi Assistance Center (IAC), where some of the names, charges, and serial numbers of detainees were listed. Going there for information became a frequent task. The IAC was an office located in a modern convention center in Baghdad where Iraqis could go to get information or assistance.

~ ~ ~

Before my arrival in early June, the four person CPT team prepared for this first CPT delegation after the invasion. Setting up appointments was not easy, because the telephones throughout Baghdad and most of Iraq were still not working. Internet service did not start until late June, so the only way to send reports and information back to CPT offices in Chicago and Canada was to call on our satellite phone. Every other evening someone from the team would go up on the roof and call Doug Pritchard at the Toronto office.

Rick Polhamus, a full-time CPTer and former horse racer

from southwestern Ohio, and I were to oversee the activities of the CPT delegation during the next ten days. Goals for the delegation were to witness the damage from the war and the conditions of post-invasion Iraq, to listen and talk to people from all points of view, to connect with newly organized Iraqi organizations, and to engage in some kind of public action.

During my first few days in Iraq, I also found time to visit the families, individuals, and church groups I had been close to last winter. At Siham and Abbas' home, I was received with much excitement and expressions of love. I was glad to see that their family had not suffered any direct harm. I told them the story of my being detained and deported with the group of eight. It seemed that no one on the team staying on or coming back had told them why or how I had left, so they were surprised to hear my story.

There was a happy reunion at Kreema's, whose family was now in their new apartment. I gave Duah and Hebe, the twins, the picture I had taken of them at their sister's birthday party during the time of bombing in March.

Our friends Amal and Safah shared that they were very thankful for their safe journey and stay in Syria during the time of bombing and invasion, yet it was also a hard time for their family. They kept worrying about family and friends back in Baghdad. Later in the summer I helped Amal get into the Ministry of Education offices, headed by a British woman, to report on corruption in the schools and to advocate changes. When she had gone alone, she had been denied entry. When I left Baghdad on the third of September, she had not received any response to the report she had carefully typed up and taken to the office.

At one of our delegation supper times, I was surprised to see Ghalia, the teacher at the Holy Family religious education school, come in to visit the team. She was one of the people I wanted to reconnect with. Ghalia invited us to come to her home, now that we could visit without endangering her family. Even last winter she had confided that her friends at the church had warned her that she might get in trouble for talking with an American so often. Fortunately, that didn't happen.

Later in the summer, Maurine and I went to Ghalia's home

and met her mother and four sisters. Her mother grew up on a farm in the mountains of northern Iraq, but later married and moved south to Baghdad. After the Gulf War they lost their land when that Kurdish territory was separated from the rest of Iraq and overseen by the UN. They are Chaldean Christians who still speak the Kildan language in their household.

At the Seventh-Day Adventist Church, friends greeted me with surprise. Many different people told me they had a hard time during the war with the lack of electricity and security. Iraqi people were still under a lot of stress. Mona and Haitham had hoped to get married that summer after Mona finished school. However, with school closed, her examinations would be late, and Haitham had lost his job and was not been able to find another one. He seemed discouraged. Others shared that they had little food or money.

Only one family at the Evangelical Presbyterian Church in Baghdad had members killed and injured. For a while after the invasion, US soldiers had been stationed near the front gates of the church building to protect it from being robbed and looted. Various church members remembered me and greeted me warmly. We had a similar welcome at the Saint Raphael's Catholic Church. It was remarkable how the Iraqi people were able to treat us without hostility in spite of the war.

Whenever I could find unscheduled time, I stopped in to see workers at the three hotels we had stayed in and was always greeted warmly. Sa'ad, a worker at the Al Dar Hotel, told us that last winter, whenever we had talked with him or after we had left the buildings to go out, government informants would ask him what we said or where we were going.

One day I went to an Internet center at the Andalus Apartments and was surprised to see and talk with our former minder, Wada. He told us his family had come through the war without any harm. He was working as a translator for a European journalist, and I saw him several times throughout the summer. I also saw another minder, Thalmer, several times. He also worked as a translator.

During one of the free blocks of time, delegation members Lee, a graduate student in theology and member of the CPT sterring committee, and Douglas McKenna duCharme, a

Presbyterian pastor from Toronto, had a taxi driver take them to various sites around the city that had been bombed. One of the places they went was the telecommunications building on Sadoon Street near the Al Dar Hotel, the one our group went to see in March, which led to our expulsion. As Lee shared her feelings about seeing the massive destruction of the building, it triggered a lot of pain and grief in me, as did many other experiences I had that summer. But I felt it was part of a healing process I needed, so I decided to go there later and see it myself.

Bakery workers and workers at the fruit and vegetable markets along Karrada street also welcomed me warmly and asked what our group was doing now that we were back.

The first time I walked into the orphanage, the children started yelling, "Peggy! Peggy!" I greeted each one, then they all started asking about Charlie. I found that little Zanib, one of the more helpless children, had died while I was gone. The sisters shared that they had gotten through the rest of the bombing and the last two months without any damage, but it had been very hard managing with little electricity and water. I knew I couldn't go and help at the orphanage as often as before, but I tried to go at least once a week whenever possible.

Later in the summer I wrote the following reflection:

A Hundred Playful Moments

Our time together at the orphanage in Baghdad this morning was full of a hundred playful moments. Achmin, usually silent and withdrawn, laughed as she tried to put a toy tree in my pocket. Yassar and Allah took turns playing the drum, but then Quar-Quar, who can't sit up or hold anything with his hands, patiently waited until the others tired of it before he gleefully grabbed it and held it between his legs as he lay on the mat and hit it proudly. Baby Nuri, with stubbed legs and arms, can now roll over back and forth by herself, while watching the others play. E'lias danced as I held her hands and sang. Every few minutes, when one would ask, "Where's Charlie?" [Charlie Litkey who also spent lots of time with them this winter/spring], I would wave my hands in the air and exclaim, "Far away!" and we would laugh. Soon we were asking, "Where's Omar?" and "Where's Amil?" etc., with lots of silliness.

When the almost twenty severely handicapped children in this matted room would start to get rowdy, I began to sing, and about four or five would join in with whatever words they remembered or were able to say. They have a repertoire of about six children's songs they know in English, but I usually add a few of my own, like "Zippidy Doo Da," or my rendition of "The Itsey Bitsy Spider," and usually have the group's rapt attention, even though most have no idea of what it means. When Fatima, who interacts very little, started crying, I picked up her stiff small body and held her, and sang "Swing Low, Sweet Chariot," and she soon calmed down. Meanwhile, Amil scooted over and had her head in my lap. I am awed by their responsiveness and trust.

In all these interactions, I try to look at each individual child in the eye, and invite them with my look to smile or respond in return. I keep saying their names as often as I can as we play. I want to say with each look or action that they are special. It doesn't matter what they can do or how much they understand, there is a special beauty, a special personality, a special gift that is there if you just notice.

These children knew very little of what was happening with the politics leading to the war, the bombing and invasion, and the difficulties of the Iraqi population around them. What they did know was their fear at the loud bomb blasts and the fear they perceived in the adults caring for them. But more than that they knew that this was their family and they were being cared for and loved.

We, who have more of a cognitive grasp of the world, have the ability to "achieve" more in life and think we understand what is going on, share the same basic fear, hurt, and lack of control over our lives, as well as the same basic needs. We're just more sophisticated in hiding or denying it. We all need to belong, to feel safe, and to know we are special and loved, no matter what our ability is, no matter whether we live in a rich suburb of Los Angeles or in Sadr City in Baghdad.

We need more moments when we realize this about all the children of the world. And we need more moments when we become as children in their delight of the simple expressions of love and laughter.

At the Al Wathba water treatment plant, where many of us had stayed in tents during the bombing, we were glad to see that there had been no damage. The "tree of life" we had planted was alive and well, just droopy in the summer's heat. Layla Al Althary, the engineer in charge of treating water, told us that a few workers spent long hours at the water plant keeping it going and providing water to their area of the city, which included twelve hospitals. Their chlorine containers leaked and they had frequent interruptions of electricity. These interruptions led to a contamination of the water supply. When the plant had to use a generator, its output was only 50 percent of its usual capability. "It's worse now than before the war with the sanctions," she said.

Along with assessing the damage, we met with a few of the many international aid organizations doing good work to increase services in hospitals, schools and water systems, and supporting Iraqi development projects. Among these were CARE International, Mennonite Central Committee, American Friends Service Committee, the Middle East Council of Churches, and Adventist Development and Relief Agency, as well as the various UN agencies. We occasionally attended meetings for international NGOs to share information, as well as the media and security briefings provided by the Coalition Provisional Authority.

Back in central Baghdad, where we lived, we had electricity for about six hours in a twenty-four-hour period, and the hours were irregular. Many businesses, hotels, hospitals, and apartment buildings had their own generators, but generators only produce a portion of the electricity needed and could operate for only a limited number of hours at a time. The average Iraqi family didn't have this luxury and spent many evenings working, caring for their families, preparing food, reading, or writing by lantern or candlelight.

The extreme heat of the midsummer was more difficult without the relief of overhead fans. With limited electricity, babies needing an incubator or patients needing emergency care could die. Electricity was also necessary for pumping water into upper floors of buildings or the amount of water that could be treated in sewage plants. When the electricity went off at water treatment plants, the pressure in the pipes diminished, causing absorption of contaminates.

Electricity was just one of the many problems mentioned when Iraqis vented their anger about post-war conditions. Repeatedly, Ambassador L. Paul Bremer, the top US civilian administrator in Iraq and head of the Coalition Provisional Authority (CPA), had responded to these complaints with "You just need to be patient!" This seemed like a reasonable request until one talked to Iraqi engineers who compared the reconstruction efforts now with the time after the first Gulf War. "In 1991, the damage was much greater, because the damage was concentrated not only on the substations, but the power stations," said Adnan Wadi Bashir, who worked as a power generation and transmission engineer for the government for twenty-four years. "We restored part of the power in 1991 within six weeks of the cease-fire, and in five months we supplied the whole Iraqi system. The job now could have been finished within a month."

At the end of the Gulf War, looters had caused a lot of damage to Iraq's electrical infrastructure. In the thirteen years after that, the electrical system had been steadily crumbling, because engineers had not been able to get most of the spare parts needed, due to the sanctions. The main difference between that war and this, as they saw it, was that in 1991, Iraqi engineers and technicians, who understood the less-modern technology and systems, did the repair and went to work immediately after the war. This time, the US government contracted the Bechtel Group for thirty million dollars to restore Iraq's electricity.

Meanwhile skilled Iraqi workers desperate for employment could have been making the repairs. Most of the subcontracts under Bechtel and other corporations working for reconstruction in Iraq were going to non-Iraqi companies, mostly American.

The Iraqi people were upset with the inefficiency of the system. Something also seemed wrong with destroying the infrastructure and creating a need for reconstruction that would mostly profit the country that destroyed it. Even those Iraqis who had welcomed the removal of Saddam were now distrustful of the US, wondering if the delays were intentional. The belief that the US had waged war in Iraq for the liberation of the Iraqi people had eroded. Iraqis were losing patience, and they wanted more than one kind of power.

In the midst of this chaotic situation, one evening in late June, we were part of a crowd of about four hundred people who came to the first performance of the Iraqi National

Symphony Orchestra. The audience was a curious mixture of Iraqi nationals, representatives of international NGOs, US military, and top US officials, including Paul Bremer. The announcer talked about music being "good for healing the wounds of war." There was something special about music at such a time, but it also seemed strange, to pretend that everyone there was one happy family.

~ ~ ~

What was happening to the Iraqi people? They were still very kind, resilient, proud, and beautiful people. However, we saw the scars in their spirit and emotions, and knew that these would not easily be healed. Children continued to respond in terror to the sound of airplanes overhead or to the sight of soldiers and their guns. Mothers were heavy with grief about their children's deaths or injuries. There was more suspicion and tension as people went about their business on the streets. The increased anger came out directly in the rise in street and domestic violence, but also individually in maladaptive behaviors. We saw more expressions of depression, dependency, feelings of helplessness, putting down one's own culture, and various kinds of manipulative behavior.

For example, families we knew who were desperate financially would put pressure on us for money. This was especially difficult for me when it came from families we had been close to. I found myself visiting certain families less often to avoid some of this. CPT had a very strict policy of not giving money or any other material relief to people we met. Our Iraqi friends wanted us to pay for them to cook for us. Here we were seen as rich Americans who should be able to help them financially. We lived very simply on a tight budget, and we also knew that if we began to give money, this would quickly change our relationship from brothers and sisters to benefactors. Besides, we could help one, but what about the thousands just as worthy?

This was one of the hardest things for me. We knew it was not any particular defect of the Iraqi people, but a casualty of war, and it would continue under the structural violence of the occupation. Yes, the woundedness of these people made our relationships more difficult, but I still loved them in their imperfections. They were still a part of me in a deep way. God gave me this gift of love, and it was still within me, giving me strength, purpose, and joy, as well as pain. One can't be prepared to die for people and not carry a deep love for them.

~ ~ ~

"*This* is Freedom?" was the theme of the delegation's public action in late June. Delegation and team members lined the west side of Firdos Square, facing the back of the Sheridan and Palestine Hotels, holding signs that asked this question in Arabic and English. On each sign, different problems Iraqis face were listed, such as hunger, lack of jobs, no self-government, and no legal process for detainees. Two of our group talked to the US soldiers on the tanks and three passed out flyers and talked with Iraqi people passing by.

Representatives from two Iraqi organizations, the Al Houza, and the Union of the Unemployed came by and asked about our group and invited us to meet with them and be present at some activities they were planning. A reporter from an Iraqi newspaper interviewed some of us. This was our flier:

"*This* is Freedom? . . .
A survey done by Christian Peacemaker Teams (Iraq) over the past month gathered responses from 700 Iraqis from all walks of life. Again and again the question came: *This* is freedom?

> 44% of Iraqis surveyed say their neighborhood is not a safe place for their families
> 86% of Iraqis say that they lack a source of income sufficient for the needs of their families
> 78% of Iraqis need medical attention or medications and find it impossible to get what they need
> 46% of Iraqi children are not attending school due to concerns for their safety
> there are also dramatically increased cases of cancer, especially leukemia due to use of depleted uranium (DU) in coalition weapons, and a lack of cancer treatment drugs for chemotherapy

unexploded ordinance continues to present a risk to civilians, especially children

courts and judicial processes are suspended

schools are not just in need of repairs, but are declared "unsafe" in the thousands by UNICEF

the impact of twelve years of sanctions means Iraq, a country of immense human and natural resource, is already impoverished and exhausted

In the aftermath of a conflict that consumed thousands of lives and billions of dollars, with massive ongoing costs to the Iraqi people, all based on a fragile promise of freedom, we ask:

This is Freedom?

CHAPTER 10

Different Voices

We know that when Jesus healed people, he often started by listening to their pain, hopelessness, or fear. Healing came after the healed took actions of faith, and sometimes it was given just in the hearing of his words.

We sought to act in the same spirit while working in Iraq. We knew that listening was an important part of our work, important for the healing of the wounds of war. We don't know fully what our listening meant for "Amira," a well-educated Iraqi woman who shared about her family and neighbors fleeing their southern Baghdad neighborhood during the bombing, because they lived near an Iraqi military base. They quickly and fearfully grabbed a few belongings, not knowing if they would ever return to see their homes intact. We visited later and saw the damage to their house from a cluster bomb explosion. The only employment her family could find was her job in one of the US administration offices. She shared feelings of pain, anger, and now fear that she has compromised her people by taking the job.

We didn't know what listening meant for a teacher in Falluja, who in May was part of the crowd protesting US soldiers taking over and occupying a local school. He witnessed US soldiers overreacting to someone throwing a stone toward them and firing into the crowd, killing eighteen and wounding about seventy-five demonstrators. He and others worked to pull out the wounded. He was not injured, but a woman near him was shot while also helping the wounded. We listened as he shared his pain for his friends and his increasing anger toward the American military and occupation.

It wasn't hard for me to listen to Iraqis share their pain and anger. I had been with them facing the coming of the war and the days of bombing. But now in mid-June I faced a bigger challenge. The hardest thing for me after coming back to Iraq was the US military presence everywhere dominating the society, and seeing the people under occupation. For Iraqis it was further humiliation and suppression of their freedom. Seeing US soldiers patrolling the streets brought to the surface my anger about all the destruction my government had unleashed in Iraq.

For my first month that summer, I continued to have difficulty connecting personally, compassionately, or caringly with soldiers. There was some kind of block or numbness inside me. I didn't know if it was frozen fear and anger from the time here during the bombing or if I just couldn't forgive them for all the destruction and chaos which resulted. But I wanted to be free to speak the truth in love, that is, to relate out of love and still stand against oppression, militarism, and world domination. I prayed for this gift.

We were in Falluja, and the delegation decided to spend time talking to US soldiers. Lee and I talked with a soldier about the war and his being in Falluja as a gunner. Then Lee began to speak more personally.

She told him that Christian Peacemaker Teams were concerned not just about the Iraqi people and their safety. "We are also concerned about *your* safety, and your soul," she told him, "because in order to kill, you need to distance yourself from the Iraqi people. And when you do that, you kill some of your own humanity as well." He was very quiet, and when we were saying good-bye we noticed tears forming in his eyes.

I walked away, grateful that God had used Lee to touch this soldier's spirit. But something had also happened to me. It began a process of melting the ice of resentment in my heart, which moved me one more step on the path of forgiveness and acceptance, preparing me for meeting "the enemy" with love.

~ ~ ~

We heard stories from Iraqi people who suffered under Saddam, as well as those suffering from the war and the occupation. We heard the corporate voices of protesters on the streets, and we listened to soldiers. All have been affected by what has happened in Iraq.

A man in Basra had served two years out of a twenty-year prison sentence in the late eighties for criticizing Saddam in a conversation with a friend. He carried a lot of hatred toward the former president and was glad the US had toppled that regime. But at the same time he was critical of the occupation, particularly that the US hadn't followed through on its promises. "Saddam took everything and didn't give us anything," he told us. "Maybe it will be the same with the US."

"There have been four rapes and kidnappings right near Baghdad University this week," Scherine, a young woman student, told us. "Most of the women my age are afraid to walk on the streets alone. I am also afraid." We knew from our experience last winter that before the war, rapes or abductions of women on the streets were virtually nonexistent. Such an increase in violence against women is common in the aftermath of war. War unleashes chaos, lawlessness, and acts of violence. Violence against women comes out of the rage and feelings of powerlessness that men experience in a war experience.

Sa'ad, another student at the university, described the US soldiers searching his house and said with intense emotion, "It's a deep shame to have authorities search your home, especially with women and children there. Our leader, Ayatollah Ali Muhammad Sistani, told us to wait and not speak out and act against Americans yet," he added. "But if Americans don't leave, we will rise up."

A member of the Assyrian Democratic Party (ADP) told us, "Under Saddam Hussein's rule we went underground because of ethnic persecution. Assyrian Christians came into central Iraq and relocated in the cities after Saddam's forces destroyed two hundred of our villages. Since then we have been able to rebuild about 150 of those villages. Most people are happy to get rid of Saddam Hussein, but not because they loved war."

Since 1991, the ADP party had been allowed to operate only in the northern directorates. Now they occupied an office complex in Baghdad. Women in their organization were actively planning various educational and cultural programs for

Assyrian women. The ADP was part of a group that met regularly to advise Paul Bremer. "Our goals are to achieve equality and full participation for Assyrian Christians and build a unified government representing all," the ADP member said. "It would be better to wait on setting up an Iraqi government until all the Iraqi groups learn to cooperate and work together." When we spoke about our work here, his response was, "Your goals are valiant, but Saddam Hussein was the greater devil!"

One of our drivers explained to us that living under Saddam's government was better than US occupation. "I think more people will be killed through the war, fighting, and resistance against America than all the people Saddam Hussein killed," he said. "In spite of Saddam's cruelty, most Iraqis loved him and wish he were back in power. A new government will have to be stronger than Saddam Hussein."

As they were preparing to send a signed petition to Paul Bremer, one ex-professor told us, "It's not right to lump us all together and dismiss us from our jobs, just because we were members of the Ba'ath Party. We are just two of the two thousand professors expelled from the universities in Iraq in this 'de-Ba'athification' policy of the American administration. This is simply collective punishment." It was common knowledge that in order to take almost any civil service job in Iraq under the former government, it was necessary to be a party member. "We are asking that authorities review each individual case and pay them the salary withheld from them when they were fired."

North of Baghdad, a tribal sheik told us his story: US soldiers, using a megaphone, woke him from his sleep. Several army vehicles and two helicopters surrounded the house. Children in the household were afraid and began crying. The soldiers came inside and began searching the house, taking Iraqi money equivalent to about seventy thousand dollars. They told him they were looking for a senior member of Saddam's regime, whom they had been told was hiding there. The sheik figured that some people in the area didn't like him and told this to the American military. He acknowledged that he had been in the same prison with Saddam before he came to power but hadn't had any contact with Saddam's family since. Before leaving, soldiers handcuffed the sheik and two members of his extended family and took them along. They released the other two, but kept the sheik in prison for twelve days.

According to the sheik, eighty men were crowed together in one room. They each had a blanket, but no beds. There were two outside toilets without walls. After he was released, he visited the Army to ask for the money back, but came out of the building without his money to find his car "accidentally" on fire. Later he told us, "When the British came as occupiers in the past, they treated us respectfully and asked us what we thought and what we needed. The Americans can stay and take our oil, if only they would give us three things: freedom, jobs, and respect."

The Iraqi head of a police station in Kerbala, appointed by US military forces, criticized Saddam, saying, "We have new freedom now and less corruption. America was just a tool in God's hands to get rid of Saddam Hussein."

For about half an hour we listened to a former intelligence officer criticize Saddam and his two sons for their arrogance and ruthlessness, and the US for the mistakes they were making, such as abolishing the ministries and firing Ba'ath Party members. Then he told us his personal story: He had worked in the intelligence department for the Ba'ath government for twenty-four years, specializing in electronic surveillance, or bugging. "You could not refuse to follow orders," he said, "or you would be killed." He knew there were problems with it, but he had to feed his family. Now he was in the University of Baghdad, studying English. He said that even though he was a former Ba'athist, he wasn't afraid for his family. We asked him, "If the Americans would ask him to do the same kind of work for them, would you do it?" He answered, "Yes."

An engineer told us his personal story too. As a teen, he was drafted into the Iraqi military for the Iran-Iraq War and became a weapons expert. But because he refused to fire any weapons, he was imprisoned for nine months. Again he was drafted in the Gulf War and was stationed near Basra. One day, near the end of the war, after going off to bring more weapons for his unit, he came back to find they had all been killed in an attack. He started walking to Baghdad, alone, in the midst of the insurrection that followed, finally arriving home in three weeks.

After the war, he graduated from Baghdad University as a construction engineer. Because he was at the top of his class, he was one of those forced to design and build Saddam's palaces. If he had refused, or didn't do his work perfectly, he would have been imprisoned or killed. Now this engineer was working for the US Office of Reconstruction and Humanitarian Assistance in Baghdad, consulting with US officials about rebuilding after the war.

"I don't love them, and I don't hate them," he said, when asked how he felt about Americans. "I will work with them, but if Americans stay too long, there will be problems, or if they don't keep their promises. Iraqi people, especially Shi'a Muslims, don't like it if they are lied to."

"US military officials came to talk to some of us," a tribal sheik from Falluja told us. He had asked the officials, "Are you coming to liberate or to rule us?" He expressed anger about the behavior of soldiers who conducted the massive searches. "Iraqis need to be treated with respect and dignity." Talking about developing a new Iraqi government, he said, "The good people of Iraq have no objection to a new leader, if it is a good person. But many of the people in the governing council are outsiders."

One day a taxi driver in Baghdad told me, "You need to hear another point of view that isn't heard in the media. I am a Ba'ath Party member," he said. "Anyone a bit higher than the lowest level of membership are being picked out and persecuted now under the American administration. Most of the Ba'ath Party members were good people and not a part of any of Saddam's cruel deeds."

"*Ahlan wa sahlan!*—Welcome!" we heard from religious leaders all over Iraq. In Christian churches and homes we were greeted as brothers and sisters in Christ. Inside or outside the mosques, Muslim leaders or lay people welcomed us as coming from one of the three Abrahamic religions. A Sunni Muslim leader in Falluja told us that the Koran says Christianity is the nearest faith to Islam and that it is wrong to hurt Christians or Jews. "We all have the same God," many Muslims told us, affirming a point of unity.

We heard about tension and violence between Christians

and Muslims in Iraq right after the invasion. In May, Muslims killed two Christians in Basra, because they were selling liquor. But at the funeral, many of their Muslim friends came to express their grief. We also heard about cooperative efforts between churches and mosques in the larger cities to give out medicines and water, and to care for indigent people.

As far as their views of the war and political situation, religious leaders differed on the extent to which they criticized Saddam and the US occupation. One Christian leader told us that at least there was religious freedom for Christians under Saddam, and any religious discrimination or persecution was illegal. "There are so many problems since the war that the new administration is not taking care of," he went on to say, "that sometimes we wish Saddam Hussein would come back."

Shi'a Muslim groups tended to be more sympathetic to the war and vocal about their experience of religious suppression or persecution under the former regime. Some of their leaders had been imprisoned, killed, or forced into exile. About a month before, Sistani, who declined to be on the new governing council, had publicly urged his followers not to resist the occupying forces with violence, but to give them at least a year to fulfill their promises. We also talked to a Shi'a ayatollah who said, "America removed Saddam Hussein for its own self-interest. Now it should get out!"

Many religious leaders were critical of the war. A bishop was the most outspoken. "It's very sad," he said.

> There are other ways to deal with dictators. How many dictators are in the world? Saddam Hussein was on his way out anyway. War just complicates things and causes more problems. Yes, we have freedom now, but it is freedom to steal and loot, the freedom that allows a few to be rich while most are poor, a freedom without justice. Bush carried out this war with a Bible in his hand. We have the same Bible as Bush used. We must use the Bible for peace!

This same bishop criticized evangelical Christians who were coming to convert the Muslims. He didn't appreciate that they often worked independently and not with the Iraqi churches, often establishing their own house fellowships by enticing members away from current congregations. He advised them not to come, saying, "Our job now is to live it, rather than preach it, and to come to unity."

Religious leaders of all backgrounds were focusing on the work of healing from the war. Whereas church buildings and mosques didn't seem to be targets, some were damaged in the bombing. We visited a Carmelite church building in Baghdad, which had its whole roof caved in by heavy bombing of government buildings nearby. Perhaps more damage occurred on a less visible level—damage of the spirit and emotional well-being of the people.

The Papal Nuncio, ambassador from the Vatican, spoke of the tremendous material needs of the Iraqi people. "But," he said, "their psychological needs are more important than the physical." He told of many humiliating abuses Iraqi people received from US forces, such as people being detained, having their hands secured behind their backs and then being thrown down on the ground "like they were just some bag, not a human being. Instead, they need to be treated with dignity and respect."

One Muslim leader expressed it well when he said, "Tell Americans, 'We have something broken in our souls, and this will take time to restore.'"

~ ~ ~

As tensions in Iraqi society increased, so did the voices of the Iraqi people being heard on the street through organized public actions. Most of these remained peaceful, but some ended in violence.

In June, a crowd of former members of the Iraqi army protested in front of the former Republican Palace, demanding jobs. Evidently the US military had told them they would give them jobs by a certain date if they did not resist the US invasion of Baghdad. The deadline had passed. We heard that during the protest one of the former Iraqi soldiers threw a rock toward the US soldiers. The soldiers responded by shooting into the crowd, killing three and wounding several other protesters.

Two days later, tensions were again high at another

nonviolent protest in Firdos Square, this time led by religious clerics calling for unity, not strife, between Islamic groups. At one point, an American soldier on top of a tank began swinging the tank gun back and forth, pointing into the crowd, increasing the tension. Team member Anne Montgomery, a seventy-six-year-old religious sister, walked through the crowd and up to the soldier and told him that what he was doing seemed unnecessarily threatening to the people and only increased the possibility for violence to occur. The soldier stopped panning the gun, and for a while the tension lessened, but then an Army jeep with a mounted gun drove directly into the crowd, causing more alarm. Skillfully, the organizers of the event brought the demonstration to a close and the crowd dispersed quietly.

On another day Handicapped International, an organization advocating for and helping victims of land mines and other unexploded weapons, gathered for a rally at Firdos Square. In the center of the square was a pile of shoes, which belonged to land mine victims who had lost limbs. There was also a display of various mines and graphic informational flyers.

Students from Al Mustansariya University invited team members to meet with a group forming a student union. In the meeting, different ones spoke about their vision for an independent organization, not under the control or direction of any existing political parties. Several problems had prompted their organizing efforts. They were upset that US soldiers had come in and were occupying one of the student dormitories for barracks. An even more sensitive complaint was that female students were upset that some soldiers were coming up to them, making lewd and suggestive comments, and taking their pictures. The group was sending representatives to take these complaints to US military authorities.

The change of government also reawakened the Iraqis' desire to speak out and be heard in a written way. An estimated 150 to 180 new newspapers started up, including two English/Arabic papers. One of these was started by Ramsey Kysia of Voices in the Wilderness. He gathered a lively group of Iraqi young adults to produce *Al Muajaha (The Iraqi Witness)*, an independent paper. For this paper, common people could submit articles and receive help preparing them for publication.

Soon after the June "*This* Is Freedom?" vigil, members of the Union of the Unemployed (UUI) invited us to their upcoming rally. We learned that they represented fifteen thousand members around Iraq and that more than 60 percent of the Iraqi workforce was unemployed, while most of the contracts and jobs of rebuilding Iraq continued to go to American corporations and other neighboring countries. The group was asking for jobs and employment insurance for those out of work.

Throughout the summer, team members took part in some of their peaceful marches and vigils in front of the Coalition Provisional Authority (CPA) headquarters. At the vigils, women on our team formed a chain with Iraqi women and sat down with the protesters behind and US soldiers in front, who were pointing their guns at the crowd and us. In this way, we acted as a peaceful buffer between the US soldiers and the protesters, hopefully keeping things nonviolent.

One week the UUI set up a tent across the street from the CPA offices, wanting to have a twenty-four-hour presence. During the night, however, US soldiers arrested twenty for

Internationals and Iraqis acting together as a peaceful buffer between US soldiers and other protesters at the Union of the Unemployed of Iraq protest in Baghdad, July 2003.

violating curfew. They were detained for a day, crowded in a small room with no food or water.

At another of their protest vigils a young man was covered by sandy dirt up to his head for about two hours. It was a symbolic statement about the severe consequences that unemployment had on their lives. Posters hung around on clotheslines, depicting the problems these people and their families faced, such as eviction, hunger, and inability to receive medicines.

Yanar Muhammad was one of those women forming a human chain at the UUI protests. She was also the founder and leader of the Organization of Women's Freedom in Iraq (OWFI). Though small in physical stature, she was very strong in vision and resolve. Because she publicly voiced opposition to the US occupation of Iraq, she was not allowed to be part of a large national women's conference in July to discuss and set the agenda for improving the lives of Iraqi women. "All the women invited were handpicked. We still don't have freedom of speech under American control," she told us. "There is freedom to agree, but not freedom of dissent."

"I just heard that an anti-Saddam group in southern Iraq killed a Ba'ath Party official and raped his nine daughters," Yanar told us. "Later other men in their tribe killed the daughters because of the 'dishonor' the rapes brought the family. There is an upsurge of the old tribal customs of 'honor killings' in Iraq since the war."

Sitting next to Yanar was her colleague, Fatima. They shared a gutted-out former bank building with the UUI. In adjoining rooms, volunteers were collating the second edition of OWFI's newspaper, *Equality*. Yanar spoke about the work and goals of this radical women's organization: OWFI was formed immediately after the war to stop the increased violence against women. The group helped women work for legal, social, and economic equality and assisted individual women in leaving abusive domestic situations. Their plans were to open a shelter for women in northern Iraq and one in Baghdad. They were working to get social insurance for all Iraqi women, to help women develop job skills, and to set up legal services for women. Then they wanted to change Iraq's constitution to give women equal rights and remove the laws that legalize honor killings.

"We were against this war," continued Yanar.

> Yes, we did want to get rid of Saddam Hussein, but not by destroying our cities. This is not a humane way. We see this declaration of "liberation" as one big lie. It is not giving us freedom or really changing the basic system that leaves power and wealth with a small minority of people. We don't hear Bremer speaking out on behalf of women's rights. Many who hated the Ba'ath Party are talking now about resistance to the occupation. We are afraid that it will mean more chaos, resulting in more raping and killing of women. The occupation has already reversed progress for women. So, working to end the occupation is part of the work of this women's organization.

Yanar suggested the next steps in the right direction would be for the United Nations peacekeeping forces to immediately replace the occupying forces in Iraq and oversee security until Iraqi society had time to organize itself without tribal leaders, politically motivated religious leaders, and the wealthy elite taking control.

~ ~ ~

Our team listened to many soldiers. Some were proud to be there, believing they were there liberating the people of Iraq. Many were questioning US policies, the war, and their staying on in Iraq, and they expressed their fear. They mentioned their buddies who had been injured or killed. All were miserable in the intense summer heat, ranging from 120 to 135 degrees Fahrenheit.

We stopped one morning at a Rafadin Bank, where teachers and other Iraqi people, employed by US authorities, had lined up since early in the morning to change the ten-thousand-dinar note they received in pay into smaller bills that merchants would accept. Moneychangers on the street would only give them seven thousand dinar in exchange.

US soldiers started yelling at the crowd. "Get out of here! If you don't leave, you will be arrested!" one called out in English to a mostly non-English-speaking crowd. We learned from the soldiers that the bank was closed and would not open that day. The people responded angrily. One soldier complained to me:

"The bank was closed by the manager, not by us. We get the blame, but we are just providing security."

We also had been listening to the Iraqi people outside the bank, who began to share their frustrations about the banks, US soldiers searching their homes and stealing their jewelry, and money, and other offenses. For them this was just one more burden. But the people were resisting leaving, in spite of the soldiers' warnings. We decided that if we walked away from the bank entrance, the crowd would follow us, and they did. This immediate problem between the soldiers and the people was resolved, but not their problems with the unusable currency.

One soldier at the Iraqi Assistance Center (IAC) warned us that it was dangerous for two women to be walking on the streets of Baghdad without a gun. We told him, "We are safer without a gun." Another soldier, who was patrolling the streets of a neighborhood we visited, was shocked to find people like us there, without weapons, and said, "You're braver than I am!" (though I think he thought we were a bit crazy too).

We had personally seen soldiers treating Iraqis in a kind and courteous manner, but we had also witnessed others being brutal, cursing or using vulgar, insulting commands with Iraqis.

For about three months we had ongoing discussions with an army colonel at a local base, about problems Iraqis experience with violent house raids, confiscation of property, and detention practices. He often spoke very condescendingly about Iraqi people. One time he told us, "Most of the Muslims can't be trusted . . . Muslim values are different from Judeo-Christian values. They don't care for other people. They just do for themselves." This was very different from our experience with Iraqi people.

"Once you are here in Iraq for a longer time, you will understand why we had to have this war," said US judge, Donald Campbell, who had been there since April 2003, heading up the Justice Ministry in the CPA offices. Two of us visited him to talk about the problems of Iraqi people detained by US forces. "Last winter, I was also opposed to the war, but I changed my mind when I started talking to so many Iraqi people who had family members tortured and killed by Saddam Hussein."

He introduced Cathy, who had just returned to Iraq through

Voices in the Wilderness, and me to an American woman whose father was Iraqi with Jewish heritage. She proceeded to talk about the persecution of Jews in Iraq—not a pretty story. Although their pain and anger was very real and justified, I also thought of the 1.7 million Iraqi people reported by UN officials to have been killed by UN economic sanctions primarily engineered and perpetuated by the US over the past thirteen years, and of thousands killed in this war. "None of this violence is right, but there were other ways to deal with brutal tyrants such as Saddam Hussein," I told her.

This was a subject I felt the need to express in writing and sent home this article:

A Better Way to Bring Change

It was easy for Americans to declare the current war in Iraq a victory and say that because Iraq is "liberated" from a terrible dictator, the war was "worth it." For people in the US, far from the fighting, exploding bombs, the burning and looting, chaos and insecurity, it has been easy to justify it and gloss over its horrors. I could make a long list of scars that the Iraqi people and the US and Britain will carry because of this war and occupation.

Probably the most devastating to Iraq is the violent rupture of its social structure. One religious leader compared the pre-war situation in Iraq to a dam, holding back the frustrations, anger, hopes, and unmet needs of the people of Iraq. "The war burst the dam," he said, "and now there are forces unleashed that seem as uncontrollable and destructive as a flood." It is the larger structural violence of war and occupation that destroyed the structures of community that provide security. Violence to end that violence of repression never ends that violence, but continues and increases it and perpetuates the desire for revenge.

The world has not caught the vision of popular nonviolent resistance, even though it has been used successfully throughout history to oust dictators who seemed just as impossible to remove or as brutal as Saddam Hussein.

Very similar to Saddam Hussein, was twenty-year Philippine ruler, Ferdinand Marcos. He shut down the press, abolished human rights organizations, arrested, tortured, and executed anyone who opposed him. In 1986, massive citizen demonstrations and world pressure shut down the society and forced his removal.

Hungary, Poland, Czechoslovakia, Bulgaria, and East Germany won freedom in 1989 from Soviet control through nonviolent movements. The Soviet Union fell by crumbling internally. In South Africa, the violent resistance was not successful, but it was the persistent nonviolent movement that finally overcame apartheid.

In the Second World War, there were many examples of successful nonviolent efforts, which kept Hitler's forces from sending Jews to concentration camps, such as in Denmark, Bulgaria, and Finland. General strikes and resistance in Norway prevented Hitler's representative from forming a fascist government there. The tragedy is not that nonviolence didn't work against the Nazis, but that it was not used enough.

In those situations, where peaceful change was considered impossible, it came without a blood bath, bombing, dumping depleted uranium, tearing apart a society, without a lengthy occupation and acts of revenge.

If unhindered, oppressive governments, such as the former Iraqi regime, sow seeds of their own destruction, and the people find ways of limiting or removing ruthless dictators. There are hundreds of examples of powerful popular movements of trained, disciplined, courageous, nonviolent people who have accomplished this.

In Iraq, it would have been better for the US not to have supported Saddam Hussein's build-up of power and brutal actions before 1991 (out of our own "national interests"). How much better it would have been to encourage and support the resistance movements to use well-tested nonviolent methods. Again it seems not to be a matter of nonviolence not working, but of nonviolence not being tried enough.

CHAPTER 11

Responding to Pervasive Violence

We heard that a mosque in Falluja had been bombed the previous night. It was July 1, and we had come to Falluja to speak with local officials about that and continue to pursue the possibility of the team or part of the team locating there.

Falluja was a tense and unsettled city. That day we had a very hurried talk with the mayor who, after hearing our proposal, once again welcomed us to come. We wanted to find various local groups or people who would support our presence, so we decided to find and meet with religious and tribal sheiks of that area.

First we went to the mosque where the bombing had happened, passing a long funeral procession on the way. At the site a large crowd of angry people showed us a small crater, about three feet wide and one foot deep in the middle of the rubble. We took pictures and recorded what we saw. The blast demolished a hall that had been built onto the side of the mosque, killed eight, and badly wounded others. We heard different theories about the source of the blast.

With funerals going on, it was not a good day to try to find the sheiks. One that we found didn't want to be interviewed by foreigners. Another welcomed us to sit and talk with him on a rug under a large shade tree. He expressed frustration and anger at the behavior of soldiers who conducted massive searches for what they called Operation Desert Scorpion. "Iraqis need to be treated with respect and dignity," he told us. He welcomed us to have a team in Falluja.

On another visit we heard that a man had been shot. His neighbors told us that someone had driven by in a car and shot some US soldiers. Another man in a nearby house heard the shots and came out his front door to see what was happening. By that time the gunman in the car had gone on his way, so the soldiers saw only the man at his door and shot and killed him.

Several times we visited the boys' and girls' schools, talking with the teachers. On one of the visits a teacher became very angry as he talked about the house searching and the brutal treatment by US soldiers. We also asked about the possibility of our living there and doing nonviolence work on the streets. "We don't want anyone to protect us. We will fight the Americans," he responded. "This is only the beginning."

We got a mixture of positive and skeptical responses. We heard from the people of Falluja that they were very independent and didn't want any outside people coming in to organize their resistance to the occupation of their city and country. They simply wanted to be in control of their own lives and community.

While walking the streets in Falluja one day, a man gave us a flyer in Arabic, which our translator read to us. It strongly denounced America, criticizing the US for its aggression against Iraq to seek control of oil and economic resources there and gain a power base in the Middle East. I had hoped we could find and talk with the sheik who wrote and distributed the flyer, but he lived more than an hour's drive from there, and we did not find the time to do it on subsequent trips.

The question for us then was, if we stayed in Falluja, where would we live? We looked at the only hotel in the city, but saw that with dormitory-style rooms and only one bathroom for all the residents, it would not be acceptable for women on the team to stay there. And, at that time, we were an all-woman team.

What about the university? Would there possibly be guest rooms there to at least stay for two or three nights in a row and go back and forth between Baghdad and Falluja? At the College of Public Administration, the friendly, American-educated dean advised us to write a letter of request to the president of the main university offices in Ramadi. We did that and on our next trip we went to Ramadi to Anbar University and talked with the vice president. They had built new buildings after the old ones had been trashed and looted in April. The vice president was welcoming, but shared his hesitation at giving us accommodations.

If they did, they would feel responsible also for our security while we were in Ramadi (even though we insisted they wouldn't).

We were disappointed that the doors to stay in Falluja weren't opening for us. We had more than enough work opening up in Baghdad and had established extensive contacts and relationships there, so at least for now we would live there. We could still take day trips to Falluja if that seemed important.

Once we had come to that conclusion, we started looking for another apartment or house to rent in Baghdad. We wanted something cheaper than our current apartment at the Zahrat Al Kaleej. Also we wanted to leave the neighborhood we were in. It was along a commercial street and right next to the Baghdad Hotel, which was now becoming fortified by walls, sandbags, and armed guards. People suspected that the CIA lived there. (Later, in September, the Baghdad Hotel would be damaged by a car bomb explosion near the entrance. In that explosion, the side of the Zahrat Al Kaleej, where we had lived, was also damaged.)

We began looking in the Karrada Dakhil neighborhood (inside of the Karrada peninsula, surrounded by the Tigris River on three sides), near the Al Dar Hotel, where we had lived the previous winter. It was a residential neighborhood where we could get to know our neighbors and was close to the Karrada Street shopping district. With the help of our translator and his cousin, we found a three-bedroom apartment just a block off Karrada Street, two blocks from the Al Dar. By July 20 we had moved in and began to meet some of the families along our block. There we had less generator back-up and so, less electricity. Most evenings we met and wrote by candlelight.

We continued to witness and speak out against the current violence and oppression, supporting Iraqi nonviolent organizations in addressing the problems in their society and responding to the problems of detainees and their families.

On July 13, we heard about the launching of the new governing council in Iraq, made up of twenty-five Iraqis hand-picked by US authorities, not chosen by the people. Some Iraqis found this a first step toward a more democratic, Iraqi-controlled government, but we heard more skepticism about it. It was made up mostly of Iraqis who supported the presence of the US and who would not challenge the occupation.

Mid-morning, on August 6, a small group of us gathered in central Baghdad to begin our Hiroshima Day march and vigil. We stopped by at the tent of the UUI protest group, across the street from the CPA headquarters. One man explained to others what we were doing and soon a group picked up our signs and came with us. Our signs listed "Weapons of Mass Destruction: the Hiroshima bomb, the August 6, 1991, imposition of economic sanctions on Iraq, the use of depleted uranium in US weapons in both Gulf wars, and the proliferation of radioactive dust all over Iraq." Estimates of how much DU was used in this latest war on Iraq differed, ranging from 500 to 1,500 tons. This was in addition to the estimated 300-500 tons used in the first Gulf War. (A British report said that in this 2003 war, US forces used five times the amount of DU than was used in 1991.)

Our group of Iraqis and internationals walked half a mile to a large shopping center smashed by US bombs, handed out copies of our press release, and held up the signs to buses and cars going by at that busy corner. For us Americans, it was a reminder of the many atrocities for which our country needs to repent.

Earlier, on July 24, our small team had made the hour-and-a-half drive south of Baghdad to the small town of Al Mahaweel. Our presence caused a stir among the people on the street. Later we found out that we were the first nonmilitary international people to come to their town since the war. We first went to the governor's office. There the assistant governor had been talking for two hours with two representatives of a US military's psychological unit. It was hard to tell who was more surprised to see us, the assistant or the soldiers. The US sergeant asked us, disbelievingly, if we often traveled around Iraq like this, without armed guards.

The soldiers were going through a long list of questions from a survey form. At one point the sergeant asked if the people in the town were able to read the newspaper. The governor's assistant winced, but replied, "Of course, this is the land of Hammurabi." (Hammurabi wrote the first code of law in the most ancient civilization in recorded history.) Another question was whether the police in Al Mahaweel had all the equipment they needed. The assistant answered, "I think you should ask the police."

Mass gravesite at Al Mahaweel.

Before leaving, the sergeant gave the assistant a new satellite radio, so he could hear special news reports (from the occupation forces) and share the news with his people. The assistant told the translator, who didn't translate this to the soldiers, that he would keep it at home, in case it was bugged. Our translator later told us what he had said.

When we expressed our interest in praying for healing and peace at a nearby mass grave, the assistant welcomed us back and helped us find local Islamic leaders of the Al Dawa party. These men welcomed us as Christians to come back in mid-August when, together, we would share our prayers for healing and peace.

On August 15, Anne Montgomery, Gene Stoltzfus, and I returned to join with local farmers and officials in a religious ceremony remembering thousands of Iraqis slain in 1991. We walked quietly and soberly through the field, among the small mounds of dug-up clothing and mementos of the people buried at this mass gravesite. We saw a man's headband, clumps of hair, red prayer beads, a pair of old shoes, and the black *abaya* of a woman who was buried with her one-and-a-half-year-old baby. Each article belonged to a man, woman, or child who had once walked this valley of Al Mahaweel, near Hilla and

Babylon in central Iraq. According to local officials, the victims were among three thousand who had been slaughtered by Saddam's forces during an uprising encouraged by the US at the end of the Gulf War in 1991.

Local Islamic groups had set up a long canopy tent, lined with chairs for this Muslim-Christian prayer vigil and memorial service. About thirty people representing Muslim leaders, Al Mahaweel and Babylon district government officials, a human rights organization, the press, and other local people gathered with us there. The temperature got up to 120 degrees Fahrenheit.

A religious sheik welcomed the group gathered, and chanted from the Koran. Then we walked out to the closest field where graves had been dug up, and we continued our prayers. We shared some thoughts and a series of short readings from Psalm 22, the Beatitudes, and the Prayer of St. Francis, which were translated into Arabic. The main text, however, was from Ezekiel 37, about the vision of the valley of dry bones and the question, "Can these bones live?" Gene suggested that these bones would rise again as those present and people around the world take a stand for justice, truth, and peace.

During the sharing, several Iraqis emphasized our common desire for peace. We prayed that such mass killings never happen again, no matter where, no matter by whom. At the close of the formal gathering, local residents led us into the field of graves, where we honored the victims and their families with prayers and silence.

Later local farmers provided the team and leaders present with a feast in a house made of reeds that grew in the marshes of southern Iraq. The hour-long service of remembrance under the hot Iraqi sun brought together Christian and Muslims, Iraqis and Americans, in a recommitment to work for a world without mass graves.

~ ~ ~

There were moments during the summer when waves of loneliness crept inside me and took over. Living in a society caught up in fear and expectations of violence, anxious about meeting daily needs, I longed for love and tenderness and open, carefree laughter. In this hot, dry desert climate, I craved beauty and color. I saw my own neediness and dryness, and longed to be filled with springs of living water. Soon I wondered if I had been giving this same love and gentleness to others around me.

The day after I dealt with these feelings, I began to see all kinds of beauty that I hadn't noticed before. I took time to savor it—a flower or plant growing up along the street, the seed pods on a tree at the university, the special kindness shown to us as strangers, people opening to us their hopes and dreams, the wide grin of a child.

In a message I sent home, I wrote:

> The realism of war, suffering, and oppressive forces are so present here, but I find it important to look beyond these things, to keep seeing the beauty of the people and culture, even in their woundedness. We receive so much kindness each day. I am fed by the beauty around me. It would be easy to overlook these things. There are many things I long to see. There are many things I would like other people and our government to see. I can share, I can act, I can speak out, but I can't make them see. I pray that we will open our hearts to God's Spirit, and for "those who have ears, let them hear, and those who have eyes, let them see!"

$$\sim \sim \sim$$

Another day we headed once again to Hilla, the modern city next to the ruins of the ancient city of Babylon. Gene and I were going with Lisa Ndejuru and Yaser Shoukry, two Canadians of the Iraq Solidarity Project, to a meeting with a human rights organization and with the governor's assistant whom we had met at Al Mahaweel. What we found there, however, was a surprise. As we walked into the offices of the governor of Hilla/Babylon, the dozen or so US Marines and Iraqi security guards seemed shocked to see us.

Minutes after we entered the building, we began to hear the chants of a protest outside the front gates of the building. Officials escorted us to a meeting room, apologizing profusely. "There are about two hundred protesting, and so far they are peaceful," they told us, seeming embarrassed and trying to allay any fear we might have.

The governor's assistant was preoccupied with what they regarded as a siege on their building. Two of us walked up to the roof, where about a dozen more Marines and Iraqi guards stood watching and taking pictures of the chanting crowd below. Their banners said in Arabic, "The people of Babylon are asking for electricity, oil, water, jobs, and civil services," and "Release the prisoners detained without any charge." We heard chants of "We don't want scandal," "The governor is skillful in robbery," and "Where is the gas and the oil stolen by thieves?"

We decided to go out and talk to the protestors. While Gene and Yaser stayed inside and talked with soldiers and security guards, Lisa and I walked out a side door of the building and out to the crowd. We asked to talk with the leaders, but they were inside negotiating with the governor and his staff. Very quickly men in the crowd surrounded us and began to pour out their frustrations and grief. They treated us with utmost respect and seemed to appreciate our willingness to listen to their concerns.

A teacher complained that only people connected with the past corrupt leaders had been hired as teachers. One man told about a former police commissioner who had lost his job and was trying to get another. A driver was suffering from the shortage of gas. Another said that soldiers detained two men who passed out a flyer criticizing the occupying authorities, but later released them.

They directed most of their anger not at the US administration, but at the governor, whom they wanted to remove from office. They said he had been a high-ranking member of the Ba'ath Party, appointed not by the people, but by US authorities. The people called him corrupt, a drunkard, a robber. We got quite an earful before we went back inside to join the others.

When we were ready to leave, officials escorted us out a back door, presumably where they felt we would be safe—far away from the crowd we had just been talking to.

~ ~ ~

For two days we visited the cities of Kerbala and Najaf, both places of major Shi'a shrines. The streets were busy with pilgrims, mainly from Iran. In both cities we visited human

Women seeking help from human rights organization in Najaf.

rights organizations where a few dedicated volunteers were swamped with people trying to get some kind of material relief or compensation for relatives who have been killed in past wars. Others were trying to locate family members who had disappeared during the recent war and occupation, or clean up unexploded weapons.

We weren't able to talk with top-level Shi'a clerics (due to a long waiting list) but met with several sheiks of lesser rank. "Saddam Hussein was just a student of the US administration," the leader of the group told us. "The US is operating out of its own self-interests. Now that Saddam no longer served US interests, we have the occupation. The sooner the occupying forces leave, the better." Their group had basically refused to meet with or work with US or British officials.

On that very hot day, the temperature was 120 to 130 degrees, and I was especially uncomfortable wearing the *abaya*. My frustration increased when the part covering my head kept slipping back, and our translator kept whispering to me that my hair was showing.

~ ~ ~

"The UN headquarters in Baghdad was bombed!" While on this trip we were shocked by the news. I was sad and sobered, having met so many UN workers there and knowing how this might affect other international workers in Iraq. The UN had done a lot of good work there through very dedicated people, but it was also associated with the suffering from the sanctions and with cooperating with US and UK policies and the occupation of Iraq. This seemed like an attempt to sabotage the whole occupation system that Iraqis feared was settling in for a long time. In the process, innocent people were getting hurt. I thought it was likely this kind of violence would continue and possibly get worse.

About a week and half later, we were again shocked to hear that Muhammad Baqir Al Hakim, one of the top three Shi'a clerics in Iraq, and about eighty others were killed by a car-bomb explosion at the Shrine of Ali in Najaf. In Baghdad the next morning, black banners commemorating him hung over streets. One group marching on a busy street chanted: "No America, No Saddam." I grieved for all the killings and loss of life there and prayed that this would not snowball into increased and continued violence.

~ ~ ~

Every Iraqi, no matter what his or her economic level, was receiving a monthly allotment of dried foods. We decided to visit a monthly food rations pick-up center. It was just a tiny, one-room storefront in a neighborhood in central Baghdad, but was the place where more than seventy families picked up their food rations each month. Women, men, and children from the neighborhood flocked around the front of the store, watching us and asking questions as we sat on crates made into makeshift chairs.

The manager listed for us the amounts of rations that one person received each month: 2 kilos sugar, 3 kilos rice, 1½ kilos cooking oil, 200 grams tea, 500 grams laundry powder, ¼ kilo beans or peas, and 9 kilos flour. That was the same amount Iraqi people had received for the previous thirteen years under Saddam's government. It was considered free, but there was actually a small service charge equivalent to about fifty cents that each family paid to the distributor for his work.

On our second visit, we watched as the supplier weighed out and bagged the goods for one family and put the bags into their pull-cart. It didn't look like very much.

Two days later, I read in a US newspaper article about the UN cutting back their staff from about four hundred to about fifty because of the bomb attack. The article mentioned that the food rations might be one of the programs that would be cut. There had already been a call to reassess the program that fall. At a time like this, when more than half of the workers in Iraq were unemployed, eliminating the program would have drastic effects on the well-being of the poor.

~ ~ ~

A day later, CPTer Jerry Stein, a Catholic priest from Texas, and I flagged a taxi on our way to make a visit. After some light conversation with the taxi driver, he looked at me and said, "You should be more careful about getting into just any taxi. It's even dangerous for Iraqis." We hadn't been doing anything we didn't normally do, but his words shook me a little. Had we been too careless in our traveling around town? I wondered.

I reported this to the others on the team to get their feedback. I had been aware of many dangers all along and wanted to be sensible and careful but not let this keep me from doing work I needed to do, so I chose to continue traveling, even if alone. With such a small team, it would be hard to always pair up. There had been other incidents that would cause us to stop and evaluate how we were operating, such as when another international woman friend of ours came close to being abducted by men with guns at about four o'clock in the afternoon along Karrada Street. She was able to run away. The next day, about that same time, I was a little nervous about walking along the same street alone. But I couldn't live with constant worry. I had to choose between shrinking back out of fear and going out to do our work. Again I chose to keep going.

I wrote back home, "We do not want to be dominated by fear. I feel led to continue doing this work in trust that God is caring for me and is with me whatever happens. There is no way of knowing where or when an attack will take place. I think we are safer than the UN or other NGO personnel who ride in marked vehicles and are more isolated from common people."

Three times during the summer I witnessed shootings. At about nine one morning, I was in my bedroom. All of sudden I heard loud shouts and arguing, then heard a shot. From my window I could see a man pointing a gun at someone I couldn't see. There was more shooting, so we ducked down to the floor and left the room. When it was quiet, we went outside and saw the owner of our apartment building with blood on his face and clothing. At first we thought he was shot. But he said, "No." We found out that two men with guns had shot into the air, trying to scare him, and trying to rob him and take his car. His head wounds came from hitting his head in the car doorway as one robber was trying to pull him out of the car to take it. Another man, from an upstairs apartment, shot a gun from the upstairs window, but, again, just shot into the air to scare the robbers away.

While driving through the city of Ramadi one day, we saw Iraqi police scuffling with some other men along the sidewalk. Ten seconds later, when we were about a block away, shots began to sound. People ran away from the scene and cars were backing up to get away.

Another time, I was in a taxi driving through an intersection near our apartment in Baghdad when we drove right through the middle of a gun battle between Iraqi police and men on the street. A few yards from my taxi, a policeman shot one of the men in the shoulder. I could see the blood coming out of his wound. I felt shaken by that for some time and talked about this with others on the team.

Each time I was reminded of the violence and danger, I had to consciously accept the risks of danger or death in order to do the work I felt called to do. I had to go back to the love I have been given for the people who couldn't leave this situation, to see their pain and remember that "nothing can separate us from the love of God."

~ ~ ~

Sometimes we needed a little humor thrown in to keep us from letting the many daily frustrations get us down.

One day while driving across Baghdad in the sweltering summer heat, our taxi driver began to expound on all the problems of the Iraqi people since the war. "I am seeking solutions to our country's problems," he mused, as we slowly wove our way through traffic snarls, at times taking fifteen to twenty minutes to get through a busy intersection. Since the war, few drivers obeyed traffic rules, and traffic lights were only as dependable as the electricity. Our translator picked up on the theme of solving problems and, wanting to bring some lightness to our traffic dilemma, began to tell a series of riddles. "What are the three easy steps to get an elephant into a refrigerator?" he asked. After all of our guesses failed, he gave us the answer: "1. Open the door. 2. Push the elephant in. 3. Close the door!"

"Easy?" we asked.

As the car inched forward again, I began to see a correlation between the traffic jam we were in the middle of—with drivers in their cars and buses coming at each other from all directions, each unwilling, and often unable, to move so the others could go through—and the tangled mess of the Iraqi society left in the wake of the war. The war resulted in massive economic, political, and health crises, and with the fall of the former regime came a lifting of restraints on lawlessness, bringing much of the society to a standstill. Iraqis found it hard to work their way through the chaos to take care of their family's needs. This sounded similar to the wider deadlocks in other international situations, where conflicts often seemed to have no good solutions.

After pondering for a moment, I decided to share my thoughts aloud. I said something like this:

The solution may seem impossible at times, but it is actually quite simple. Simple, but not easy, because the rich and powerful countries don't have the will to do it. Their foreign policies involve programs like economic globalization in third-world countries and free trade agreements, which provide the legal structures for large international corporations to move into and take over major economic operations in these countries. They end up taking much of the wealth and natural resources out of the country and displacing the poor from their land. US policy toward Iraq included helping build up the power of a local dictator who carried out his own oppressive agendas among his people.

The way to start solving these problems is not to focus just on the symptoms of increasing violence against the US and stamping out "terrorism," but to completely change this greedy foreign policy and pursue new policies that establish justice with and within those countries.

Simple? Yes, it would make a huge difference. Easy? No. To change the will of the rich and powerful may be like trying to force the elephant into a refrigerator, or "through the eye of a needle," as someone said years ago.

CHAPTER 12

Disappeared

Let us rededicate ourselves in the long and bitter, but beautiful
struggle for a new world. If we but make the right choice, we
will be able to speed up the day, all over America, all over the
world, when justice will roll down like waters, and righteous-
ness like a might stream.
—Martin Luther King Jr.

As the summer progressed, more Iraqi people came to us for
help finding information about family members who had been
detained by the US military. Often their fathers, sons, or brothers
had been missing or arrested for two or three months, and they
still didn't know where they were or what they were charged
with. Most had heard about detainees being treated brutally
and kept in horrible living conditions, and so they worried
about their loved ones' safety. The following are a sample of the
kinds of cases reported to us:

A dentist, who didn't want his name to be used, came to us
distraught because his brother, a fourth-year engineering
student, had been arrested. He told us that his brother and two
friends had just left their classes and had been walking home on
June 23 when they saw a fight break out among some Iraqi men
nearby. His brother went to see what was happening, heard gun-
shots, and ran. US military police caught him and at first were
going to let him go, because he had no weapon. Then they found
a weapon on the ground in the area and accused him of firing it.

I am reading an Iraqi man's written complaint detailing human rights abuses, August 2003.

Soldiers took him to an Iraqi police station for questioning and arrested him. He had been scheduled to take his final exams the next day. At the end of August, when we got the lists of detainees from the CPA, we found Ameer was being held in Um Qasr. When I left Iraq two months later, he was still in detention.

Ramuydh, thirty-nine, left his job as a guard at a chicken farm between Falluja and Ramadi as usual at 6:30 a.m. on July 13 and started home on his motorcycle. He carried a gun that he used to protect the chicken farm. Later, when he didn't return home, his brother and friends went to find him along his usual route. They found tracks in the desert, some remnants of food he had with him, and small, broken parts of his motorcycle. There were other tracks there, so they assumed US soldiers had arrested him. His brother went to the governor's office in Falluja, where we met him. We tried to find information about Ramuyd at the Iraq Assistance Center (IAC) in Baghdad, but had no success.

The family of another detained man told us his story: The father had been an officer in the Iraqi army. After the invasion of Baghdad he was afraid and stayed mostly in his home. US soldiers came to his home at midnight, started shooting at his house, then blasted the door open and came in. They searched the house, destroyed furnishings, and stole money and gold jewelry. In the process of shooting at the house, they shot the man's wife in the face, arm, and leg, and later she lost one of her eyes. The man was still detained and the family did not know where he was.

An assistant dean of the College of Languages, his wife, and another man came to us, asking for help concerning their sons, who had been arrested on July 22. American soldiers had rounded up thirty-five men in the area near a military base where a mine had exploded. Later an Iraqi policeman came to tell them of their son's arrest, that he was charged with exploding the mine and was at the airport detention center.

Suhail, a veterinarian, told us the story of his detention. On May 16, he and his son, Ahmed, had gone out of curiosity to see one of Saddam's palaces. There was a truck nearby, which the US soldiers thought belonged to the two men. Soldiers initially arrested just his son, but Suhail, who spoke some English, decided to stay with him and was arrested too. Suhail had high blood pressure and was on medication.

They were detained at the airport, but later moved to Abu Ghraib prison. They were in tents and slept on bare ground, with no mats or blankets, with about a hundred men in each tent. On June 13, the prisoners shouted, "Freedom!" repeatedly and the US soldiers opened fire on them, killing four and wounding three. Suhail knew one of those killed, a man of nineteen who had been married four months. He held the young man as he died. The next day soldiers gave Suhail clean clothes, told him not to speak about what he had seen, and then released him. We helped find where his son had been transferred, and later, when his son was released, he came to thank us.

"This whole experience is so unreal, it's like science fiction," an Iraqi science professor told us when recounting to us his three-month ordeal being interrogated in more than a dozen meetings with the US "Scientific Assessment Team." Many other scientists he knew had similar experiences. One professor he knew was taken away and detained for two weeks. Another was still in detention. "I wish there was something I could do to close this file," he lamented.

"It started with a polite interview," he said, "and then the interrogation became more harsh and threatening. We were guilty until proven innocent." They demanded that he tell them where weapons of mass destruction (WMD) were. When he told them he didn't know about any, interrogators insisted he was lying. "They asked me over and over, telling me I was lying. That was the hardest part. When they asked why I wasn't telling the truth, I answered, 'Are you interested in the truth, or just in what you want to hear?'

"We explained in detail how our systems work. The judgment of all scientists I know is that WMD do not exist here or elsewhere in the country. The interrogators referred to a 'reliable source' claiming the existence of a secret underground laboratory. We were honest. We knew of no such place. I finally said, 'Then bring that person here and let *him* find it for you!'"

When we first started looking for information about the detainees, we would mostly go to the IAC, where officers were friendly and helpful and would look on computer lists to try to find their names, charges, and location. Even then, however, we were only able to find information in about ten percent of the cases we brought. When we told them of the stories the detainees and their families told us about the physical and psychological abuse and theft of property, the officers were concerned but said they didn't have any power to make changes. In one of the earlier cases we went to an Iraqi police station with an Iraqi man and found out the charges against his brother. When we pushed the US Army captain in charge at that station about any due process or timeline for a trial, he told us, "This is a war. We don't have to give them any rights."

Later in the summer, Cathy and I went through a lengthy process to get into the main CPA headquarters. Just being in that place was an amazing experience, seeing the opulence and power of the former regime, but now it was the center of power of the new regime. It was like a village in itself, cut off from the real world of Iraqi society. Initially, we went to take part in a meeting set up by the Justice Ministry for Iraqi human rights workers. Because it took us so long to get in, we missed the meeting, but decided to use the opportunity to talk to various US officials working there.

We talked to Sandy Hodgkinson, director of the human rights office of the CPA, who expressed concern, but said his office was mostly focusing on human rights abuses of the former regime.

Then we talked to Judge Campbell and told him about our work with families of detained Iraqis. When we talked about the abuse of detainees, their lack of legal rights, and the theft of money and jewelry, he expressed concern and frustration. He described the situation as terrible, disorganized, and inadequate. But he said, "This is the best we can do right now." Then he proceeded to have his staff photocopy two huge documents, one in English and one in Arabic, listing about six thousand names. "These were men arrested for anything from curfew violations to murder," he said. It did not list men accused of violence against US troops or ones currently being transferred from one detention center to another.

We went away, glad to have the lists of detainees. It would help us with our work, but it was tragic to realize there was not much hope for the system of justice in Iraq being changed or improved in the near future.

This also meant we needed to take further steps to deal with the problems of human rights in Iraq. We decided to take one case and see how far we could go with it in dealing with US authorities. In late August, Gene Stoltzfus, director of CPT, Jerry, and I visited the home of Dr. Talib, a retired physician and his wife, Nawal, a dentist. They told us their story:

Just after midnight on August 1, 2003, they woke to the sounds of shooting and the crashing in their outside door. Their first thought was that it was thieves, so the oldest son shot their gun into the air to scare them away. The response was heavy firing on the house from every direction. They then realized it was American soldiers. For the next two and a half hours Dr. Talib went toward the door and called out in good English, "Come in. We are not violent!" and every time he did this, the shooting would start again. The family members were afraid they would all be killed.

Finally, at about 3:00 a.m., Dr. Talib crawled near the door and called out, "I am coming to open the door." One soldier answered nervously, "Open the door!" When he did, the soldiers

Dr. Talib and his wife, Nawal, at their home in Baghdad.

rushed in and started hitting and kicking Dr. Talib and his three adult sons, knocking them to the floor, now covered with kerosene from a punctured tank. The soldiers handcuffed their hands behind their backs, stepped on their heads, and continued to kick them. Meanwhile other soldiers ransacked the house, destroying household furnishings. The only weapons the soldiers found were a legally permitted small pistol and automatic rifle.

One of the soldiers asked the father if his name was Akif. He replied, "No, my name is Talib. Akif's house is further down on this street." The soldiers realized they had made a mistake. The captain apologized. Then they got into an incredible conversation. Dr. Talib asked the soldiers, "Why didn't you just ring the doorbell? We would have let you in."

The captain replied, "We were scared." He then asked Dr. Talib, "Do you like America?"

Dr. Talib said, "I did until this happened." Then he said, "I thought you were from a country of freedom and democracy. Is this freedom? Is this democracy?"

The captain replied, "You don't know how many of our people are being killed each day."

When they were ready to leave, the captain said he would have to take the three sons. All of Dr. Talib's pleading did not stop the soldiers, and they took them away. We were there one month later and the family still didn't know where the sons were. We saw the physical damage done to the house, but we saw a deeper damage in their faces. Their eyes carried the strain of fear, pain, and worry for their sons.

We decided to try to find where the three were being held, so two team members spent an entire day accompanying the family to a Civil Military Operations Center (CMOC). We finally were able to learn that the sons were incarcerated at Um Qasr in southern Iraq. The family filed an appeal for their release.

A few days later, in early September when I was preparing to leave Iraq, Jerry drove with Dr. Talib and his wife to the prison at Um Qasr. Other Iraqis were waiting in the hot sun, also trying to go in. After three hours, they were able to see the three brothers. They also talked with Major Stacy Garrity, who was helpful and said she would recommend they be released. But she said the process would take at least two weeks. The three were not released until the end of October.

We were horrified, not only at the brutal treatment in the house raids and detention process and the detaining of innocent people, but also the lack of a process for determining guilt or innocence or releasing information to families about charges, location, and well-being of the detained. Though many of the US officials expressed concern to us, we saw little evidence that they were taking steps to change the situation.

Earlier in the summer when we had started working with detainees, we wondered if these were a few exceptions or if the dysfunction of the system was just a natural part of the chaos that normally follows war. As fall approached, however, we saw that the problems seemed consistent and the system did not improve. There were a few successful inquiries, where the family was able to find and visit the detainee, and even a few were released. But for the most part, this didn't happen. It became increasingly clear to us that the problem was not just a few bad people in the system, or the violent nature of an occupation, but an explicit policy being put into practice.

The team continued to document such cases in order to expose what was going on in Iraq and to explain it to the American people and government officials. We found it a continual challenge to find creative ways to confront US authorities with the truth and call them to a radical turning around, a way of respect and justice. It seemed to me that the occupying forces were generally not "winning the hearts and minds" of the Iraqi people. Toward the end of that summer I put some of what I was seeing and hearing into writing:

Navigating the Dilemmas of Power and Fear

US and British occupying forces in Iraq are facing some difficult challenges. The attacks against soldiers have not only been increasing, but seem to be coming from a more organized resistance. As Army Staff Sergeant Hubert Howell recently said, "A lot of people might think it's calmed down, but it's just beginning."

The military has responded in turn with increased raids into Iraqi homes, desperately attempting to find Ba'ath Party leaders, "terrorists," and "weapons of mass destruction." On the streets our team sees more rolls of razor wire, sand-barrel walls built to protect the military posts, and coalition provisional offices.

All this "protects" occupation forces, but does not deal with the underlying causes of the increasing anger and frustration of the Iraqi people that fuels these attacks. There is rising anger about their unmet daily needs, lack of regular electricity, running water, and jobs.

Unfortunately, what our team sees on the streets of Iraq is not a well-organized, concerted effort to repair, rebuild, and quickly transfer political or economic power so forces can leave. We see slow, disorganized structures and processes. It is the picture of an occupation that has no plans for leaving soon, but intends to stay and reap economic and political benefits from this country.

We see fear driving people on all sides. We see Iraqis rebelling against foreign rule and US forces responding with increased ruthlessness to internal rebellion, and labeling it "terrorism." But this is the nature of occupation, which sets up this inevitable escalation of violence. And this cycle of violence will likely continue to escalate unless something new is given.

Something new could be a change of direction and policy of the occupying forces, leading to a quick rebuilding and transference of power and control. But it could also come out of the increasing number of grassroots Iraqi organizations springing up, with a vision of confronting the problems and the occupation through nonviolent action. Combining boldness of speech and action to seek justice for the Iraqi people with a vision of the power of nonviolence, they have the potential to give constructive leadership to rebuilding and reclaiming their society without more bloodshed in this land.

On September 3, after another full and powerful three months in Iraq, I left the country. I would often think about the people of Iraq and the team as I traveled around the United States, telling these stories and writing this book. I would continue to carry a deep love for this war-torn society.

PART 3

Speaking Truth to Power

December 25, 2003—March 24, 2004

I knew that I could never raise my voice
against the violence of the oppressed in the ghettos
without having first spoken clearly
to the greatest purveyor of violence in the world today,
my own government.
—*Martin Luther King Jr.*

CHAPTER 13

Tell Me, Is the War Over?

I slept little the night of December 15, 2003, anticipating leaving my family and friends, and the hills, fields, and woods of southeastern Ohio the next morning to go back to Iraq. One month earlier Art and I had made the decision that we would both go at the same time to the Middle East to work with CPT that winter. He would go for two months to Hebron, where he felt called, and I, for three months to Iraq.

How could I explain why I was returning? It was clear to me that a piece of my heart was still there with the Iraqi people, whom I love and care about. For me, it was important for people of peace to be present there and in other conflict situations, working in the spirit of love. I wanted to be part of a group seeking to find and practice nonviolent, life-giving ways of intervening in violent situations. When I have taken risks or stepped out in faith to work with others for love, justice, and peace, God has always been there with us, working through what we do. And though it's not easy, it's been life-giving and has strengthened my faith.

This time I flew first to Tokyo for a week of speaking about the Iraq Peace Team and Christian Peacemaker Team's experiences in Iraq and meeting with peace and human rights organizations. For the work of IPT and CPT in Iraq, I received the Yoko Tada Human Rights Award, established in honor of Yoko Tada, a Japanese human rights lawyer who died at a young age. Masakazu Honda, a Japanese reporter from the *Asahi Shimbun* newspaper in Tokyo who interviewed me in April 2003 in Amman after I was expelled from Iraq, had been impressed by our team's work and had submitted my name.

Like people working for peace in the US, many of the people I met in Japan said they felt their organizations were small and weak in dealing with all the problems they saw. Being with them and witnessing their work and dedication for peace encouraged me. My way of encouraging them was to tell the stories of how many had worked for peace in Iraq. It was a gift to learn from each other.

In Hiroshima, a visit to the Atomic Bomb Museum and Peace Park had special meaning to me after having experienced the bombing of Baghdad. Here, with the horrible reminders of the consequences of war, had emerged the powerful voice for peace of the first and second generations of atomic bomb survivors. They work so that nuclear weapons are never used again.

In June 2003 the Hiroshima Alliance for Nuclear Weapons Abolition had launched a project called the No DU Hiroshima Project. As a part of this group, Haruko Moritaki collected dust samples from Iraqi tanks, water, soil, and urine from around heavily populated sites in Baghdad bombed by American forces in March and April 2003, and took them to Hiroshima. By the time I left Iraq in late March 2004, the study had not been completed, but the samples analyzed so far were found to contain DU at 10 to 100 times normal background radiation. This group also looked at studies by Iraqi and international scientists showing the correlation between the increase in cancers and birth defects and increased amounts of DU present since the first Gulf War. Out of this work they published the book *Hiroshima Appeal to Abolish DU Weapons*, a vivid and compassionate description of the nature and problems of DU.

Members of the Article 9 Society had worked to preserve Article 9 in the Japanese constitution, which declares that Japan will not prepare for war or have a standing army and that it will promote peace around the world. Over the years the commitment to this constitutional document eroded as Japan's leaders began rearming and formed the Japanese Self-Defense Force. They fostered an interpretation of Article 9 that gave Japan the right of self-defense.

As I arrived, Japan decided to send Self-Defense Forces to Iraq to the southern city of Samawe, where they would help US troops transport supplies into Iraq from Kuwait. Japan's government also decided to develop a missile defense system, saying that their biggest national threat was North Korea's ballistic missiles. The Article 9 Society saw these steps as violations of Japan's constitution and wanted to maintain its clear pledge for world peace.

~ ~ ~

From Tokyo I flew to Chicago, where I met Art and three others who would be joining the team in Iraq. These included Sheila Provencher, a full-time CPTer from South Bend, Indiana; and Haven and Rose Whiteside, part-time workers from Florida. Together we flew to Amman, where we met Maxine Nash, a full-time worker from Indiana, who had just come from working with CPT in the West Bank.

After a day in Amman, Sunday, December 28, Art traveled west to Hebron, while the rest of us headed east to Iraq. The Al Monzer Hotel staff in Amman, whom we had come to know well, helped us find a bus to Baghdad. Because all the buses going that way left in the evening, we traveled overnight.

Crossing the border went slowly with about thirty passengers on board, but without any problems. This time, Iraqi soldiers and guards replaced US troops there. I was too sleepy to think or feel much about where I was headed.

In the darkness of the night I woke from time to time, but didn't see much of the road or terrain. By daylight we had passed Ramadi, crossed the Euphrates River with the expanse of vegetation on either side, and passed Falluja without any problem. By nine we were finding our way through the heavy morning traffic in the western neighborhoods of Baghdad. It felt like coming home when at about ten o'clock we reached our Karrada apartment, meeting Cliff Kindy and Allan Slater, both of whom had been in Iraq before the war and had now been back in Iraq since November 2003, the only team members in Iraq at that time.

It wasn't long before we were at work. Three of us went with Cliff that afternoon to a meeting of a coalition of international and Iraqi groups working at human rights issues, coordinated by a lively Italian human rights worker, Paula

Gasparoli. Because I would be coordinating the detainee campaign, I thought I might as well get started. Later I would find time to get settled into the apartment and visit Iraqi friends, the orphanage, and Iraqi religious leaders. I also wanted to pray and worship with Iraqis and catch up on what had changed since I left. Then there would be other team work, such as responding to immediate requests for help, listening to people on all sides, writing their stories and other articles, distributing *Hiroshima Appeal to Abolish DU Weapons* and doing household tasks. There was no gradual immersion.

~ ~ ~

A loud boom interrupted our CPT team meeting at about nine Tuesday morning, December 30, my second day back in Iraq. As we left our apartment, neighbors in our building told us that a grenade had exploded two blocks away on Karrada Street.

Three team members went to see what had happened. First we saw broken windows in the buildings for about a half-block on either side of Karrada Street. The falafel shop and the date store were among those damaged. A crowd of about three hundred people gathered. Women stood around crying; school children dismissed from their school because of the explosion stood around with fearful expressions.

Several people told us that an Iraqi man had been killed as he had been taking money to a bank, and a street vendor was wounded. They said the glass of one US military Humvee, which had been the target of the bomb, was damaged, and an Iraqi translator inside was wounded. No US soldiers were hurt.

We saw the dead man's body covered by a large piece of corrugated cardboard. People we spoke to did not know his name, because he was not from that neighborhood. The next day, however, neighbors told us that the street vendor had died and that up to five people had been injured.

That morning, Iraqi police came, followed by about twenty US soldiers, who sporadically yelled to the crowd, "Get away!" and "Get out of here!" in English, but did not really enforce their threats. Soon Iraqi men broke through the crowd, put the man's body in a simple wooden coffin, lifted it to their shoulders, and took it into the nearby mosque. Fifteen minutes later the men brought the body out again, covered with a black shroud, put it into a pickup truck, and drove away, escorted by an Iraqi policeman on a motorcycle.

Meanwhile we took pictures and talked to several people who spoke English. One man was very angry and said, "This was the work of outsiders. Iraqi people wouldn't do such a thing! The US is the most powerful country in the world, and people around the world are now coming into Iraq because this is where they can attack the US."

Ayad, a local welder we had known over the past year told us, "Iraqi people don't hate American people, but they do not want US soldiers here because of what they are doing. We don't like our country occupied. Americans also wouldn't want soldiers from outside coming into their towns."

Back at the apartment we reported to the rest of the team what we had seen and experienced on the street. We observed that this attack had been clearly directed toward the US military and did not represent any particular escalation or change in the type of violence that had been occurring. This situation reminded us that it is risky to be in close proximity to US forces.

We also felt grief and pain for the Iraqi people and for the soldiers who had been targeted. This act of violence not only killed and injured a few; it killed part of the spirit of a whole community. It increased the fear, rage, and feelings of being powerless and violated, which in turn produce more acts of violence. We were part of this community caught in a tragic cycle of violence. We saw the need for healing among both Iraqis and soldiers, and the need to claim the value of each life involved in this struggle.

∼ ∼ ∼

On New Year's Eve, Siham's house was decorated and alive with laughter and reminiscing. With Sheila and me, from CPT, were Kathy Kelly (back in Iraq for two weeks), Rick McDowell and Mary Trotochaud of AFSC, and Jerry Zwada, who had lived with us at the Al Dar Hotel the winter before, until just after the bombing started. We ate *dolma* (vegetables stuffed with a rice mixture), fish, and chicken briani, topped off with a variety of sweets different guests had brought.

Unfortunately, later that evening a car bomb blast damaged a restaurant about eight blocks away, killing five, including a pregnant friend of our landlord, and injuring thirty-two. Five of the victims were internationals.

New Year's Day included an afternoon of visiting and feasting with newer friends of the team, Basima and Ra'ad, and their four children. The fact that Ra'ad was Muslim and Basima was Christian didn't seem to cause any conflict in their progressive household. Along with other special food, they cooked two sheep heads, traditionally served at the New Year. Ra'ad took the sheep heads outside, broke them open, and came back with the cooked brains on a platter. I managed to eat some, but didn't relish it the way the family seemed to.

Another new family I met was Musa, Shema, and their son and daughter. I fell in love with four-year-old Fatima and played with her whenever they came to visit. Musa was Muslim, but Shema was from a religious group called the Sabeans, descendents of the followers of John the Baptist. When we visited their home, Musa told us the story of his persecution under the former regime.

Between 1996 and 1998, secret police came periodically to Musa's home to interrogate him. He first suspected that neighbors had accused him of speaking out against Saddam. Then he thought it might be because as a printer he printed world maps with Israel and Kuwait on them.

While imprisoned for thirteen months in 1991 and 2000, he was tortured by having several toe nails pulled off, being hung by his arms pulled behind his back, and being burned on his leg with a hot prod. In spite of what he had experienced, he had a good sense of humor and usually expressed a positive viewpoint about the US presence.

After the invasion, he saw the man who had tortured him in prison and told him, "You're an animal! I could kill you, but I'm not an animal, so I won't." His former torturer nervously replied, "Thank-you."

Sa'ad Kadhim, another man we met at one of the Iraqi

human rights organizations, also had a story to tell: He was nineteen years old in 1994, when he refused an order from his military commander to fight the people of Kurdistan. "I told them those people are Iraqi and Muslims, and if I kill them, God will be angry," he said. "But it isn't only Muslims; I can't kill anyone. War is wrong."

When pressed further on how he came to this belief, he said, "There is a chapter in the Koran that tells us not to kill when we haven't been attacked. But it is something innate in me. I don't like to shed the blood of others. I have always been peaceful by nature."

He was imprisoned for two and a half months, during which he was beaten, kicked, and whipped with a cable "until it cut the meat." His arms were handcuffed behind his back in the "scorpion" position, one arm with elbow pointing skyward and reaching behind his neck, the other arm bent behind his back and pushed upward to meet the other hand below the neck. Sa'ad was suspended in the air from his bound hands for up to two hours at a time. While Sa'ad was in prison, his father died. After he was released on July 31, he didn't go back to the military, as he was supposed to. His stepmother informed on him and he was arrested a second time.

In August 1994, the Iraqi government passed Resolution 115, which added cutting off part or all of the right ear and having a line tattooed on the forehead as punishments for those refusing to follow military orders. Those with these marks would lose privileges such as being able to complete their education, buy a house or car, or receive monthly food rations. Their families were forced to move to one of two designated places on the edge of the desert and live in a tent. About 3,600 men refused to cooperate with the military, including some sixty-year-old men.

Sa'ad got out of prison after two years. "I thought my tragedy would end when I left prison, but it had only just began. Some people looked on me with pity, but others ridiculed me, calling me a coward or traitor. I got depressed and stayed in my room for four months. We are not cowards; we faced the possibility of death. I couldn't get a job, but friends took me in and gave me occasional electrical work around their houses." Then with intense emotion, Sa'ad said, "One day I asked to marry a young woman, but her family said no, because of the dishonor it would cause their family."

Since the fall of Saddam, Sa'ad had been volunteering with the National Association of Defense of Human Rights in Iraq (NADHRI) in Baghdad. He was part of the seven-person Committee of War Refusers established in October 2003. The committee helped other such men find jobs and receive corrective surgery and possibly compensation. They were also working through the Iraqi governing council to repeal Resolution 115. In a week, the group planned to have a press conference and celebration at the Al Kindi hospital, where one of the scarred men would receive the first cosmetic surgical operation.

When we commented on the courage and strength he displayed in making his decision not to go to war in spite of all the horrible consequences, Sa'ad told us, "What I want most is to live in peace and for there to be peace in all the world." He shared how much it had meant to him to be able to work with the human rights organization. "It helps me to be able to help others find help and hope. Now my clipped ear that was once a sign of disgrace is instead a badge of honor."

~ ~ ~

On January 3 we heard the sounds of a lot of bombing in the distance and later found out that it was from US military artillery and mortar fire on agricultural areas around the Al Dora area of southwest Baghdad. Military officers we talked to that day said that these were well-planned strategic strikes in response to attacks on US military units and were based on careful intelligence work. Residents of Al Dora later told us that these seemed to be random, blanket strikes that caused heavy damage to whole neighborhoods and farmland.

~ ~ ~

About twenty-five Iraqis and internationals gathered at the Al Wathba water treatment plant on January 10. CPT team members came with an eight-person, short-term delegation to plant a memorial commemorating the one-year anniversary of

George Weber's death in the automobile accident north of Basra. The words on the memorial read, "Tree of Life, in honor of George Weber, 1930-2003, CPT volunteer, and CPT presence here during "Shock and Awe," March–April, 2003."

Cliff talked about the time around George's death. Then he read from his journal about the beginning of the bombing of Baghdad in the early morning of March 20, 2003, when our team had set up the Peace Encampment at the site.

Then Layla Al Athary, engineer at the plant spoke. "Tell me, is the war over? I don't believe it is. Look at what is happening in our country. People are being killed every day. The common Iraqi person doesn't know what decisions other people are making about our future. We don't know what is going to happen to us. We feel very powerless. We are hungering for the time when we can make decisions for our own country and when our children can live in a peaceful society."

Being there was like coming home for me. The bombing of Baghdad and George's death were the two most dramatic and difficult times we had faced as a team while working in Iraq during the past year. We faced the death of our fellow CPTer, and we faced the possibility of death and destruction of thousands of Iraqi people and of our own team during the bombing. Our lives were linked with George's, as well as with these people standing with us.

Our prayer then was that the people of Iraq be spared this war, and our prayer now was that this war be over. But it was not over.

~ ~ ~

In the next two weeks I felt more deeply integrated into Iraqi life and culture, catching up on what people were thinking. I got used to being constantly watched and stared at when walking on the streets and open to the different ways people might react to me as an American. They might idolize or defer to us as members of the group in power, appreciate our work and presence, or hate us and see us as their enemy.

I wished I could say things had gotten better since I'd left in September. In a few ways they had. More Iraqis were doing the police work, physical clean up, and repair of city streets; there was some reduction in looting and robberies; and more commercial products were for sale in shops. But the phone system still didn't work, and water was occasionally shut off for days at a time. There was not much difference in the amount of electricity since the previous summer, about eight hours in a twenty-four hour day. The only difference was that the generators at the apartment building were working better so that in the evenings we had power for our computers and light to work by.

A doctor told me hospitals were getting some medications donated through international humanitarian organizations, but only had about 40 percent of what they needed to take care of all their patients. There was a new Iraqi Health Ministry, but it was not able to provide medical equipment and supplies, and was not receiving such supplies from the US. Instead, any material aid was coming from other international aid organizations and governments.

When thinking about the quality of life—people feeling safe, being able to provide for their family's needs, having a sense of hope for the future—things were worse. I sensed more anger and discouragement.

What I saw when walking down the streets of Baghdad hadn't changed a lot either. I saw the same busy streets and markets, unemployed men hanging around talking or playing backgammon, and children coming to and from school. There was still a lot of rebuilding and repairing of old and damaged homes. Some places where the sewers were not working, pools of smelly greenish water collected around the curbs. It was common to see median strips crushed from tanks driving over them. Everywhere armed guards in front of businesses and organizations held their automatic weapons. You could not assume that you would be walking on smooth pavement on sidewalks or streets, but had to watch for holes, rubble, or ditches dug for repairing pipelines. When crossing the street or riding in a car, you could encounter cars going in the wrong direction in your lane. And at any time a peaceful street scene could be interrupted by a convoy of soldiers in Humvees or tanks rumbling by with their guns pointed at you as they passed.

~ ~ ~

After I had left in September, the strength of the Iraqi resistance increased. Not only were US military posts and caravans targeted, but also some international agencies and individuals. In September, a car bomb had exploded at the Baghdad Hotel and damaged the Zahrat Al Kaleej apartment building next door, where our team's apartment had been located between May and July.

In late October and early November there was a wave of suicide bombings or other bombings in Baghdad, killing Iraqis and internationals. This was not only at places where American officials were living, such as the Al Rasheed Hotel, but also at humanitarian organizations, such as the International Committee of the Red Cross (ICRC). This led to the closing of the ICRC's main headquarters, leaving just a few workers scattered in unpublicized locations. In the week of November 2-8, resistance groups killed thirty-five US soldiers and two Japanese diplomats.

~ ~ ~

Economic occupation of Iraq went forward another step on September 19, when Ambassador Bremer instituted a new Iraqi law (Order 39). This law unilaterally privatized 200 Iraqi state companies (mines, banks, factories, etc.) and allowed foreign corporations to take 100 percent ownership of them. _The Economist_ called this "a capitalist dream."

Order 39 also violated international law (the Hague Regulations of 1907, ratified by the US) that said an occupying power must respect the laws of the country it occupies. Iraq's Constitution outlawed the privatization of key state assets and barred foreigners from owning Iraqi firms. This new law also violated the US Army's Law of Land Warfare, which states "the occupant does not have the right of sale or unqualified use of (non-military) property."

A number of economists, commenting on this move by Bremer, said that Iraq's new government could still overturn such privatization and takeover of Iraqi businesses. To those of us in Iraq, this economic interest seemed to be one reason why the US was concerned about maintaining control over the process of forming the new government and writing a new Constitution. We saw laws being written for US economic interests and the increasing control of Iraqi essential services by foreign companies such as Bechtel and Halliburton.

~ ~ ~

In early December, the Iraqi governing council announced that Iraq would hold its own tribunal to try former Ba'ath Party leaders involved in atrocities against the Iraqi people. Then on December 13, US military search teams found and captured Saddam Hussein. President Bush appeared triumphant.

Many people expressed their feelings to us about that. A few people still maintained admiration for Saddam. Most were relieved that his whereabouts were known and that he might be brought to justice. Many people were upset, however, about the way the US had handled his arrest. Iraqis were offended by the US publicizing the picture of Saddam in a disheveled, unkempt state and describing him as being in a "rat hole, covered with lice and body sores." This seemed disrespectful to a man who had formerly been the leader of their country. Such disrespect directed toward Saddam felt like disrespect toward them. One person said, "Whether you loved him or hated him, he is still a member of the Iraqi family."

~ ~ ~

One day, Maxine and Sheila, two teammates who were spending six weeks in Arabic language study and living in an Iraqi household, rushed into our apartment, saying there were soldiers in a tank and a couple of Humvees stationed near our apartment building on Abu Nawass Street. When I got outside, we saw them but couldn't see any problem. I asked them if there was something wrong, but got no answer. Later we found out that Um Hani, our landlady, had flagged down a patrol to check out a suspicious car parked in front of the apartment building. The soldiers hauled the car away. Any car like that is automatically suspected of being a car bomb.

Um Hani recently asked us not congregate in groups around

the front entrance or along the street near our building when we have delegations with us. She was afraid that the presence of our team and several other international media groups in the apartment building could attract a vengeful attack.

On Sunday, January 18, at eight in the morning, a loud blast shook our house. We found out later that two car bombs had exploded in front of the CPA headquarters, killing at least twenty-four and wounding at least 120. Because of the bombing, US forces closed the street in front of the headquarters and the nearby Jumarriyah Bridge for over a week, causing even worse traffic jams around central Baghdad than usual. We heard that, except for November 2003, January 2004 had been the month with the most deaths of US soldiers in Iraq.

Throughout the winter months it was common for us to hear loud explosions of bombs in the distance. Often we would run up five flights to the roof to try to see smoke and guess where the explosion had taken place.

On February 24, our friend Musa, usually optimistic and generally supportive of US troops being in Iraq, told us that a shopkeeper who worked next to his print shop had been killed that week. The shopkeeper was driving past a convoy of US troops, and a soldier shot him. Musa said he felt a dramatic change in the climate with the turnover of US troops. He thought soldiers were harsher with Iraqis and that Iraqis were reacting with more hatred and frustration toward US soldiers and the occupation. I had not seen this change personally, but other Iraqis told us the same. In spite of our friend's perception, there was statistically less violence in February.

One deadly incident shook our team and worried our families and colleagues back home. The report went out in mid-February that an attack on three US pastors traveling near Hilla killed one and injured another. CPT director Gene Stoltzfus called us that evening to make sure it wasn't members of our group.

One day Le Anne Claussen, a full-time CPTer who had been in Iraq on delegations before the war, for three months this past fall, and had just returned for another three-month stay, and I went to the IAC to meet with the new director. When we got ready to leave, soldiers outside the building told us that no one was allowed to leave, because there was a car near the outer gate that might have a bomb in it. We waited two hours before the crowd of people we were with, trapped inside the barriers and the building, were allowed to go.

~ ~ ~

Another teammate reported one day in mid-January: "Two US soldiers were killed and three wounded today in a mortar attack on their compound. A whole family was killed when their car tried to pass a US military convoy on a highway near Tikrit today and US soldiers opened fire on the car." Tears came to my eyes. Suddenly more emotions rushed to the surface. "Why more innocent deaths?!"

For two weeks I had been on edge, trying to adjust to the life back in Iraq. I found myself being more uptight and standing back watching, not fully involved. Are people really more hostile toward any American? Without realizing it, I had been holding my deeper emotions back and trying to be strong until I became more grounded. It didn't mean I didn't care. I cared too much!

While participating in an Iraqi church service, I got in touch with my feelings. I'd been feeling plunged back into a different world, finding what I was to do there. "Okay, God, if I am supposed to be here, give me more peace about it, give me understanding, give me love!" I found myself praying the prayer I had prayed many times the winter before: to be able to open and give myself to whatever God had in mind for me, that I would once again be willing to give my life for the people here. That night I let the wall around me melt, allowing myself to do more than observe. Now I felt more keenly the pain and grief, as well as the love I carry for the Iraqi people.

CHAPTER 14

Our Own Brush with Danger

When we talked to women in Iraq, they reminded us that the security of any society is intertwined with the security of the women of that society. One test of democracy is how women are being treated. Upon returning to Iraq, I was sad to see that security for women had not improved much since the summer. Under the former regime crime against women and street crime had been almost nonexistent. I remember hearing women talk about feeling safe on the streets of Baghdad at two in the morning before the invasion. Now women were still hiding in their homes rather than venturing out to work or school, or playing an active role in rebuilding Iraq. "This is liberation?" many asked us.

Security is more than whether one feels safe to venture out and participate in society. Security also means being able to feed one's family, have clean water and adequate shelter, and care for one's health needs. The lack of these things, in turn, fed into the desperation that fuels crime and violent resistance.

What we were seeing in Iraq was partly the unleashing of violence that set up a whole cycle of responses of violence from the war. It was partly due to the devastation caused by the war, which knocked out all Iraqi civil structures and authority, as well as communication, health, and sanitation systems. It was partly the result of years of oppression under the former regime. And it was partly the result of current oppression, evoking revenge and a desire to throw off the oppressors.

At one of our vigils a man said to me without much emotion, "Your cause is a heavenly one, but this is not the reality we live in. The first time I saw a dead body, I was so upset I couldn't sleep all night. Now it seems like normal to us. Recently, I helped carry away ten dead bodies and a bucket of body parts, and it did not bother me. I didn't care. It is now normal life for us. We smile and go on with life. We have to. But, thank you for what you are doing." What could I say, but, "This should not be normal! There must be something better for Iraq."

What we were seeing was the emergence of a culture of violence and the acceptance of automatic weapons and hand-guns being held by guards in front of businesses, apartment buildings, banks, and organizations; being carried openly on the street, inside shops and offices; and being aimed at passersby by convoys of US soldiers.

Early in my three months in Iraq this winter, I would react more emotionally when I heard about people being killed. Toward the end of that time I too had become used to the frequent killings and sounds of shooting and explosions.

~ ~ ~

Before returning in December, I had heard from other team members in Iraq that it was more dangerous to be there as an American than it had been. I took this seriously, but didn't really know what it meant. Did that mean it wasn't safe to walk on the streets or that women couldn't go anywhere alone? Would we even be able to work? Was I walking back into the fire, as one of my friends had told me? All this made me feel a little uneasy. During the first two or three weeks I carried an under-lying nervousness or fear, but this gradually diminished.

On February 8, I tried to share with family and friends back home about security in Iraq when I wrote:

> In spite of the ongoing violence, I have become more relaxed being here. Part of that is having a greater internalized sense of what the dangers here are for an international civilian and what are reasonable limitations on our mobility. Part of that is feeling more and more a part of this society, and part of it is accepting the dangers as part of my choosing to be here.
>
> We are in more danger being here in Iraq, especially as Americans. There is always the possibility that we are in the wrong place at the wrong time. We could be targeted, yet there is

less chance of this for our group because of our living openly in a residential neighborhood where people are familiar with us and our work, and because we don't travel around in nice new vans. Anyway, safety is something we think about, yet try not to be preoccupied with.

As time went on, I realized that even though I felt more grounded, I also took an automatic internalized sense of vigilance, being more aware of what was going on around me.

Another issue of safety for CPTers going to Iraq was DU contamination. Those of us who were there during the bombing were in greater danger of contamination. But even those CPTers who were coming later for delegations or longer work on the team had to decide whether to take the risk. This was especially a concern for team members of childbearing age. Because we didn't really know how much we may have been contaminated, CPT staff was considering having some team members tested for DU in their urine.

We talked one evening with Canon Andrew White, who met and worked with religious leaders of all faiths in Iraq and moved in and out of the Green Zone in his work. He and his colleagues had considered living at the Palestine Hotel, which is protected by armed guards, tall concrete slabs, and razor wire, plus a checkpoint and search to get in. But they chose to live in a smaller hotel in a residential area. "We are safer living among the people," he told us. "The more security you have, the less secure you are, and the less security you have, the more secure you are." We agreed.

One day when our team was preparing to leave for Kerbala, Jane MacKay Wright, a media arts teacher from Ontario, who had also come to Iraq with the October 2002 CPT delegation, asked me, "Is it safe going there?" I answered without hesitation, "No. It isn't. It's a risk going anywhere in Iraq." Later in the day, after we returned from a very fruitful day in Kerbala, participating in a vigil concerning the problems of detainees, Jane told me, "Sometimes it seems like someone is watching over us."

"Yes," I said, "more than we ever know."

Just two days later, our CPT team became the victims of violence. On Monday evening, February 9, we faced the possibility of our death.

At about nine at night, two men came to our apartment to visit us. Stewart Vriesinga, a full-time CPTer from Ontario who had been in Iraq during the bombing and invasion, and had just returned, met the men earlier in the afternoon on the street. They seemed to know about CPT and expressed interest in our work with detainee issues. Now they were with us, having a friendly visit . . . at least at first.

One told us that in late April 2003, he had come home from work to find all of his family dead, killed by some US military action. It was devastating for him; life no longer had purpose and anger overwhelmed him. He became part of the resistance against the US. Woven into their stories, both men said repeatedly, "We have killed and bombed many people."

We acknowledged their anger, but as avid promoters of nonviolence, we also expressed the concern that the US may actually use the increase of violent resistance to justify prolonging their brutality and occupation. They acknowledged this and seemed to know about Badshah Khan, the great Muslim Pathan nonviolent warrior and a contemporary of Gandhi.

Cliff brought out videotapes of the TV series *A Force More Powerful,* ready to give it on loan. I expressed concern about what killing and bombing people did to them in their spirit, their soul. One said they already knew they were going to hell. Stewart told them, "You have a purpose to die. I hope you can someday find a purpose to live."

But then the conversation shifted. I wondered why they were getting so nervous. I first realized they were there for something other than a friendly visit when they told us to each put our teacups on the table. Their manner changed, and their expressions became more sinister. "We are on a suicide-bombing mission tonight," the one with fluent English announced. "Our assignment is to blow up this building, and the bomb is set to go off in twenty minutes." One pulled up his shirtsleeve very quickly to give a brief glimpse of a black box strapped around his waist, not enough time to really see what it was.

At first it was hard to believe it was really happening. I felt stunned. Then a low level of fear crept over me. I wanted to get out of there. But I reined in my feelings. It was imperative that I stay calm. I want to handle this with strength and love, I thought, to get through this without anyone getting hurt. Things I had learned in nonviolence trainings went through my mind. We must keep them talking.

"But we don't really want to hurt you good people, so you will get out of this alive if you cooperate," one said as he pulled a pistol out from his waist. The other took out a knife. "What does cooperating mean?" I asked. He seemed annoyed, but answered, "That's all right, you'll soon know." We were not supposed to ask questions. It was obvious they were frightened too.

They took computer cords and tied the hands of Jim Loney, a writer from Ontario who had been on a prewar delegation and had been back working on the team for two months this winter, Cliff, and Stewart behind their backs and sat each on a chair on one side of the room. They ordered Jane and me to sit on the couch and all of us not to talk loudly or scream. Everybody cooperated. I was thankful they didn't tie our hands, and thought, "What would they do with us?" I decided not to think too much about that.

I realized that we could all die that evening. It hadn't happened last year, but maybe it would this time. I felt a deep sadness as I imaged my boys and Art and thought of each of my companions. "God, give us strength and wisdom!" I silently prayed. "Please touch these men; change their hearts." In the midst of this terrible situation I was given an acceptance of whatever might happen, and with that, a kind of peace.

Then they asked for money. We remained calm, but kept talking, mostly expressing our concern for them. But we also complied with their requests. One of the men went with Jane into our bedroom to get the money. "This isn't very much, there must be more," he said as he made threatening motions with his knife pointed near Stewart's neck. Jim explained that the delegation had just been there and we didn't have much money left.

They finally left with two computers, two cell phones, two digital cameras, and about six hundred dollars in cash. As they left they warned us our lives would be in danger if we screamed, shouted, or left the room. We said we would pray for them. We were greatly relieved as they ran out of the building, looking very frightened. No one had gotten hurt. It was all over!

We were all in shock, but we knew we must talk about it. Several of us thought that the story about the suicide mission, the bomb, and threats to kill us was fabricated to scare us into submitting, that this was really just a robbery. The twenty minutes had gone by without an explosion. Some were not sure, and none of us could definitely know. Maybe the way we related to them did save our lives. One team member surmised that maybe when the one man who had the contraption strapped to his waist had gone to use our bathroom earlier in the evening, he had defused the bomb, because he decided not to carry the bombing out. We asked ourselves what we would have done differently, if we could. And did our actions or words plant any seeds in them?

It was a shaking experience and we regretted the material loss. We felt angry about what they had done, but were also very grateful for each of our lives. We had not been hurt. We experienced in a small way the vulnerability and lack of safety that the Iraqi people feel in their occupied society. We expressed the desire for this to make us wiser but not substantially change the ways we operated in Baghdad. Stewart pointed out that as long as they didn't steal our trust in people, we hadn't lost too much.

What did this mean for us? We all continued to be shaken by it, and we each found our own ways of dealing with it. I had to find some time and space to cry and sort out feelings of fear and anger that came up. I felt more vulnerable. The possibility of being hurt or killed seemed more real to me now. I had to keep going back to affirming God's love and care for me and others and my sense of calling to be there. The question came to me once more: "Am I still willing to die here if that is what working here means?" I never felt I should go home early. It helped to remember that the Iraqi people were much more vulnerable than we were, and most did not have the option to stay or leave.

We found ourselves talking about the incident in the following week, sometimes comparing our memory or perceptions of things that had happened that night. I found myself asking what I would do if a similar situation would come up again. One time several of us informally started brainstorming things we could have done to disrupt the robbery attempt if we had been more aware earlier in the interaction, before the gun and knife came out and things escalated.

Things we thought of included making an excuse to open the curtains and windows so we were visible to people walking by; going out the front door and inviting the two building guards in to join us for tea; two people getting up and leaving early, saying they were going to get some of our friends; one person making a phone call and audibly inviting other people to come over right away; one person having a coughing fit and going out the door to get fresh air; all getting up and going out with Stewart when he went outside with one of the men toward the beginning of the time; and other ideas. Obviously these had more chance of working in the earlier stages and not all these would have. And maybe none of these would have made any difference, but it was helpful for us to think creatively about it. I think we all became more thoughtful about inviting people in and sensitized to warning signs of potential danger. I began to have feelings of suspicion coming up more quickly in situations and started thinking about what I could do if my suspicions began to be confirmed.

One evening two weeks later, after Art arrived from Hebron to spend a week with the team and me, we were riding home in a taxi. It was dark and I was in the back seat and wasn't watching closely. I soon realized that we had passed the street of our apartment. In my broken Arabic I told the taxi driver to turn right, but he nodded and kept on going up Karrada Street. I felt afraid, thinking he might be intentionally driving us onward. I thought that if he went much further, I would tell Art to quickly open the door and we would both jump out together when the driver slowed down. But then the driver turned right toward Abu Nawass Street and then right again toward our apartment. Soon we were there and paying him for the trip, and all was well. I had overreacted.

A couple of days earlier, when our team was returning from Ramadi, a van pulled up close to the right side of ours and drove close to us for about five minutes. Then it fell back and pulled up to the right side of our van. Cliff waved and smiled at the passenger, who looked angry, but the passenger didn't smile back. Then the van drove in front of our van. Many of us watched this scene, thinking that any moment we might be pushed off to the side of the road in an attempted robbery. But our driver kept calm, and when the van went ahead, he slowed down until we lost view of the van. We felt a wave of relief and thankfulness.

When we were passing the huge Abu Ghraib prison, we saw flashes of light to the south. Then we saw what looked like fireworks going into the sky. About a minute later a few loud explosions in front of us shook the van. At first I thought we were hit. Our driver immediately turned off a dirt road to the right and waited a few minutes until all was quiet before continuing our trip. We could see smoke billowing up near the prison. Later we learned that five rockets and thirty-five mortars had been fired at the prison that night, with no casualties.

∼ ∼ ∼

While Art was still with us, several team members and our translator went to visit Imam Sayyid Ali Mussawi Al Waahd, caretaker of the Kadhum Shrine, in the Kadamiah area of Baghdad, and assistant to Sistani, the top Shi'a leader in Iraq. Sitting on the floor, he welcomed us warmly and asked about former teammates he knew.

Also with him was a professor of Arabic language, who told us that the Shi'a were very patient, but their patience was running out. The professor translated for Ali as he told us that the Shi'a didn't agree with the acts of terror on September 11. Osama Bin Laden was created by the Americans, and used as a stooge to remove communists from Afghanistan. "These are bad people," he said. "That is not Islamic jihad. Bin Laden, like Saddam, was working for the CIA. Al Qaida misuses the Koran. Yes, we are to use power, but there are many kinds of power. We should not be killing people."

Art asked Ali what the essence of Shi'a Islam was. Ali said, "Forgiveness. We need to forgive." After expressing his respect for Christianity, he said, "Bush could not possibly be a Christian. If Bush followed Jesus, there would be no problem in

Iraq. But Bush is not a Christian. We have no problem with Christians. All religions are welcome in Iraq."

We got into a discussion of nonviolence in which he acknowledged that there were many forms of force and resistance. We mostly listened. He already knew about CPT and what we stood for. As we sat with him, I was impressed by his gentle spirit, humility, and the loving way he related to the men and women coming in and out to ask for help and advice.

US analysts describe the situation in Iraq as a choice between US forces staying in Iraq or internal fighting among Shi'a (the majority people group in Iraq) for power, or between Shi'a and Sunni, or between the various factions. US policy makers also use the fear of there being a Shi'a-run Islamic state to justify not allowing free elections. The longer I am in Iraq, the more I see and experience a deep desire for democracy, peace, and cooperation among different Iraqi groups. Iraqis do not want more fighting. When I talk to leaders such as Sayyid Ali, it makes me less fearful of the Shi'a taking power and trust that Iraqis have compassionate and competent leaders ready to help make the necessary transitions to a peaceful self-rule.

~ ~ ~

During my last two weeks in Iraq in March, there was an upsurge in bombings and killings. Four CPTers were on the scene when three bombs exploded on March 2 in the courtyard of the large Kadhum Shrine in Baghdad, during special holy days for the Shi'a Muslims. More than ten thousand Shi'a pilgrims gathered there at that time to commemorate the death of Imam Hussein, the grandson of the prophet Muhammad. By invitation from Shi'a cleric Sayyid Ali Mussawi Al Waahd, four CPTers were present as peaceful observers at the shrine during those holy days. Earlier they had gone to the nearby base and asked the US military commander there not to enter the area around the shrine, because it might provoke unnecessary violence. He agreed.

After the bombing occurred on March 2, Le Anne videotaped part of the aftermath, and the others helped to comfort some of the bystanders and care for the wounded. Shortly afterward, a convoy of US army vehicles, tanks, Humvees, and two medic vehicles drove toward the shrine's main entrance and blocked the road, trying to provide security. But angry pilgrims ran toward them, throwing shoes and stones. US soldiers escalated the angry response by firing into the air. At the urging of Iraqi guards, the soldiers finally retreated and left the area.

"It was frightening," Sheila told those of us who had stayed back to do other work that day. "The US soldiers were probably just coming to try to help and didn't realize how much danger they were in. I was just praying that both they and the crowd would stay calm so there wouldn't be a massacre."

Sayyid Ali then sent a message to be read over the loud speaker, appealing for calm and forbidding revenge attacks on soldiers, police, or other authorities. To prevent further violence, security officials joined hands, creating a human chain to keep the crowd away from the shrine's entrance, while workers cleaned the plaza. US military personnel at the base later sent a letter of thanks to Sayyid Ali for alerting them to the danger to their troops.

A half-hour before this bombing, there was also an attack on a Shi'a shrine in Kerbala, where millions of Shi'a pilgrims from all over the world were gathered. The Iraqi Health Ministry reported 185 people killed and more than 300 wounded.

In the week that followed, a group of four American, Southern Baptist men and their driver, were killed near Mosel in a drive-by shooting.

There were two bombings near our apartment on March 17. A smaller bomb exploded about four blocks away on Abu Nawass at around 4:30 p.m., injuring a boy's face. By the time Cliff and Sheila found their way to the site, the boy had been taken to a hospital, but they saw shattered glass and windows broken in houses nearby.

Our apartment building and homes all over the area shook when the next big bomb exploded at about 8:30 p.m. Most of us rushed up to the roof, where we saw a huge cloud of smoke billowing over buildings to the north. Later we heard that the bomb had left a huge crater in front of the Mount Lebanon Hotel, about six blocks from our apartment, killing twenty-nine and injuring many others. The talk this time was that resistance fighters were now going after what were called "soft targets." Soft targets tended to be places not heavily fortified, civilian rather than military, or Iraqi people working with or for the CPA or US military.

The next day we heard a number of explosions throughout the day, and I wondered if this sudden increase had to do with the approaching anniversary of the beginning of the 2003 Iraq war.

Rumors were going around that the US military was behind these attacks, that they had made it look like Iraqis did it. Some said that car bombs were really cars hit by missiles shot from US helicopters. Other rumors claimed that US casualties were much higher than we were being told, that many Americans were quietly buried in graves and not counted in the tallies.

In the past most Iraqis had found it hard to believe the US didn't have their best interests in mind. But even this goodwill was eroding and more Iraqis were becoming angry. Most angry Iraqis, however, were not yet involved in violent resistance, as generally they were a patient, generous people, ready to give what they had to us and welcome us as foreigners. But we knew that the time could come when even the more patient ones would join a general revolt against the US occupation.

~ ~ ~

"You shouldn't be traveling around Iraq without a gun," a US military intelligence officer in Balad told us. "I know where you can get inexpensive flak jackets." Other international NGOs had hired armed guards and closely followed US security reports. It became obvious to us that our view of security did not match the view held by most US personnel in Iraq.

We asked ourselves, "Whose security were the house raids and detentions for?" It seemed to be for the security of US troops or the CPA, rather than for the Iraqis. What was the source of the security problem? Would there be the kind of violence that is happening now without the occupation? Did security require US soldiers to round up masses of men, kill many innocent people, and terrorize a whole community in order to catch four suspected resistance fighters?

Iraqis got a mixed message when they saw, as we did, two signs on the back of a US military convoy, one saying, "Back off or I will shoot you," and the second saying, "Have a nice day."

Yes, what you saw depended on where you stood. The policies of the occupying powers were based on a view of Iraqi people as "enemies" and "terrorists." The military's response was to use excessive force. Iraqis respond to how they were treated and retaliated accordingly. This set up a self-perpetuating chain reaction.

We believed that security started with assuming people were friends and then treating them in open and respectful ways. If the CPA saw Iraqis as equal partners capable of rebuilding and running their own country, it would involve them in decision making and in reconstructing their society. It would use security procedures that would win their hearts and minds.

CHAPTER 15

Campaign for Justice

When I left in September 2003, work with detainees and their families had become the main focus of the team. This developed into what became called the Campaign for Justice for Iraqi Detainees. Its goals were to expose the injustice of the detention system and to advocate for the rights of detained Iraqis. During the fall, the team continued to contact and arrange for meetings with US authorities in Iraq. (There is more about this process in chapter 17, "Speaking to Those in Power.")

Human rights violations often involved house raids using excessive force against unarmed civilians, theft and destruction of personal property, mistreatment and torture of detainees during interrogation and in prison, and the withholding of information about detainees' whereabouts and well-being from their families and human rights organizations. In general, the detention system offered no legal representation or clear judicial process.

In partnership with Iraqi leaders and organizations, our team recorded and publicized the stories of Iraqi detainees and their families. We also documented the accounts from neighborhoods or villages where violent house raids, home demolitions, or other acts of collective punishment were carried out by the US military. We also accompanied family members to CPA offices to search for information and justice for their loved ones.

After being released, one Iraqi man told us that soldiers used an electric cattle prod on his genitals. During the winter, a number of people told us there was sexual abuse of men and women in the prisons, and that prisoners were kept naked in their cells. We knew it would be difficult to find people willing to be interviewed about this because of the shame and fear of ostracism from their own people and retaliation by the US authorities. Our team continued, without success, to try to arrange such interviews to verify the credibility of these particular claims. Since we could not verify them, we did not include them in our official written reports.

In December, as the number of detainee families we were working with increased, it seemed helpful to write a written report to summarize the team's findings. Matthew Chandler, a full-time CPTer from Oregon, took up the challenge and compiled a report on seventy-two cases. I quickly got involved in all these activities after returning in late December.

We sent our report to US officials in Iraq, and met with them as well. We expressed concern, not only about the widespread abuse of prisoners, but also the injustice of detaining innocent people. We passed out flyers to US soldiers to educate them about human rights of a people under occupation. We also carried out public vigils and marches and hosted press conferences to bring attention to these issues.

The campaign also involved the efforts of people in North America who would bring these stories and issues to the attention of the general public and US government officials for this purpose. Many of the stories were posted on the CPT web page. We asked people around the world to pray for the safety and health of Iraqi detainees, their families, and coalition soldiers and officials who carry out the detentions of Iraqis.

In Baghdad, the groups we worked with more closely were the Human Rights Organization in Iraq (HROI); the National Association of Defense of Human Rights in Iraq (NADHRI); the Society for Human Rights in Iraq (SHRI); and Sheik Moyad, imam of the Abu Hanifa Mosque and advocate for the people in the Adumiyah District. We also had ongoing relationships with human rights organizations in Balad, Al Jazeera village, Najaf, and Karbala, and with individuals doing advocacy work.

We didn't want to do what Iraqis could do better, but we wanted to be supportive of their work. Often that involved using our privilege as North Americans to gain access to information or resources for them. This included sending information home or around the world. It meant building bridges between US policy makers in Iraq and the Iraqi human rights groups, such as we had attempted in Baghdad and Balad.

Different team members took on the role of liaison to different groups and met regularly with them. They shared about their organization's activities and concerns, and discussed how we could work together. Sometimes they brought cases to us to help with; sometimes we referred cases to them.

One day we were meeting with the director of NADHRI, discussing how we might work together on a public action. He suggested that we protest a sign put up by the CPA at the Jumarriyah Bridge that Iraqis felt was offensive. It had a picture of an Iraqi man on the ground being detained, his hands cuffed behind him, and a US soldier pointing his gun at him. We said we would look at the sign and consider this, but when we looked for it, the sign was gone. We didn't know whether it was from vandalism or if the CPA had taken it down, but a different sign had appeared a week later at the same spot.

We were part of an informal association of Iraqi and international groups and individuals working on human rights issues. This group organized meetings and invited families to come and share about the rights violations they had experienced. One of these gatherings was a large press conference in which International Occupation Watch released their report documenting cases of abuse. I attended and also handed out our report.

This was one of many occasions when international and Iraqi press interviewed team members about the problems of detainees. For a time, Maxine was our primary spokesperson with the media. Later, Jane took on the role of contacting media with stories. In early March she arranged interviews with families for reporter Jeffrey Gettleman of the *New York Times*, which contributed to his front-page article about detainees in the March 7, 2004, Sunday edition.

In addition to interviewing new families and released prisoners, I reconnected with a couple of the families we had begun working with the summer before.

During my three months in Iraq I had several opportunities to visit in the home of Dr. Talib, his wife, Nawal, and their family. These were happier occasions than those during the past August. The three sons had been released by October 28 and were back with their family. All three told us the stories of their time in detention. The following is a shortened version of one of the sons' story, corrected to make his English smoother. (See the father's version of the story in chapter 12.)

Through the entire first night and into the first day for a total of about fourteen hours we were held blindfolded and forced to kneel with our arms tied behind our back. I can still see the places on my arms where my handcuffs cut into my arms. At one point they placed a smaller handcuff, wire-like device on my arms and twisted them. A soldier said, "Tie it until you can see blood." They tightened the handcuff so that my hands swelled up and blood came out. The scars remain even now.

During that day the guards shouted at me. "You want to kill the US army! I will take you to Guantanamo." I told them I did not shoot at the US army. Then a soldier came and said to us. "Everyone is going to die."

While we were still blindfolded, a soldier came and took my brother away and shot a bullet into the air. That soldier then went to my brother and told him that they had killed me and said that he is next. He told him that he is going to die. The soldier made sounds like he was reloading the gun. And then said, "Say good-bye because you are going to join your brother and you are going to die." Several times he put the gun to my brother's head after making sounds like they were loading the gun. During this whole time we were blindfolded. Each brother was sure the other was dead. Then someone came and hit me on the shoulder.

Then they took us to another building where they put us in a small prison-like cell. There were three other people there too. The keepers were told to give us water every hour. Finally another soldier came and removed our blindfolds and handcuffs. Until we reached the cell we had been given nothing to drink and hand-cuffs and blindfolds had been in place since our arrest.

The next day they took us back to the place where we had been terrorized earlier. Two of the Akif boys were now released. Then they put us in the truck for transport to the airport where a woman detective questioned us. We were asked, "Why are you here? What do you do? Are you a Ba'ath Party member? What was the occupation of your father?" I told the detective exactly what happened and the detective was a little surprised. The detective said to me. "Your record says you resisted US forces."

Then we were processed into the camp at the airport and assigned a capture tag and numbers for Camp Cropper in the airport. We were there for fourteen to fifteen days. The water was terrible. Food was military rations, two meals per day. It tasted terrible but we were forced to eat it. Some people vomited it right back up. The number in our four-by-seven-meter tent varied between thirty and forty, so it was crowded and hot.

Two days later I was transferred to Bucca [Um Qasr]. At the airport before departing, a doctor checked me, including my blood pressure. The doctor asked me what kind of water I was drinking and I told him that I drank what they gave me to drink. The doctor said to me, "You need a lot of water."

On the way to Bucca we stopped for one night at Nasariya. I was so happy to get away from the airport because we all know that no one ever gets released from the airport. Other detainees had told me that the road to release goes through Um Qasr and I was on the way there. The food was better and the water was better. My total time in detention was sixty-six days. During that time I lost twenty kilos (about forty-five pounds). There was a man in our group who was suffering from diabetes-induced coma, but the guards refused to get help for him. We prisoners managed to revive him.

At Um Qasr a detective with the same questions interviewed me again. The woman detective told me that I was not a criminal, a terrorist, or a supporter of Saddam so I should be patient and I would be released. Persons in Bucca with charges of being connected to Al Qaeda described how they were beaten but otherwise many of us were treated well. I was happy to see my parents when they came.

~ ~ ~

On January 26, Dr. Ali Al Za'ag, an Iraqi science professor at Baghdad University, was released. I had met and interviewed Dr. Ali back in the summer, after he had been interrogated fifteen times. This time he was detained when he went to a General Information Center (GIC) in the Karrada District of Baghdad. He had been urged by US forces to go there and get a gun permit in order to protect himself from the threats to the scientific community. He was arrested by a US soldier who refused to listen to his argument that he had been interrogated fifteen times already and had been declared "clean" by weapons inspector Scott Alcott.

A neighbor who went with him reported that Dr. Ali never came out of the office. After visiting the GIC several times and receiving no information, the family approached CPT and International Occupation Watch (IOW) for assistance. For several weeks CPTers and Eman of IOW went with family members to various CPA offices, trying to find out where Dr. Ali was, what the charges were, and to protest the arrest. Major Scott Peterson, head of the GIC told them, "This is not a case of Big Brother. He will not disappear down some black hole. In one week we will be able to tell you whether he will be held or released." Weeks went by and the family still received no further information. Several of us joined in a vigil at the university, sponsored by faculty and students on his behalf.

The family believed Dr. Ali was arrested because another American weapons inspection team had returned to Iraq for another search for WMD. US forces had arrested at least six other scientists in this latest search, despite the fact that the head of the previous inspections team had recently returned to the US, declaring that there were no such weapons, that they were destroyed in the early to middle 1990s.

On March 4, we got a call saying that after thirty-eight days, Dr. Ali was free. A week later he told us his story:

From the GIC he was taken to the Green Zone where soldiers put him in a three-meter by three-meter wire cage that he likened to an animal cage. It was out of doors, unprotected from the weather, and next to fifteen to twenty other cages that held prisoners. "I was treated like a dangerous person," he said. He was there only until dark, when US military police in two Humvees transported him to Camp Cropper at the Baghdad Airport.

Dr. Ali assumed that the camp he was taken to was under the auspices of US military intelligence. Upon entry, guards took his picture, did an eye print, took fingerprints, and printed out a wristband that gave him a prisoner-of-war number.

While he was there he tried to find ways to resist being dehumanized by his experience. Guards put him in a small cell about the same size as his earlier cage. "As a biologist I prefer not to call my humiliating confinement a 'cell,' one of the essential building blocks of all of life which God called 'good.' And I made friends of the guards. I refused to call them my enemy."

For five days he stayed in solitary confinement before he was able to question guards about the reason for his arrest. Ten days later, guards gave him a pencil and paper to write the anonymous person in charge to ask that same question. "Two men came the next day and told me, 'We didn't know you were here. Sorry, you shouldn't be here.' I replied, 'So, let me go home.' They answered, 'This bureaucratic system won't easily get you released.' 'Will I be here for days or weeks?' I asked. They said, 'We don't know.'"

Some time later, after he had given up hope for an early release, guards took him to another location where three people questioned him for two hours. One he knew as Brenda, one of the interrogators from the summer before. They admitted that some of the questions were the same. After they asked questions, he wrote the answers, and they sent the report to Washington, D.C. Dr. Ali commented after his release, "They are looking for 'true lies,' which don't exist." This was the only time during his thirty-eight-day confinement that he was questioned.

Some days later, guards came to his room and said he could go home. He arrived on his doorstep and greeted his surprised and delighted wife, son, and daughter. At the university, colleagues and students sacrificed three sheep to recognize his return, a ritual reminiscent of Abraham's sacrifice and often done in Iraq after a person had gone through a grueling event.

~ ~ ~

We listened to the stories of men who had recently been released. On February 13, a group of us went to visit "Achmed," a fifty-two-year-old farmer who lived on the outskirts of Baghdad. (He asked us not to use his real name for fear of punishment from the US military.) He was detained and tortured by US forces at the end of January. The following is a summary of his story:

> One day, at the end of January, I was inside my house when there was an explosion about two kilometers away. We went to the mosque to pray because it was a Friday. When we finished the

prayers, we saw helicopters everywhere and we heard the news that the Americans came to my house and arrested my nephew, who was visiting from another city. I told everyone in my family we did nothing, so they would release him.

My son lives in the next house. They searched his house and took his money. When they finished checking his house they were waiting for us. They arrested us and asked us if we did this explosion. We said no. They asked us do you know who did it and we said no. The soldiers said either tell us you did it, or tell us who did it.

They handcuffed me and pulled me by the back of my collar to their car. They beat us and kicked us with their shoes. They put bags over our heads so we couldn't see who was beating us.

On the way to the camp, I asked for water and they beat me on the head with the bottle of water. I fell down when I was getting out of the car and somebody lifted me under my arms and threw me to the ground. They lined us up against a wall. Somebody kicked me, my head jerked and banged into the wall. I fell down.

They took us at 1:00 p.m. and we reached the camp at 5:30 p.m. For four days we only had water, no food. And for all this time we were outside, not under a roof, and we can see nothing because we were wearing hoods.

After I hit the wall with my head and fell down they handcuffed me with my hands behind my back lying on my stomach. [Achmed showed us his wrists. They were ringed with pink scar tissue.] They kept me in this position through the night and into the next day—almost twenty-four hours—and we weren't allowed to move our legs in that time. We could not sleep during that time because they always kicked us. I don't know for sure, but I think they did this for a purpose, as a way to torture us and not give us a chance to sleep.

Look at this. [His wife brought in a white tunic. Numbers were written in black marker across the front of the tunic.] This is what they wrote on me, to identify me.

During these twenty-four hours, they brought some dogs. I could hear them searching and doing things with them. They didn't bite me but I could hear the screams of other people, so thought they were being bitten.

There was a translator and I tried to tell him that we couldn't feel our hands—it feels like they are cut—and he said "That's the way it is." The next day, they made us sit cross-legged with our hands handcuffed behind our backs and hooded. The soldiers came and kicked us on the kneecaps and you could hear them laughing. I was so tired, but if I started to fall asleep they kicked me.

When you asked the translator to go to the toilet the soldiers shouted at you and kicked you. You had to ask ten to fifteen times before they let you go. When you reached the toilet, they released your hands but you could not use them—they had no feeling in them and wouldn't bend—so sometimes you couldn't control yourself.

For all this time there was no food, only water. It did not rain, but it was cold. We had to sit this way all through the night until the next day. This is the mark it made. [Achmed showed us a quarter-sized, red scab on the outside bone of his ankle.] Then they made us stand. And so it continued this way for four days.

Sometimes they would take me to another place and let me walk into a wall. They interviewed me three times. Each time they took me inside a room before someone with a translator. They lifted the hood from my head. It's made of the same material they use to make sandbags. They asked me for three to five minutes if I knew someone who did it and then they took me back.

After four days, they told me I would have lunch. They took me in front of the wall and beside me was a dog. A soldier had a biscuit to give the dog and a piece of meat to give to me but I couldn't eat the meat because of its smell. So I told him give me the biscuit and give the meat to the dog, but the soldier gave the biscuit and the meat to the dog. They put the bag back on my head and took me back to my place.

On the fifth day, again taking me by the neck and hitting me into walls, they put me in a car and took me to Scania, a huge military base they built in Al Dora [a suburb of Baghdad]. I could hear other voices with me. They searched me, took my cigars and my lighter and my money, and put them in a bag. They said I would get it back.

One of the soldiers spoke to me in Arabic. He said he would help me. He said he would put me with the group that has already been tortured. They took off the bag and freed my hands.

They took our group inside a room and closed the door. There were beds and blankets so you could sleep. I slept inside this room, but there was no food until nine in the night. They brought us the same bags of dried food they make for the soldiers, which is difficult for us to eat. There we spent all of the night until the next morning. In the morning you could go to the toilet if you wanted. About twenty of us spent three days in this room.

After the three days, they took ten of us and stood us against the wall outside. They said they would release us. They said when you reach the main road, stop a car and tell them you have no money and that you will pay them when you get home. They did not return my ID or my cigars or my money. I went to the main road, found a taxi, and drove home.

God says you have to tell the truth. For that reason I am telling you the truth.

"Ali," Achmed's twenty-six-year-old son, told his story next. Like his father, he had been hooded and handcuffed, and had received no food for four days.

They put us in a dark room and we were sitting cross-legged on the floor. They took the bag off my head and an officer who was doing the investigation asked me with a translator about the explosion—who did it, where I was. Then they put the bag over my head again and took me back [to where my father was].

At the second time, they took my father first and then they took me. They told me that my father told them everything so now we want to hear the truth from [me]. I replied to them the same: "I don't know anything about the explosion."

The third time, they put me inside the same room with the officer and the translator. They took the bag off my head and put me against the wall. He came really close to me and told me not to look to the left or to the right, to just look at him. He said you will answer my questions. But first he gave me four points to remember. Because I was nervous I forgot the fourth point and he beat me with his hand and I fell down. He asked me the four points again but I forgot the fourth point again so he kicked me in the groin and I fell down.

He kept asking me about the explosions. He put his hand under my chin and lifted me up from the floor. While he was doing this to me he said if you vomit you must swallow it—don't spit it out. Then he hit me with his hand and I fell and he kicked me with his shoes. Then he said if you refuse to answer my questions I will take pictures of your wife and your mother and your sister naked and I will put them on the satellite as a sex film. The last time he beat me I collapsed and I couldn't remember anything after that.

The next day they used something like a needle on my neck and my back. I couldn't tell what it was because I was hooded, but it felt like they were poking me with a nail.

When we were released after four days, they took us to the outside gate and left us with our hands handcuffed behind our backs. We were eleven persons. We had to go to someone with a shop nearby and ask for a knife to cut our handcuffs.

When they released me, they took 400,000 dinars (about 280 US dollars) and my ID.

~ ~ ~

Two brothers from the city of Samara came to our apartment to tell us the story of the death of their father while he was being detained. The following is a shortened version of the story according to Abdulkahar:

On December 21, 2003, at 9:30 p.m., US soldiers surrounded our house and crashed in the front gate with a tank. When we opened the house door to see what was happening, about fifteen soldiers rushed inside, broke open cupboards and cabinets, and ransacked the house. We saw soldiers dividing up family money they took during the search. Soldiers pushed around our seventy-year-old father Mehide Al Jamal, who had recently had a hip replacement operation and had difficulty walking. Our father was a former surveyor and planner for the rural areas around Samara and was well respected in the community.

Soldiers handcuffed four of us: our father, our uncle, my brother, and me. They put plastic bags over our heads and took us away in an armored military vehicle.

Our father started gasping for breath and called out "Help me! I can't breathe!" The soldiers responded with "Shut up! Shut up! F— you!" When I pleaded for the soldiers to loosen or take the bag off my father's head, soldiers cursed me and hit me in the chest with a rifle butt. I heard one soldier say, "The f—ing old man may be dead."

My uncle, brother, and I were then transferred to another vehicle and taken home and released. There we found the body of our dead father. A soldier told us that our father had died of heart failure, but I responded angrily, "No, you killed my father. You soldiers treat us like animals!"

After the funeral service, we filed a claim against the US military and a man in our community who we believed accused our father falsely. Many in the community hated him because he had been an informant for the former regime. Now he was doing it for the US. Colonel Nate Sassaman, commander of the unit involved, told us he would bring the informant to us, but we said,

"No, we don't want revenge. We want justice." Sassaman then said he would investigate the informer, but later told us that he was innocent.

At the time we heard this story, we had a plastic sandbag that Theresa, a woman working to help families of detainees, had brought to us, saying that soldiers had used it to put on the head of a four-year-old boy when his father, the imam of a mosque, was detained. On the bag was written with a black marker pen, "Wrongo, Dongo, Captain Stupid." We showed this bag to Abdulkahar, and he said, "Yes, this is the kind of bag soldiers put on our heads when we were detained." He put it on his head, and we could see how tightly it fit.

~ ~ ~

In our team worship one night, Jim read the familiar story from Luke 21:1-4:

> [Jesus] looked up and saw rich people putting their gifts into the treasury; he also saw a poor widow put in two small copper coins. He said, "Truly I tell you, this poor widow has put in more than all of them; for all of them have contributed out of their abundance, but she out of her poverty has put in all she had to live on."

We listened to this story in a meditative way. At first it simply spoke to me of my own lack of generosity, my fear that my own needs would not be met. But the words hit harder when Rose talked about listening and writing the story of the woman who came to our apartment that today desperately wanting help to find out what had happened to her husband. He had disappeared last April 9, the day US troops invaded Baghdad. She was probably a widow, but she hoped her husband might be found among the thousands of Iraqis currently detained in prisons by US forces. We felt very sad for her, but did not really think we could help her, other than write up and share her story.

In some ways she was like the widow in the story, not so much that she gave away all she had, but that she was very poor and insignificant to those in power. Other matters, like security, had been considered more important than dealing with her problems.

What hit me that evening was that in the midst of all my efforts to get organized, I was beginning to look at our list of seventy-two cases in our report as cases to be dealt with. Sure, when this woman and others came in, I could feel a part of their pain as I looked into their eyes and listened to their stories. But there were so many, and those I had not seen were starting to become, for me, numbers that we would report.

My hope is that we may be able to see the people we work with as our sisters and brothers. I pray that we will refuse to measure their value by their ability to contribute or their bigness or smallness of status. Yes, I pray that we can do this difficult work with love.

CHAPTER 16

Collective Punishment

Among the stories we heard about US military violence against Iraqis were many we would call "collective punishment." Sometimes when one member of the family or village was suspected of violent resistance, other members would also be arrested or killed, or the whole family would have its home destroyed or ransacked and property stolen. This kind of punishment, technically called "collective penalties," was prohibited in the Geneva Conventions. It was not unlike some of the horrible things that happened under Saddam. In fact, many Iraqis said to us, "Thank you for getting rid of the old Saddam, but now we have the English speaking Saddam!" The following accounts describe some examples our team witnessed in three locations.

~ ~ ~

It was January 12, 2004, and we were traveling to Balad, a city of ninety thousand about fifty miles north of Baghdad. After a half-hour drive out of Baghdad we passed a huge garbage dump. Scattered among the piles of trash were small shacks and tents, along with sheep and goats. We could see people picking through the piles. We passed several long US military convoys. Two trucks loaded with Iraqi soldiers, totally unprotected, were part of the line, along with armored Humvees and tanks filled with American soldiers. The US soldier in the last vehicle was on top with his gun pointed at traffic following the convoy. It was hard to understand how that made the convoy safer. To me he looked more like a sitting target. In fact, we felt more danger being near the US soldiers and all their "protection."

In the courthouse of Balad we sat with about eighteen Iraqi lawyers, members of the Balad branch of the Human Rights Organization in Iraq (HROI). We listened as they shared their frustrations and concerns. Along with the usual complaints about the lack of electricity, water, healthcare resources, and jobs, they told about frequent house raids and bombings, mostly in the rural areas surrounding the city, sometimes in response to attacks, sometimes seemingly at random. Two lawyers in their organization, Imad Abdul Raheen and Kamel Hassen Kkhoumais, had been detained in December. The group of lawyers believed it was because they were legally representing men suspected of violent resistance, and US intelligence was trying to get information about their clients. Other lawyers had tried to visit Imad and Kamel at Abu Ghraib prison, but as of mid-March had not been allowed in.

After we checked carefully with the group of lawyers, three of them decided to go with us to the Paliwoda Forward Operating Base, a US military base on the edge of Balad named after a soldier who had recently been killed in an attack. We wanted to see if there were Iraqis detained there, learn how they were being treated and processed, listen to the perspective of the military concerning these problems, and try to establish a channel of communication between the military and these lawyers.

Once inside the base, we walked past a bulletin board of pictures of soldiers doing their work and a picture of the September 11 attack, linking that tragedy to their mission in Iraq. For about an hour we listened and talked with Colonel Nate Sassaman and two intelligence officers. They were surprised to see us and hear that we were traveling around Iraq without weapons or guards. Sassaman proceeded to tell us that his unit was trying to reach out to the local Iraqi people and to minimize the more violent forms of operations that had been used back in the spring and summer to stabilize the situation. "We don't search many homes anymore and haven't done any in the last two weeks," he said. "We never keep detainees here over twenty-four hours, but release them if there isn't any evidence against them."

It sounded good, but it contradicted what we were hearing and seeing. In the course of the meeting, the three Iraqi lawyers brought up a case in which US soldiers from the unit had fired on a car carrying six local Iraqis. The car caught on fire and one of the passengers ran from it. The lawyers said that the soldiers chased down that man and threw him back into the car. All six died in the fire. At that point Sassaman didn't deny the story, but got angry, and said, "Let's not bring up something that's already been dealt with."

He then attempted to discredit the lawyers, saying, "They don't know Captain Gembarra, and they aren't registered with our office. I don't think they are good lawyers." He also said, "Ninety-five percent of the Iraqis who come with complaints come with false claims." Later it became clear to us that lawyers who worked with cases of men detained in raids were not considered reputable because the men they were representing were considered terrorists.

On our way out of the base, we saw about twenty Iraqi men,

Children of Abu Hishma standing behind wire that was put up around their village as a collective punishment.

obviously detainees, held in an unsheltered area. And we had just been told that they had not done any raids in the past two weeks!

Before we went back to Baghdad that evening, we stopped outside the entrance to Abu Hishma, a village of around twelve thousand about twelve miles from Balad. Abu Hishma had been surrounded by razor wire since November 17, after a US soldier was killed on a road next to the village. In retaliation, US forces carried out several raids and detained 182 Abu Hishma men.

Sassaman had earlier told our team that the razor wire would come down when villagers turned in the attackers. We talked to many people milling around outside the front gate. One man poured out his anger against the US military and government. Before we left we met a journalist, Aziz, who invited some of us to come back to the village and spend the night.

The next day we heard a knock on the door, and there was Sami, one of the three lawyers from the Human Rights Organization in Iraq (Balad chapter) who had gone with CPTers to talk to Sassaman. With him was Abu Mohanned (meaning "father of Mohanned"). Mohanned was one of the other three lawyers who had been with us in the meeting with Sassaman.

Abu Mohanned told us the following story: At four that morning about one hundred soldiers from Colonel Sassaman's unit had surrounded Abu Mohanned's home and carried out house raids in his village. First they crashed in the door and broke the TV and some other furnishings. Then they rounded up all the men, taking all six of his sons (including two other lawyers) out into the yard dressed only in lightweight sleeping clothes. They were forced to lie down in the mud and rain with their hands tied behind their backs until they were taken to the military base and detained with about fifteen others from the village.

At around 8:30 that same morning, Abu Mohanned and Sami went to the base to ask for the release of those just detained. Abu Mohanned brought along medicine for his epileptic son, but Sassaman refused to give it to the prisoner. Sassaman told them that the detainees would be released in two or three days and that he wanted to have a meeting with the lawyers and with CPT.

*Meeting between human rights lawyers (Suhaib and Hamdi)
and military officers (Nate Sassaman and translator, Thanna)
at the courthouse in Balad, January 2004.*

Three days later, on Saturday, January 16, six of our CPT team returned to Balad to meet with Sassaman and these lawyers. Mohanned and his five brothers had been released after being held for seventeen hours. Even though they would have liked to have had made a legal complaint, there was no legal process in place for them to do so.

Mohanned was willing to be one of the four lawyers to speak out on behalf of the Lawyers Guild and the HROI. We spent time discussing the agenda with the lawyers beforehand, and they were clear that their first priority for the meeting was to establish an ongoing communications process with US military authorities. We also set the date for an overnight stay at Abu Hishma.

Sassaman and Judge Advocate Captain Vivian Gembarra came to the Balad courthouse for the meeting, representing the US military. A CNN reporter and a cameraman were also there working on a documentary. After introducing the lawyer groups, CPTers Cliff, Jim, and I facilitated a discussion, which resulted in a decision to meet together twice a month to discuss problems in the detention process. Both groups expressed satisfaction with the outcome. Our work as CPT was described as building a bridge of communication between the two groups.

These meetings did take place on a regular basis. After our team stopped attending them, however, the lawyers told us the military officers wouldn't talk about the problems and negotiate with them. We realized the imbalance of power between the military officers and the lawyers was too great for real partnership and negotiation. There didn't seem to be enough incentive for the officers to give up any of their power. So we started meeting with them again. Later, when team members met with the Balad lawyers and new officers rotated into the base, we expressed concern about the need for a liaison between the lawyers and someone from the base who was not both carrying out house raids and judging any appeal or claim against the actions of his unit. Sassaman's role in both those tasks was clearly a conflict of interest.

Eight team members went back to the Balad area on January 27 for a two-day visit. First we went to the village of Abu Sifa to visit the families of the two lawyers, Kamel and Imad, who were still detained in Abu Ghraib since December. We stopped first at the home of Kamel and met his wife, Hania, and other relatives who warmly welcomed us.

With her husband in prison, Hania now cared for her six children alone. She and her children feared that once more US soldiers would return and terrorize the family. She had tried to visit her husband twice, but was turned away each time. She asked if we could help get her husband released, since there were no charges against him.

Muhammad Al Tai, Hania's cousin and one of the only two men left in the village, described the raid on December 16: The villagers awakened at two in the morning to find their homes surrounded by military vehicles and helicopters overhead from the army's fourth infantry division based in Balad. Tanks tore up the fields and destroyed fences. Soldiers kicked in the doors of the houses and bedrooms, and herded people outside in the rain while they searched. Soldiers gathered all the men and beat them. When Hania refused to hand over the key to her car, a soldier broke her finger grabbing for it. Her seventy-year-old uncle died after soldiers put a plastic bag over his head. Soldiers took an equivalent of seventeen thousand dollars from the homes.

On December 31, US soldiers returned and demolished several other homes. Two days later they came again and caused more damage. Villagers took us to see two of the three demolished homes. We saw where tanks had blasted massive holes in the front walls of both homes and sprayed the inside walls with bullets. We saw a crushed car parked in the yard.

According to Sassaman, the December 16 raid was aimed at capturing a high-ranking Ba'ath official from Tikrit thought to be in the area. Documents found with Saddam linked this official to him. Evidently they found the wanted man, but still rounded up the others. Muhammad said, "Because of this one man, the US detained eighty-three men, including two attorneys, fifteen school teachers, a blind man, police officers, men in their eighties, and six teens. According to Sassaman, the second raid was done because his base had been mortared from that area. Most of these eighty-three had still not been released by the time I left in late March.

After leaving Abu Sifa we went to Abu Hishma. Because we were told it was considered dangerous for internationals to be in Abu Hishma, the team had earlier chosen three to go in. But all eight of us went in because we arrived at the guarded gates just before the 5:00 p.m. curfew and the road to Balad was about to be closed. The man who invited our group wasn't there, so we were brought to the home of a tribal sheik, who welcomed us to spend the night with his family. "We don't know who did the attacks on US soldiers," said Sheik Mohammad Abbas Alawa. "The people here are generally peaceful."

While we were walking around to see the village the next morning, residents took us to a huge crater where ten days earlier a US bomb had completely destroyed a small house. We met a twenty-two-year-old man who had been blinded in one eye from the bomb's shrapnel.

One family told about Widad Salih, the wife of the school-master. They said that on October 16 she had walked out of her

Jane MacKay Wright, Rose Whiteside, and I with women at Sheik Mohammed Abbas Alawa's home in Abu Hishma.

front door to get some water. Then, without warning, US soldiers shot her in the neck and killed her.

Another family told about Aziz, a fourth-year English language student, shot in a spray of random fire by US soldiers approaching the village. When his sister-in-law bent down to help him, she was also shot and killed. Aziz died two hours later, after soldiers prevented the family from getting him medical care. A week later, soldiers came back and detained the husband of the woman killed. The family suspected it was because they feared he might seek revenge against the troops.

A second tribal sheik told of his experience of being detained with about one hundred other men in an unsheltered area of the nearby military base. They had to sleep on the ground without blankets. For three days it rained on them. He said that soldiers beat and kicked him and dropped his special headdress band, a sign of his position, in the mud. The detainees were given no water for washing. "Is it acceptable behavior for soldiers to put me, an older man, on the ground and put their boot on my head?" he challenged us.

The cousin of Yassin Tada, a former ambassador under Saddam who then became a merchant, told us that Yassin had been wanted by the US military. Soldiers came and took three of his brothers hostage until he turned himself in. Though Yassin did turn himself in, the brothers still had not been released.

Many others crowded around us, clamoring to be heard. We heard story after story of abuse and injustice. These weren't just isolated incidents or accidents, but seemed part of an ongoing "security" strategy.

People in Abu Hishma were angry about being enclosed by wire and having curfews every night. But one resident said, "No, we are safer with it around our village, because if there is an attack on US soldiers at night, we will not be blamed." This made sense, but I also found it disturbing. Things were so bad that they would rather have the barbed wire around them than be accused of being terrorists.

By the end of the day I was feeling heavy emotionally. This was more than I wanted to hear. I felt angry and full of grief. How could I write and share about this? People would not want to believe it. I didn't want to believe it. But it was there, and I, as an American, needed to witness it.

~ ~ ~

Two weeks later, February 10, two team members returned to Abu Hishma and recorded the following events which, based on the villagers' reports, happened over a sixty-hour period:

On Friday, February 6, there was a rocket-propelled grenade attack against a US position. About the time of noon prayers that same day, US forces opened fire from a helicopter on Ali Hameed Mheu, a Baghdad college student who later died. He had been walking along the road in Yithrub, just west of Abu Hishma village.

Two days later, two sheiks came to the CPT apartment in Baghdad to report that tanks, helicopters, and jets had fired weapons around Abu Hishma through the previous night. They said, "The shooting seemed to be to scare people or keep them awake." That same night a Tomahawk missile dug a fifteen-foot crater in Rabah Auda Kaliph's citrus grove inside Abu Hishma.

US forces closed the roads around Abu Hishma until 8:00 p.m. Sunday, so the travelers to Ali's funeral could not return to the razor-wired village until after dark. Taha Rasheed Lateef and two passengers passed through the checkpoint in his pickup. He was between the entrance and the nearby mosque when a helicopter fired three bursts, according to a police officer at the entrance checkpoint. Hospital staff in Tikrit, where his body had been carried, reported that the bullet had entered his back and killed him.

~ ~ ~

On one of our visits to Balad and to the Paliwoda Forward Operations US military base, some of us, including Art, who had left the West Bank and come to spend a week with the team and me in Iraq, waited in the van while Cliff and two others went to find Sassaman. An Iraqi guard came over and talked with us. He put his gun down in our van and even let one of the journalists we brought with us hold his gun. He was quite friendly. I thought how a man with a gun is dangerous in a tense situation. A person without a gun will use his or her mind, speech, or some other tool. But a person with a gun is less likely to take time to think creatively of how to deal with the problem. He or she is tempted to use the gun first.

We saw Cliff talking with Sassaman, so Art and I decided to walk toward them. The guard accompanied us. Sassaman had been in a tank, part of a small convoy heading out of the base. When he saw Cliff, he had the tank stop, jumped out, and talked with him. He was upset about an article someone from the previous delegation had written about him. Cliff mostly listened.

Then Cliff said some things he had wanted to say. He seriously invited Sassaman to quit his work with the military, join CPT, and move into nonviolence work. Sassaman responded, "I'd have to ask Mrs. Sassaman," adding that he only had eighteen months to finish up with the Army. The conversation ended, Sassaman climbed onto the tank, and the convoy took off to some mission. Cliff later wrote him a letter by e-mail, expanding his invitation.

~ ~ ~

Despite prior warnings, we did not consider Abu Hishma a hostile place for Americans to visit. Generally, Iraqis liked and admired the US and its culture so much that they had a hard time thinking badly of it. A relative of one of the people detained in the Balad area, referring to the US soldiers who were terrorizing their village, told us, "People like this shouldn't be called Americans."

The US could so easily win the hearts and minds of most Iraqis. But the horrible acts of violence by its military in the name of security were eroding that initial goodwill. The team asked the questions, "Is there some reason the US military continued to provoke an angry and violent response from the Iraqi people? Could it be a deliberate strategy to justify an indefinite period of occupation?" If so, this is an even greater tragedy.

~ ~ ~

I first went to Al Jazeera, a small village eight miles from Ramadi, on February 12, with a vanload of CPTers. To get to the village we drove along the Euphrates River, where we saw lots of fields with women and men planting and building up the carefully raised garden beds. Between the beds were ditches for irrigation water. Unlike much in this region of Iraq, many houses were built with rock.

On our way, Cliff reminded us of the history of this village. Our team had been there on three previous visits after hearing the story of the tragedy that had occurred there on November 22, 2003. At 5:00 p.m. that day, Ibrahim, his brother, Sabah, and Muhammad, a guest, arrived at their house and found it surrounded by US soldiers. The soldiers handcuffed them and sat them on the ground. Suspecting that there were armed resisters in the house, the soldiers divided up and entered from two different sides. There was no electricity and, apparently, in the dark, one group mistook the other for an enemy and opened fire. Four US soldiers were killed by friendly fire. The remaining soldiers were very upset when they came out of the house. They took out their anger by killing the three handcuffed Iraqi men and ordering the house destroyed, which was done later by

Children near demolished home in Al Jazeera village.

helicopter and tank fire. The soldiers also assassinated five other Iraqi men who arrived at the house later. Eight days later, CPTers went to meet the survivors, see the demolished house, and record the story. Then, on December 28, the team went back to Al Jazeera for a press conference, set up by the HROI (Al Jazeera branch), at which family members shared the stories of the killings and home demolition.

This was my first visit to Al Jazeera, and I found it horrible to walk around the piles of rubble with parts of the original walls standing. This was where a family had once lived, and this was all that was left of their home. What could we say to Muhammad's wife, holding her fifteen-day-old son and standing beside her two-year-old daughter? Near them was Ibrahim's nine-year-old son. Did the violence that occurred here bring any more security to the Iraqi people or the US military?

We found Taha, one of the lawyers the team had worked with in the past, but soon realized that something was wrong. The people did not greet us, but stayed at a distance, looking at us suspiciously. Even Taha was reserved. "Where are the results of your visits?" he asked. "There has been no change in their situation or compensation given for all the damage and pain they suffered. There is still a lot of anger and pain. The family needs money to buy materials for continuing with the rebuilding." None of the internationals who had been there had even come back with copies of any articles written or pictures that had been taken.

We said we were sorry. We would try to get copies of reports and pictures to them. Also we had sent messages to Sa'ad, another lawyer from Al Jazeera, asking to be able to come and spend some days working to help rebuild the house, but never got a response. We weren't able to give them money or supply them with materials, but we wanted to go and give some labor. After visiting with Taha longer and greeting the women and children, we arranged to come back the next week for two days of work.

One week later, on February 18, we returned to Al Jazeera. Again the villagers were reserved and not welcoming. The mother of two of the men who had been killed, however, came to us and voiced her anger and grief, accusing the US soldiers of taking her sons away from her and leaving her homeless. It was an awkward moment, but we needed to just listen to her. They didn't seem to have work for us. Finally Taha told us we could break up rock into smaller pieces for the walls of the new building. Later some of the young men in the village joined in helping us split and haul rock. Some of our group started talking to and taking pictures of the children, and women CPTers visited with the women. Gradually, they became friendlier. The angry mother even calmed down and started helping us with the rocks. We ended up being there only a day, and our work was just a small token, but by the time we left there were two big piles of rocks and heartfelt good-byes.

~ ~ ~

Weeks later, on March 17, two team members went to Ramadi to sit in on a session of the court where a US lawyer dealt with compensation cases for one morning a week. On the wall was a list of 1,400 cases dating back to April 2003, claiming damage done by US forces. In most of these cases, compensation was denied.

The captain explained that the US government was under no obligation to pay for any damage caused by its troops. The Foreign Claims Act (FCA) had been established for accidental damage to property by troops conducting exercises in countries such as Germany and Korea. He considered granting FCA money for a few deserving claimants as a goodwill gesture, but didn't see it becoming a widespread policy.

Iraqi lawyers were not convinced that this was goodwill. They did not see the economic benefits of occupation. There was not a system of law that allowed them to help their clients, so they received little respect for their profession. Iraqis believed that if US forces killed someone during a house raid, shot at cars, or broke the walls of a house, they should pay compensation. Lawyers told us, "Surely international law required the US military to pay for its actions."

But the US military thought otherwise. They believed that they operate on intelligence and that every house raid was justified. House raids were considered combat operations, and no compensation would be paid for damage during combat. If the family being raided was found to have no weapons and was not harboring resistance fighters, it was still considered a combat operation and Iraqis had no legal recourse. "We don't want to become a life-insurance policy for bad guys," said the captain.

Iraqi lawyers were frustrated and angry. "Many times soldiers opened fire on Iraqis," one said. "The Iraqis were given no rights in these cases."

~ ~ ~

"They are all terrorists," one or two Iraqi men called out to us each day as they passed by a team vigil in central Baghdad calling for justice for Iraqi detainees. They pointed to our poster-size pictures of detainees, but usually rushed on, leaving no time for dialogue.

After hearing the stories of each detainee we represented and the circumstances around their detention, we knew that was not the case. Many were rounded up with all the other men in their neighborhood or told the raid on their house or the shooting at their car that wounded them was a mistake, but then were not

Bullet holes in door and room of house in Abu Sifa, from a US military raid, December 31, 2003.

released. Some were simply driving by when others shot or detonated a bomb aimed at a US military patrol.

We had written the stories of some of the eighty-three men rounded up in the village of Abu Sifa, and of 182 men from Abu Hishma. There seemed to be great injustices in these cases. We had brought attention to the families of the men killed in the village of Al Jazeera. We had seen and heard the stories of the suffering that military actions had caused Iraqi individuals and families.

But what if the attacks against the Army patrols and base nearby were from the men of Abu Hishma? What if the men rounded up at Abu Sifa or Al Jazeera village were resistance fighters? What did that mean for our telling of these stories and protesting what the US military was doing? Did that mean we were being used by these groups of people to cover up their crimes, as some people suggest?

No. Even if some of these men were part of the Iraqi resistance movement, they should not be treated with excessive force, abuse, and humiliation, but with the same respect and dignity we would want for our family members. Legal rights would allow them to have their cases settled and for them to be released if innocent. This is especially important given the claims of the US government to be bringing freedom and democracy to Iraq.

Many of us also saw the war and occupation of Iraq as illegal and unjust. It had spawned both violent resistance and an increase of crime. I remember what one of the human rights lawyers we work with told us: "There were no terrorists before the war. The war created terrorists. Give the people their rights and there will be no terrorists."

Real peace and security in Iraq will only begin to take root when the injustices of the occupation are gone. The purpose of our work concerning the problems of detainees was not to try to make the occupation a little better. It was to respond to the suffering it caused and to witness to the destructive powers of war and occupation. We don't want to be trapped in the mindset that we need to keep increasing protective walls and violent procedures in the name of security. We need to try to break down the walls and remove the bonds of oppression.

CHAPTER 17

Speaking to Those in Power

When we extend our hand to the enemy, God reaches out for both of us.

    —*Thomas Merton*

Being North Americans in Iraq carries a lot of privilege. On the street our lighter skin, our hair, and our clothing made us stand out in any crowd. We had access to information and resources from back home that helped us rise above some of the limitations and chaos of post-invasion Iraq. We were able to get into CPA or US military offices and talk to personnel whom Iraqis didn't have access to, because of our passports, English language, and some knowledge of how these systems operated. We also had some power as voters back home. We wanted to use this privilege, not only to help Iraqis speak out or to help them access what little help was available, but also to speak directly on their behalf to those in power.

Often our contacts with US officials in Iraq came in the process of getting information, advocating for particular families, or just traveling around the country. But we also made special appointments or contacts with certain officials to share what we had learned and to give our suggestions. All through our time in Iraq, over the span of a year and a half, we tried to offer and demonstrate alternatives to the use of violence in Iraq—before the war, during the war, and in the post-invasion time. We tried to point to ways of moving out the escalating spiral of violence.

Everywhere we went we encountered soldiers—soldiers who believed that their presence was important and helpful to the

Iraqi people. There were also soldiers who believed the opposite or didn't want to be in Iraq. Most were stressed and afraid; many were traumatized by what they were experiencing. Even though we opposed the occupation, we did not want to see them as our enemies or demonize them. Most American youth deployed in Iraq went there as good people with positive intentions. They were caught up in a violent system, and were also taught to be brutal and abusive. We wanted to support soldiers in their struggle to retain their humanity and not dehumanize Iraqis. We wanted them to see that it is not necessary to use excessive force to maintain security.

We saw that the use of excessive violence put them in more danger. We wanted to listen to their concerns and pain, but also share with them what we were experiencing and learning. In early December, the team decided to develop and pass out the following leaflet to soldiers:

Coalition Forces and the Human Rights of Iraqi Citizens

Like all human beings, Iraqis have a right to just treatment and respect. Yet many Iraqi families have shared with us their stories of US troops violating their human rights and dignity. As a result, support is growing among Iraqis for violent resistance.

If any coalition soldier mistreats an Iraqi citizen, it endangers all coalition soldiers. For your own safety and for the well-being of Iraqi citizens, we invite you to abide by these principles taken from the Geneva Conventions, the Universal Declaration of Human Rights, and related humanitarian and human rights law:

> Soldiers have a duty to protect civilians. Care must be taken not to harm those who are unarmed, or women, children, and the elderly or sick. Force should be used only when absolutely necessary and in proportion to the level of force threatened.
>
> Coalition forces, as the occupying power in Iraq, are ultimately responsible for ensuring that family members of detainees are notified as to where they will be detained.
>
> It is against international law to punish a group of people collectively (such as reprisal assaults on a family, neighborhood, or town) because individuals within that area have attacked coalition forces. Only those who are guilty of wrongdoing should be punished.

Soldiers shall respect the property of civilians. If property is confiscated, a receipt must be issued with explicit instructions for how it may be retrieved.

From the CPA Office of Human Rights and Transitional Justice:
No Iraqi citizen shall be subjected to:

Arbitrary arrest or detention
Torture
Cruel and inhuman or degrading treatment or punishment
Arbitrary interference with privacy
Attacks against honor and reputation

Iraqis detained by coalition forces have been held for months without charges, without legal counsel, and without contact with their families. The loss of husbands and fathers and the income and security they provide creates terrible hardship for families. Often men are detained on the basis of false information and malicious rumors. Please remember that suspicion is not proof and that the men detained may be innocent of all wrongdoing.

Coalition forces are obliged to respect the provisions of international human rights treaties to which their home countries and/or Iraq have signed. The "Rules of Engagement" are not the only rules which apply.

You can be held liable for your actions in Iraq, even if you are obeying orders from your commanding officer.

When you return home, will you be able to tell your families that you acted with honor and compassion?

~ ~ ~

Responses to the flyer were mostly positive, but occasionally soldiers got defensive and angry, especially those who had been in Iraq a long time and had been under a lot of stress.

One time, on the way home from Falluja, the team stopped at a large US Army base. While trying unsuccessfully to get in, the team members passed out flyers to guards around the entrance and to soldiers on convoys as they came through. Another time Cliff was walking near the Palestine Hotel and offered flyers to two soldiers on a tank. One refused to take it, but the other took it gladly and wanted to talk. It seemed that he was considering trying to leave the military.

In February, when Art was in Iraq for a week, he went with Cliff and an Iraqi man to Abu Ghraib prison to try to help him visit his detained brother. After walking through openings in the razor wire in front of the prison, a guard told them, "He is not allowed any visits."

Art and Cliff challenged this and told the Iraqi guards they wanted to talk with an American official. That is when they met "Tony," a US soldier about twenty-two years old, short, and good-looking. "I like to work out in the gym, but most days I am too tired to even think after standing guard in front of the prison for twelve hours every day," he said.

He told them he was only a common soldier. He had no authority and there was nothing he could do to help them arrange a visit. Then he opened up. "The situation is a mess in Iraq, and the American military is making it worse. I can understand that the Iraqi people are angry. Under Saddam," he said, "families could visit their loved ones once a week."

Tony expressed a lot of frustration with the military. He was eager to leave Iraq and the military, and said he could be killed any day. He was wearing a ragged piece of cloth as an armband in remembrance of a buddy who had been killed a few days earlier. Tony said, "If you try to do what is right, you get kicked. I tried to do what is right, and I got knocked down into the cellar." He didn't explain what he meant.

He was fighting back tears as Cliff and Art told him they wanted him to be safe, that they cared about him. Here was a good person, caught in a force he could not control, trying to preserve his integrity, trying to keep his heart from becoming hard and cold, trying to do the best he could.

~ ~ ~

The team continued to meet with US officials. Officers at the IAC gave us lists of detainees when higher ranking officers wanted those lists tightly controlled. In late October, the team unsuccessfully tried to set up a meeting with General Janis

Karpinski, who had oversight of all the prisons. None of the officers would give the team her contact information. So they met with Colonel Ralph Sabatino, who had worked with the CPA Ministry of Justice to classify names of detainees. Members of our team also met with Major Clincy, the liaison between the combined joint task force at the airport and the Ministry of Justice, and Lieutenant Colonel Fisher. These meetings were opportunities to report on the injustices and abuses the team was documenting in the detainee system.

Once the CPT report of the seventy-two detainee cases was completed, we used it as a basis for discussions with US military and civilian officers who were influential in carrying out detainee policies. The report was quite long, so in January we made the following two-page summary, written to address such officials:

CPT Summary Report on Iraqi Detainees

Introduction

CPT has maintained a peaceful presence in Iraq since October 2002. Presently, CPT is working with Iraqi people and human rights organizations to monitor various interactions between coalition forces and the Iraqi people. CPT is particularly concerned that any mistreatment of the Iraqi people could lead to long-term problems including:

1. Increasing numbers of Iraqi people joining resistance groups

2. Increasing danger of attacks against coalition soldiers

3. A growing record of human rights violations against the Iraqi people

Since the fall of the Saddam Hussein regime on April 9, 2003, the Coalition Provisional Authority (CPA) has imprisoned thousands of people. The CPA, the current governing body of Iraq, now has the responsibility of housing those prisoners and separating the guilty from the innocent. The CPA also has additional duties because the International Committee of the Red Cross has left Iraq due to the lack of security. These additional CPA duties are to inform family members of the whereabouts of imprisoned relatives, to report on prisoners' health and well-being, and to arrange family visits.

Summary:
CPT has already presented the CPA with some statistical data that we compiled of seventy-two case studies from our files. Our conclusion is straightforward: The *military actions designed to ensure short-term security are in fact compromising long-term US security interests.* The following notes highlight problems that need immediate attention and policy development.

1. Violent house raids. House raids include soldiers breaking furniture and TVs, kicking and beating people, terrifying Iraqi children, and heaping shame on Iraqi women who are pulled from their beds wearing only nightclothes. *CPT strongly recommends ending such midnight raids, and all use of excessive force and degrading treatment.*

2. Lack of family visits with prisoners is causing frustration and anger. In addition, many families trying to visit prisoners receive misleading directions. The waiting time for an appointment is six months. *CPT strongly urges the CPA to model to the international community the sort of transparency and ease of access to both detainee information and visitations that are warranted by basic human rights.*

3. Health concerns. Families have no way to inquire about the health and well-being of prisoners, even when their detained loved ones were injured at the time of their arrest. Family members often report that detained relatives have chronic health problems such as diabetes, heart disease, or high blood pressure. *CPT urges the CPA to allow family members access to all information pertaining to the health of detainees.*

4. Mistreatment of detainees. All the released detainees that CPT volunteers have talked to reported that they were housed in overcrowded tents without proper clothes or toilet facilities, particularly in the initial detention centers to which they were taken. They reported physical and psychological torture or abuse. CPT volunteers saw handcuffed prisoners being led around with black plastic bags over their heads at an Army base near Balad on December 24, 2003. Released detainees often report this sort of treatment and worse. *Such treatment violates the Fourth Geneva Convention (Article 85). Training for new troops should train soldiers to stop cruel and humiliating treatment and use minimal force.*

5. Theft of property. CPT has heard many stories about coalition forces confiscating money and property during house raids. We have heard Iraqis refer to this confiscation of money and property as "theft." We have not heard of any instances in which coalition forces gave the owners receipts for confiscated property. We know of only one incident in which confiscated property (a computer) was returned. *CPT urges coalition forces to cease unnecessary confiscation of property, to issue receipts when confiscation is necessary, and to return all property that has been unjustly confiscated. If possible, have a local civilian authority present as a witness of any property taken.*

6. Ineffective application process for confiscated property. Many people who have applied for compensation for damaged and confiscated property have not received any written proof of their application. They have not received any documents communicating decisions on compensation. Because there is no paper trail, CPT has no evidence that the CPA has paid any compensation to families, even when CPA officials have made verbal agreements to do so. *CPT urges the CPA to develop a systematic and transparent process for compensation, to document and follow through on all requests for compensation, and to give families copies of all documents relating to compensation.*

7. Inaccessibility of information. CPT has no evidence to suggest that the CPA has ever initiated any communication with Iraqi citizens about imprisoned relatives, the return of confiscated property, or compensation for damaged property. Iraqi citizens have to be extremely persistent to get any information from the occupying forces. Iraqis are increasingly frustrated and angered by failed attempts to get straightforward, truthful answers to questions asked of coalition officers. *CPT strongly urges the CPA to share information with families and legal representatives of detainees.*

8. Lack of security. Iraqis live in fear because of the lack of security. They say that the criminals arrested every day by Iraqi police are then freed within a few days by coalition authorities. Meanwhile, innocent detainees are held for months. Iraqis' perception is that the CPA is targeting the wrong people. *The CPA still needs to convince Iraqis that it is doing all it can to free the streets of common thieves, while releasing innocent detainees.*

Conclusion:

The development of a process for handling detainee issues that is transparent, efficient, and that upholds basic legal rights is essential for establishing a secure and democratic society. The Coalition Provisional Authority can best lay the foundation for policy by working in partnership with Iraqi human rights organizations and with lawyers who have been responding to the problems of detainees. A more open approach that attends to the concerns of families and more freely shares information will, in the long run, provide better security for both Iraqi civilians and coalition soldiers and personnel. The CPA should model the sort of justice system most desirable for a future free, democratic Iraq.

In late December, lower-ranking military personnel at the IAC urged us to take our recommendations to the policy makers to deal with a problem situation "much bigger than the Iraqi theater." Later when we looked back, we wonder whether they were trying to help us expose the abuse scandal to the public. The first one they suggested that we talk to was Colonel Sabatino.

Our first recommended meeting with higher ranking officers was on January 3, 2004, with Col. Sabatino, Major Clincy, and SSG Berlo. I summarized our concerns about excessive violence used in house raids, abusive treatment of detainees, and unjust confiscation of property. Sheila outlined our concerns about inaccessibility of information and poor visitation policies. Allan shared specific examples that he had observed.

Sabatino stated right out that night raids would continue, because they were military operations procedure. The "bad guys" operate at night, he explained, and that is when military forces have the best chance to capture them. "It is safer to hold such raids than to try to dialogue," he said. CPTers suggested that in the long run, the trauma to families and the resulting resentment and anger compromised security.

Sabatino confirmed that the house raids were often timed to be less than forty-five seconds, and there were usually twenty-five seconds of "absolute fury," when soldiers physically pushed and subdued people who "did not comply" quickly with orders (shouted in English) to get down. He clearly supported this use of force, despite acknowledging that sometimes military units raided the wrong house. This was the area of our greatest disagreement.

"Abusive treatment of detainees is a training problem," he said. "Detainees or their families who have been mistreated should file a complaint. It will be investigated and prosecuted." He then outlined the proper steps for filing a complaint. When we related the extreme difficulties families were having in trying to go through these steps, he acknowledged that: "Yes, there isn't a good way for an Iraqi civilian to report a military crime."

Sabatino defended the practice of confiscating property, but agreed with us that there were many problems connected to this. Soldiers were not following the official policies for issuing receipts. He admitted that he had never seen any soldier issue a receipt. He suggested that the head attorney at the HROI request a meeting with staff judge advocate, Sharon Reily at the airport detention center to discuss the claims procedure.

On January 9, the CPT team sent reports and a letter to Bremmer; Sanchez; Colonel Jerry Phillabaum, an officer under Karpinski; and Sandy Hodgkinson, director of the CPT human rights office, requesting meetings to discuss the report and our suggestion. CPT agreed to draft the letter of request for the HROI. Meetings were eventually scheduled with assistants of Bremer and Sanchez, and later in April with Hodgkinson's replacement, but we did not get a response form Phillabaum or anyone else at Abu Ghraib.

"Yes, a four- to six-month wait for visitation at Abu Ghraib prison is poor policy, but we are trying to work on it," Sabatino told us. He also said it was unlikely that international NGOs or Iraqi organizations would receive access to the lists of prisoners. CPA's plan was to update the list, translate it into Arabic, and make it available to every Civil Military Operations Center (CMOC). He suggested we write letters to Ambassador Paul Bremer and Lieutenant General Ricardo Sanchez, asking for meetings if we wanted to pursue the issues of inaccessibility of information.

Less than two weeks later, Allan briefly took our advocacy work another step further when he had a short "sit-in" and fast at the IAC. He had been working hard to help a family go through the system to try to reclaim property that had been confiscated by US soldiers when their houses were raided in September, or at least to get compensation. They had gone more than five times to different offices since October and had received a letter from a US colonel saying their case should be investigated. Each time they were put off, until finally they were told there was nothing US agencies could do for them.

Allan felt pain and frustration with the injustice of this

dysfunctional system and the unnecessary suffering it was causing this and other Iraqi families. He felt this so deeply that he decided to stay at the offices until the officials investigated this family's request. He called on officials to provide a more consistent, well-defined, efficient, and just system of responding to claims.

Allan sat at the offices overnight and started a liquids-only fast, which he kept for four and a half days. From several Iraqis working in the IAC Allan heard the following comments: (1) There is no peace or justice here in Iraq, (2) Only 5 percent of the Iraqis who come to the IAC actually receive assistance, and (3) Your friend will never get his confiscated pictures and money returned; US soldiers conducting house raids keep the money they find and just throw family pictures in the garbage.

Three of our team were talking with him when the head of the IAC asked him to leave and threatened arrest. When he didn't leave, the official brought over three military police to escort him to the door and tell him he was barred from the building. For a couple of weeks after that, CPTers were not allowed entry into the IAC.

Two weeks later, on January 24, Sheila, Cliff, and I met with Ambassador Richard Jones, Deputy Administrator and Chief Policy Officer of the CPA; Scott Norwood, liaison between the military and CPA; and Ronald Schilcher of the Office of Provincial Outreach, who had known CPT team members in Hebron when he worked at the US Consulate in Jerusalem. Jones was personable and expressed respect for CPT's perspective, saying, "The detainee issue is of great concern to us." He said that the CPA had "competing interests": security, public relations, and humanitarian. He said that until November the priority was security, but now they needed to work on relationships with the Iraqi people.

He described the steps they were taking to resolve some of the "horror stories" of human rights abuses and detainee injustices. Such steps included creating an executive board to work on these issues and reducing from twenty-four to fourteen days the time detainees spent "in limbo" in holding areas before they were assigned to a detention facility. He pointed out that this was then the policy, but that it remained to be seen whether or not the policy would be carried out. Bremer announced the planned release of five hundred detainees and ordered that an information center be created in a trailer outside Abu Ghraib prison to assist families in finding information.

Sheila, Cliff, and I then summarized CPT's report of abuses against Iraqi people when detained and the lack of a clear, consistent, transparent process for families to find information or to make compensation claims, giving some examples. The men seemed surprised by what we described. We gave suggestions for policies that would reduce these abuses and would be more respectful of the Iraqi people, as well as increase the security of international people in Iraq. We suggested that their staff arrange for regular meetings with Iraqi human rights lawyers to discuss these problems and involve them in the planning for the new justice system of Iraq. We left information with them about contacting three such groups that we worked with on a regular basis and offered to help make initial connections with them.

In response, Norwood suggested they were in the process of setting up a website, which would list the detainees, so that family members could go to the Internet and check for themselves. He suggested we contact his office to get more information about filing a report on abuses by the US military. We continued to set up meetings with other officials in the military and the CPA.

Our team began a series of follow-up steps. We began to funnel information of claimed abuses to their offices by e-mail, the way they had suggested, but by the time I left in late March, we had not received any responses. We arranged for a meeting with Jones and three Iraqi human rights organizations. This meeting was postponed three times immediately before the meetings were to take place, and as of April, had still not happened. This was especially hard because, with the phone system still not working, it was difficult to contact the people invited to participate. Each time they showed up at our apartment ready to go, we had to tell them the meeting had been postponed. It seemed to hurt our credibility with their organizations. The promised releases of prisoners had been slow and small compared to the amount of new prisoners detained each day.

~ ~ ~

Our next meeting was on February 14 with Colonel Marc Warren, Chief Judge Advocate under Sanchez. Two military personnel picked us up at the IAC and drove us to the Republican Palace. As we walked in, Warren rearranged the furniture in the cramped office so that he was not sitting behind a desk and we were all in a circle on the same level. When we each introduced ourselves, he shared openly about missing his family.

Sheila, Cliff, and I presented CPT's report and summary of the report and shared our concerns, citing examples from Abu Hishma and the Al Dora suburb of Baghdad. Warren responded, saying that he thought our report was well written. In response to some of the stories of the men we had interviewed in the Al Dora raid, he said, "You can't believe everything you hear."

"That's true," I answered, "but we have been hearing similar stories widely in different areas of Iraq, so we have concluded that these are not isolated incidents or accidents, but general practice."

Warren told us that his job was to see that the US forces followed the law. They would work on correcting abuses by improving the training of the new soldiers who were being rotated into Iraq. They want to train them to be more culturally aware, to use precise force, and to restrain their use of force.

He mentioned the book and movie *Algiers*, a story from the Algerian revolution against French colonization. What struck him in the account was that the French started using extreme interrogation tactics and used extreme counterforce measures, which seemed effective in the short run, but increased the resistance and later "blew up" in their face.

"It's instructive for the situation we are in right now," Warren added.

"Family visits are a real concern of mine," he said, then acknowledged that they had done a poor job of disseminating information and that the process of moving detainees through the system was incredibly slow. Soon, however, the CPA website would include a list of lesser security prisoners, he said. "Information about high-security guys, we will keep under our control."

One other improvement Warren mentioned was that more judge advocates had been commissioned to work on the review board to make decisions on individual cases. Instead of only two days a week, they would work seven days a week and each week try to process at least one hundred cases.

In response to our talking about prisoners' legal rights and referring to the Geneva Conventions, he said the Geneva Conventions allow occupying forces to hold security detainees "forever." "But we will try to cull out those amenable for trial." When we asked if they would give the oversight of security detainees to Iraqis when the transfer of power came on July 1, he said no.

After our talk, Warren's assistant, Rob, took us for an extensive tour around the building, Saddam's former Republican Palace, showing us the chapel, the cafeteria, and the notorious huge swimming pool outside. What I will always remember, however, was the beautiful, large, spreading shade tree near the pool, the mural on a wall in a lounge depicting the bombing of the Twin Towers with the caption "Thank God for the Coalition Forces and Freedom Fighters at Home and Abroad," and a bulletin board displaying Valentine cards from home. On the way out of the Green Zone, Rob asked us questions about why we were there and whether we felt safe. We had a good talk

Because of new military troops rotating in during February and the CPA's work on reorganizing the detainee lists, we did not receive any more updated lists. In early March, Cliff met Edward Schmultz, the former US Assistant Attorney, who told him, "There are thousands of Iraqis being held who should be at home. We're working on a list to get all the names straight."

Stewart began to study more closely the last list we had received, dated December 30, 2003, which included 8,855 names. We were aware that there were thousands more detainees, considered high security, not on this list. He found that of those on this list, 453 had no charges listed, 22 were held as a kind of hostage (that is, held because they were relatives or friends of a suspected person and their detainment would hopefully cause the suspected person to turn himself in voluntarily), and at least eighty-nine were listed as being detained because they were at or near the target of a military raid, and the charge of 79 was listed as being a Ba'ath Party member. He took this study to various journalists.

There were many good people in this horrible system, many who wanted to do things differently but were under orders or felt they had no power to change things. Talking with the US military and CPA officials seemed important to do, but we didn't have very high expectations for what would come from it. We didn't know how much influence our work had on the recent increase of releases of security detainees or on the CPA's investigations into allegations of abuse by US soldiers in detention centers. We would continue to seek out meetings with people in the system, working toward establishing the new justice system. We would still urge them to give decision-making power to the Iraqi human rights workers in this early stage of the process.

Any change, however, was fairly small, not really addressing the basic structural violence used to maintain security for the occupying forces and prop up the system of occupation.

～ ～ ～

"What is the next step for me in speaking to those in power?" I asked myself as I was nearing the end of my three-month stay. Once I went back in the US there would be not only government officials to communicate with but also the general public as I travel and speak. Most people back home don't realize the power they have in granting or removing their support for policies and for government officials.

My work in Iraq was difficult, but probably the hardest work I do is to speak to the people in the US who don't want to hear anything different from what the mainline media is reporting or anything critical of our government. It is especially hard to speak to Christian people who don't want to try to view the war or occupation in light of the way of Jesus, the way of nonviolent, suffering love. They fear that any criticism of US policy in Iraq or of what the military is doing in Iraq would be equated with not caring for the hundreds of men and women who have died or been wounded there. They are accustomed to accepting what the government says, that violence and war are the only ways to deal with evil, even though this is a contradiction of the gospel message. I pray that somehow God will use what I say to open their minds and hearts.

CHAPTER 18

Lenten Fast

*Is this not the fast that I choose: To loose the bonds of injustice,
to undo the thongs of the yoke, to let the oppressed go free.
Then your light will break forth like the dawn and your healing
shall spring quickly, your ancient ruins shall be rebuilt, you shall
raise up the foundations of many generations.*
                                    —Isaiah 58:5-6, 8, 12

We were not surprised with the inflexibility of detainee policy.
It was part of a bigger occupation system. Lawyers and human
rights workers had been doing good work, but it took something more. This was also a spiritual struggle, and we invited
others to join us in that struggle. With the help of the staff in
our Chicago office, and Sheila's coordination here, we launched
a fast in conjunction with a letter-writing campaign. We would
start it on the first day of the Lenten season, and it would last
at least forty days.

The theme became "Break Every Yoke: Iraq Fast for Justice
and Healing." Healing was needed for all who had participated
in the war and its aftermath of violence, for Iraq as a country,
the Iraqi people, and the coalition soldiers.

In our announcement and invitation to join the Lenten
campaign, we said the following:

Break Every Yoke: Iraq Fast for Justice and Healing
*There are 11,000 to 13,000 Iraqis languishing in detention
centers. Due process for the detained is unbearably slow, and
many suffer abuse, hunger, and psychological distress in prison.*

Their families struggle to get by and wonder if their loved ones are dead or alive. Thousands of families—both US and Iraqi— ache for the wounds of war to be healed. It is time to ask for miracles. It is time to empty ourselves and beg for God's mercy and compassion. It is time to proclaim a fast.

Christian Peacemaker Teams (CPT) members living and working in Iraq will spend the season of Lent in a Fast for Justice and Healing. We fast to set the oppressed free and to break the yokes of injustice that keep thousands of Iraqis imprisoned without due process. We fast to become more vulnerable to God's presence, to beg the God of mercy and compassion to break the yokes of fear, violence, and injustice that imprison all of us. We fast to seek the miracle of forgiveness, peace, and healing of all the terror of war. (CPT members will fast in a variety of ways, including the liquids-only and Ramadan-style fasting. They will engage in public witness daily at the Tahrir Square in Baghdad.)

Please JOIN US in whatever way you are able. There are many ways of fasting:

- Give up a meal, a TV show, or a favorite pastime.
- Write letters as part of our Adopt a Detainee campaign; Go to www.cpt.org for the names and addresses of detainees, the Coalition Provisional Authority officials who are in charge of these detainees, sample letters, and other relative information.
- Hold a public vigil to draw attention to the plight of Iraqi detainees. Bring candles or posters of pictures of detainees, or wear handcuffs and head-shrouds to graphically depict the situation of Iraqi detainees.
- Join with a group of friends, church community, or family to eat a simple meal and pray for peace.
- Devote an extra fifteen minutes daily to silence: fasting from the TV, phone, or other distractions.
- Join with a group to fast in a particular way for the whole of Lent, each person taking one day per week.
- Go to www.cpt.org to share your prayers, actions, and experience of fasting with Christian Peacemaker Teams and others around the world.

The Adopt a Detainee letter-writing campaign would be a joint effort between the team (coordinated in Iraq by Jim) and people in North America. We would prepare stories and information about detainees to be sent out to groups such as churches, mosques, synagogues, and peace organizations in North America. Each member of a participating group would write at least one letter to a US government official and one to Paul Bremer, head of the CPA in Iraq, on behalf of that detainee. This would result in these officials receiving hundreds of letters urging a fair trial, family visits, legal representation, release of those found innocent, the establishment of a transparent and accountable judicial process for security detainees, and investigation into the mistreatment of prisoners.

We chose many of the detainees we already had in our files. Then we went to the human rights organizations and asked if they would work with us to prepare more stories. The director of the NADHRI said they didn't have people with the time to write about cases, but they had eighty-eight cases they could give us. That sounded a little overwhelming, but we knew we could take on a few new ones.

And some people came to our door with new detainee cases. Theresa, a Polish woman in Al Dora who had lived in Iraq for many years and spoke Arabic fluently, came to us saying that she had been working with many families in her area and wanted to work together with our team on those issues. The next time she came, she brought along Hameed, from Falluja, who wanted to work with us not just for his nephew, Yasser, who had been detained April 4, 2003, but also to help other detainees. We decided to include Yasser's case and enlarged a picture of him into poster size. We also interviewed Salah, Yasser's friend who had been detained with him but was later released. Here is a summary of his story:

> On April 4, 2003 [shortly before Baghdad was invaded by US forces], Yasser and Salah were traveling home in a pickup truck on the outskirts of Baghdad [Radwania]. As their car approached a bend in the road, US soldiers opened fire on their vehicle. Both Yasser and Salah were wounded: Salah in the head and right thigh, Yasser in the leg and hand.
>
> After searching the vehicle, the soldiers administered first aid and transported them to a helicopter, which then took them to a hospital. Salah, who was the most severely injured of the two, fainted at some point during the trip. His recollection of that

hospital is foggy, but he thinks it was on a ship in the Gulf. Salah and Yasser were separated when Salah was transferred to a hospital in Nasiriya, already under US control at the time, for further medical attention. When Salah made inquiries, the hospital staff said no one by the name of Yasser had been admitted.

Salah left the hospital early against medical advice in order to reassure his worried relatives. He also met with Yasser's family after returning home. It was through Salah that Yasser's family finally learned what had happened to him.

Equipped with this new information, Yasser's family and friends began a search. They inquired at the Iraqi Assistance Center. They went to the Red Cross and the Red Crescent. They sought out translators who worked in the prisons and, through conversations with released detainees, they learned that Yasser had been seen in three different prisons. More recently, a detainee released from Abu Ghraib prison on the outskirts of Baghdad also reported seeing Yasser.

~ ~ ~

Here is an example of one of our cases, written up for our letter-writing campaign:

Wisam Adnan Hameed Ismaeel Hussain

Wisam is a twenty-two-year-old-taxi driver from Al Dora, a suburb of Baghdad. He disappeared in his red Volkswagen on August 7, 2003.

The Jordanian embassy was bombed on August 6, 2003. US soldiers determined that a red Volkswagen was involved in the bombing. Subsequently, all red Volkswagens and their drivers were swept up in Al Dora. Wisam was last seen in his taxi at 6:30 p.m. He did not come home that night and has not been seen since.

Wisam is unmarried and is his family's sole breadwinner. His father has back problems and cannot work. He supported his father, his mother, four sisters, and two brothers, ranging from four to eighteen years of age. Wisam's uncle describes him as a good boy whose aim was to help his family. He did not carry a weapon in his taxi. During the former regime, Wisam was in the military and served as security for the Russian embassy in Baghdad.

When Wisam disappeared, his family checked the handful of hospitals open at the time but did not find him. Later, an Iraqi soldier the family knows found Wisam's car at the Baghdad airport and saw his name on a list there. When the family checked at Abu Ghraib prison they were told that Wisam's name was not there. They last visited Abu Ghraib prison in October 2003 and were told they needed Wisam's identification number to find him. The family has no other information about him and no way to find his identification number. They are pleading to find out what has happened to him, what he is charged with, and how they can visit him. Wisam's uncle said they just want to see that he is all right.

Context

In CPT's view the American invasion and occupation of Iraq was, and remains, an illegal and unilateral projection of US power. The war on Iraq has nothing to do with its stated objectives: saving the world from weapons of mass destruction and delivering the Iraqi people from the tyrannical hands of Saddam Hussein. Every action the US takes to defend its ongoing occupation, including house raids and security detentions, is similarly illegitimate.

Some of the detainees CPT has included in this letter-writing campaign may have been involved in armed resistance to the US occupation. However, for CPT the issue is human rights—not the "guilt" or "innocence" of a particular detainee. Every detainee, regardless of what they may have done to whom, is entitled as a human being to certain protections and rights. As a signatory to the Geneva Convention on the Treatment of Prisoners of War, the US is obliged to uphold the minimum protections and rights outlined therein.

Despite the occasional exception, security detainees as a group are systematically denied access to legal representation and visits with their families. Many families have had no news about their loved one since the date of their arrest. Many detainees are being held without formal charges and many are not even registered. All are being held indefinitely without access to a transparent judicial process. CPT also hears reports from released detainees about mistreatment, abuse, torture, and substandard living conditions.

Action Request

- That Wisam's case be processed immediately so that, if innocent, he can be released to care for his family.
- That regular family visits be instituted immediately for Wisam while he is imprisoned.
- That Wisam have immediate access to legal representation.

I am holding a poster of detainee Yasser Al-Mohamedy at a Lenten vigil in Tahrir Square in Baghdad, March 2004.

- That a transparent and accountable judicial process be established immediately for security detainees, or they be released.

On February 25, the beginning of Lent, our team began to fast and hold vigils five days a week from noon to two. Three days a week we stood at Tahrir Square in the center of Baghdad. Other days we would move to other locations either in Baghdad or other cities where we had been working with Iraqi human rights organizations. Many people came to the vigil asking us what they can do to help. We wrote a list of suggestions we could give those who ask:

- Come to the vigil, especially on Thursdays. Bring a banner or picture.
- Join a human rights organization, such as the Human Rights Organization of Iraq (near the Ministry of Justice on Haifa St.), the National Association for the Defense of

Human Rights (on Rasheed St. near Jumarriyah Bridge),
or the Society for Human Rights in Iraq (on Rasheed St.
near Jumarriyah Bridge).

•Get to know families of detainees in your community and
go with them to the Iraqi Assistance Center to insist on
justice for detainees.

•Visit Haifa Street during Solidarity Week, March 16-19.

•Organize a support group for families of detainees.

•Ask your imam or pastor to talk about it to the community.

•Write an open letter to Americans and bring it to the vigil.
We will send it to our political leaders and home communities.

•Help your neighbor of a different faith.

~ ~ ~

Crowds gathered tightly around our group of six CPTers, as
we stood in front of our tent on the wide walkway under the
Liberty Memorial at Tahrir Square in central Baghdad. This was
the third day of the Lenten Fast Vigil, and we estimated that up
to six thousand people had come through that square each day.
Faces full of curiosity and suspicion stared intently at us, and
people reached out to get a flyer as they tried to figure out what
the presence of these international people meant.

"Those men are terrorists," one man told us, pointing to the
poster-size pictures of detainees. "They deserve to be executed!"
Another man asked challengingly, "Where were you when
Saddam was putting the Iraqi people in prison and torturing
them?" "Why do you have pictures of mostly Sunni men and
not Shi'a?" Others gave thumbs up or thanked us for being
there. Occasionally some would start telling about a friend of
theirs or someone in their family who was also detained or hurt
by US forces.

Two journalists stopping by for interviews warned us not to
continue to come back to that site to protest. We had planned
to do this for four days out of each of the next few weeks. "This
is a dangerous part of the city, and there are many gangs and
thieves around here. They know when you plan to come back."

Because our regular translators weren't there that day, various
men came by and began interpreting conversations between

team members and people in the crowd. A professor from Al Mustansariya University talked excitedly about his hopes for the future, the importance of work for justice, and his desire for us to come to talk to students. A deaf-mute man protectively tried to keep the crowd at a distance if they pressed too close. Another man was a member of the HROI, one of the Iraqi organizations we had been working with since the previous August. Taking us under his wing, he confronted and sent away men who were harassing CPT women, and he defended our positions to some of the critics.

"Some of these men are accusing you of being supporters of Saddam Hussein, or of being paid by the CIA or US military to do this," he told us. These accusations sounded ridiculous, but we took seriously the potential threat embedded in their statements.

Later we evaluated the three days of vigils. Would it be wise to move to another location, or were the warnings coming from the prejudices and fears of a few? We needed to get more pictures made of Shi'a men on our list. Would it be possible to do some of the street theater we had envisioned? Would we be able to keep up the strength to be there for two hours a day for four days a week and at other locations the other three?

We affirmed that the vigils had attracted the attention of and opened a dialogue with thousands of people passing by and many media personnel. It was also evident that in the midst of the various dangers and unknowns were "guardian angels," people who unexpectedly appeared and who watched over and assisted us.

~ ~ ~

After the bombings in Kerbala and Kadhamiyah on March 2, we held a large photo of Kadhimiyah as seen just after the bombing and a large banner that read in Arabic, "We mourn the loss of life at Kadhamiha and Kerbala, and we mourn for all the victims of violence in Iraq. NO MORE VIOLENCE." This brought a very positive response from the people who gathered around us at the vigil. "Thank you for your feeling," one man told us.

Midway through our vigil on March 6, we noticed a car

Two women at a Lenten vigil in Tahrir Square in Baghdad holding photos of a detained family member, March 2004.

awkwardly parked on the street right in front of the vigil site. People began to wonder if it might contain a bomb, so the vigil moved underneath the freedom mural nearby, while police towed away the car. Later, when people recommended we stop vigiling there, Jane commented, "We know it's risky but it's important work. We need to keep doing it."

At first, when some would ask angrily, "Where were you and your group or others around the world when Saddam was torturing or imprisoning us; why didn't you come to vigil then?" I would answer defensively that we were concerned or that we wanted to see that the same things don't happen again under the Americans. But then I switched my response and started saying variations of "Yes, we failed to speak out adequately for you during that time. I'm sorry." They would usually still need to say it over and over to us, because the pain was so deep—and we were just scratching the surface. But I realized that in these situations, they needed us to listen and acknowledge our complicity to the violence they had endured— and to care.

Saying "Yes, we failed you" was probably too simplistic and inadequate. I would have liked to have said more: "We failed to speak out adequately for you when you were being tortured." But it is more than that. "Yes, we failed you when the US helped support Saddam Hussein all those years leading up to the Gulf War and put the economic sanctions on Iraq in August 1990, which killed over a million people."

A man from Basra came up to Cliff one day and said he had worked with Northrup Grumman, a large US military contractor. He asked a number of questions, trying to understand what we were doing. He stood there listening to other Iraqis tell their stories of abuse during the former regime and under the present occupation. Cliff acknowledged the oppression of both regimes and said that we wanted to work so that such injustice would not happen again. The young man from Northrup Grumman said more than once to Cliff, "What you are doing is *very* important!"

Azmar, an intellectual in his forties, stopped to talk for more than half an hour. He shared many things (including that he plays the electric guitar), but emphasized up front that he didn't think that the vigil and fast would do any good, that we could not change policies. Also he said that he was very glad the US had invaded, that the horrible bombing was worth it, and that the first days when Saddam was gone were the best days of his life. He was disillusioned about the current situation, but still felt that the war was right and that we could do very little to change any problems nonviolently.

Azmar told us that after September 11, he had read an article from the US entitled "Why Do They Hate Us?" He said to me, "I'll tell you why people hate America—because of the foreign policy." And he said that for a long time he hated not only America, but also Americans. However, when the soldiers first invaded Baghdad, Azmar spoke one-on-one with a number of them. He found them to be very friendly; they let him sit in the tanks, even in the driver's seat. "They showed me pictures of their families, saying 'This is my daughter, this is my wife, this is my father, this is my mother.' And suddenly I realized that they are real people, human beings, and I no longer hated them."

Lenten Fast Vigil for Iraqi detainees in Kerbala, March 16, 2004.

After hearing this story, Sheila wrote the following in her journal: "While as a pacifist it is painful to think that such human connection happened at the expense of all the people who died under bombs and who die in the prisons today, Azmar's transformation and realization of the soldiers as human beings *is* at the heart of peacemaking. How would we ever send young soldiers off to war if we really deeply realized they were human beings sent to kill other human beings? We would all have to go ourselves, nonviolently."

One day, US soldiers came by while Cliff was setting up for the vigil. After looking at the banners and signs, one soldier told Iraqis standing nearby, "Don't listen to them; these people are just talk. We are the ones who got rid of the butcher." Then he told Cliff, "But you do your thing here; you have freedom of speech."

On most days, there were some people who came with stories of their own, of family members detained. We encouraged them to come join our vigil with pictures and be available to talk with reporters. Some of them did return with pictures. On Thursday, March 18, our vigil was one of the activities scheduled for Solidarity Week, sponsored by the coalition of human rights

CPT workers with Iraqis at a Lenten Fast Vigil for Iraqi detainees at the demolished house of Muhammed Abdula Wahad, a teacher in Abu Sifa, March 9, 2004.

organizations we were a part of. About 150 other people joined us. At the end of our time, more than a hundred members of the group marched over the Jumarriyah Bridge and stood with banners and posters across from the Republican Palace in the Green Zone. We represented ten different countries.

Meanwhile, we heard reports from CPT's Chicago office that a number of staff workers had spent several nights in near-subzero weather in tents at the Chicago Federal Plaza as a way to dramatize the harsh conditions endured by Iraqi detainees at the hands of US forces.

Our first "vigil on the road" was in Abu Hishma, the razor-wire surrounded village, where some of the campaign's detainees and families came from. Our vigil turned into a march down the middle of town, toward the checkpoint entrance of the town when the Iraqi men holding pictures all started walking. Just before the entrance, Iraqi Civil Defence Corps (ICDC) officers stopped us. They insisted the group not go any further, but had no problem with us staying there or marching back into the village. Soon they posed for pictures and joined in the enthusiasm of the crowd.

The next day we took the vigil to Abu Sifa, home of about eighty families of detainees and the place where almost all of the men of the village were detained at one time. As usual, the people welcomed us warmly. Several members of a family who had been displaced when US soldiers had demolished their house, and some of their neighbors, joined in our vigil held in the ruins of the house. The walls were pockmarked with bullet holes and the entire second floor was collapsed. Fifteen-year-old Muhammad, who had been released from detention ten days earlier, told his story to some of the team, while other team members played with the children.

When we took the vigil to Kerbala on March 16, Husain Al-Ibrihimi, founder of the Kerbala Human Rights Watch, arranged for banners, carpets on the pavement and a sound system, and brought dozens of people from their organization and a lot of energy. Achmed Fakhr Al-Dein Zeni's four small children were there holding posters asking for their father to be released. Genia Muhammad Ali, a sixty-five-year-old widow whose two sons and nephew had been detained in the summer, sat in a wheelchair and wept as she told her story. She still did not know the charges against her sons.

We stood on a plaza between the two holy shrines. Scores of people stopped and listened to readings from the Koran, deliberately chosen to emphasize the brotherhood of Christians and Muslims, and speeches about the necessity for human rights for detainees. Others joined the demonstration, holding signs and pictures. Husain spoke and invited the people there to work together to build a just society. He pointed to our team and said, "These people come from very far away to help us, so we must help ourselves!"

As I stood there, mesmerized by the crowds of people coming and going, my thoughts flashed back to the summer before, when we were exploring living in Falluja, looking for housing and sponsorship. The door hadn't opened, partly because of the higher level of anger already built up toward Americans, but it was more than that. In July, we had not yet had the months of working with detainee cases with human rights organizations, and thus had not yet built credibility and trust with the local people. By now their experience with CPT spoke louder than any words of intention we had given them before. Now there were many doors we could walk through if we were ready.

Later, at his home, Husain shared his thoughts with us about the day, democracy in Iraq, and his hopes for the future. "Iraqis need more education for democracy," he said. "The people there found it hard to believe that you as Americans could speak against the American government policies. For thirty-five years of dictatorship, if you saw a demonstration like this against Saddam, everyone would be killed, immediately. So it will take a long time for the people to overcome that fear." But he was also positive and excited about the challenge ahead. Some of his students saw him at the demonstration and asked why he did not tell them about it; they wanted to join.

On the last vigil I took part in, two days before I left, a large group of men crowded around us to express their strong opinions. I realized that I was getting stressed, caught myself, and prayed for love for the people. For the rest of the time, I was more relaxed, but felt a heavy weight inside. There was so much pain there.

Next to me, Sheila was talking to a man who had brought a list of eight things written in Arabic that he wanted us to deal with. He said to her sternly, "You must listen!" He read the list of tragedies that had happened to him and his family during the Iran-Iraq war, the 1991 Gulf War, and since. One concerned a village where he lived where many people were killed, including his parents and brothers. He told her that we should not just stay here, but must go to these other places and do something about them.

"I started to defend our group, but then realized I had to listen," Sheila explained afterward. "I said a quick prayer for help. I told him, 'I wish I had the power to change all these things,' but as I said this, I couldn't hold back the tears. Then he started crying too. I wanted to run from the pain, and he did too, but he stayed there with me. He kept nodding when I told him 'I am just one person, but I will do what I can and will pray for you, for healing.' It was a moment of communion. We both knew that we would pray for each other and work for peace and healing in Iraq."

CHAPTER 19

Where Do We Go from Here?

It was early March and our team of eight gathered to look at where we were in our work and in the situation in Iraq. We asked ourselves many questions: What did we hope would come out of our being and working here? How were we to carry this out? What part of our work do we affirm? What do we want to do better? How do we nurture nonviolence and loving alternatives in this situation? We brainstormed possible changes in the situation, such as scenarios of increased tension and violence, or scenarios of positive change. How might we respond? How could we best prepare for the post-vigil phase of CPT's project?

We shared a lot of thoughts, hopes, and concerns. We affirmed many basic aspirations, such as working out of love, being guided by God's Spirit, being willing to take risks, and balancing nurturing with action. But we also affirmed some other goals. These included working in partnership with the Iraqi people, building bridges between Iraqi groups in tension or between Iraqis and US officials, nurturing grassroots and nonviolent approaches to dealing with the problems there, finding more Iraqi advisors, testing a project located outside Baghdad, and being proactive in exploring risk-taking direct action.

What we do depends on the circumstances and what doors open. Sometimes it means getting out of the way, letting Iraqis do it, just as we recommend that the US allow the Iraqi people to do the rebuilding and reshaping of their own country. We don't want our actions to support the legacy of oppression and corruption of either former regimes or the new regime thrust on Iraq. We don't have all the answers. We are still learning.

We hope to try to incorporate these goals in the Lenten

campaign and other work with detainees. We will continue to pursue meetings with a small group of the Najaf human rights group, which wants to explore forming a Muslim Peacemaker Team. Then with the changing situation, new tasks and ways of responding may be given.

~ ~ ~

At times during the winter I thought over my time in Iraq. God had given me this quest—a quest I still didn't fully understand. I came to Iraq feeling a deep caring and longing that Iraqi people might experience a fuller love, joy, and laughter—that they can be free of the fear and pain they carry. I wanted them to feel safe and not have to worry about survival, so they can be free to give.

I wanted to be able to give them this freedom and peace and to take away their fears, but I knew it wasn't in my power. All of my work, any sacrifice, any risks I had taken, couldn't do it. Others may continue to control them, use them, take their resources, and give them little in return. I could never give them what they need, but I could care and love deeply. I could put my longings, my understanding of their suffering and their hopes and dreams into action and prayer for them.

Jesus walked amidst an oppressed people in an occupied land. He struggled with what his role there was. He realized it was not to meet all those physical needs or to take political power and force a change. He realized his was a path of humility, of servanthood, not of winning the admiration of others. He was open to God leading him. He had compassion on the poor and suffering. He loved, healed, and gave himself. He called other to join him in living in a new order, but doing that challenged the old systems of injustice and oppression.

So we want to follow this path in Iraq or anywhere we are. It involves compassion, humility, and servanthood while challenging the powers of evil, living under different loyalties, and not accepting the commonly held myths of power and violence.

In many ways, working in Iraq that winter was harder than at previous times. The occupation more entrenched, more volatile, and could have blown up at any time. The situation was more confusing and complicated. We wrestled with how we could help without being dispensers of material goods or just making the occupation better? How could we work with those Iraqis we disagreed with about the means of resistance, or when we did not support their desire to adopt western economic values?

Our relationships with the local people, and being with them in their struggle remained a priority. At our team retreat on March 10, I was able to see that I had been carrying too much worry and sense of responsibility. I had been too task-oriented and had left less space open for relationships.

I saw the US military and other internationals removing themselves from daily contact with the Iraqi people and building more protective walls and barriers to ward off violent attacks. I even felt a bit of pride in our refusal to do the same. But what I came to see was that I was also withdrawing at times and using different methods of protecting myself. I found myself continually putting up protective walls around myself, not so much from the dangers of violence from Iraqis or US soldiers, but to protect my own inner strength.

We found that when we did express love and concern, people would bring even more needs and demands to us. It would increase their expectations and frustration with us for not being able to change their situation. Closing myself off emotionally from other people, either Iraqis or teammates at times, was my way of protecting myself from the overwhelming needs and demands that I wanted to meet but never could. I wanted to be friends and express my love to Iraqi people without immediately having strings attached. Sometimes I also pulled back emotionally so that I didn't sink down into the despair myself and take on more pain than I could carry.

I felt that my relationships were in the process of becoming less romantic, healthier, more honest and real. There was less affirmation and appreciation of our presence and work. Our relationships would include hearing more of their anger, frustration, confusion—and their challenges about what we were doing.

Even within our apartment, I would still feel "on call" all day long and was with people constantly. I needed to tune out some of what others were doing. Sometimes it became necessary to go up to the roof to get that quiet moment to think and pray, or to use the time before rising in the morning to become more centered. I shared with people in the February delegation how being with the children at the orphanage replenished my spirit, but I couldn't find time to go there very often. Bob Holmes, leader of the delegation and pastoral care worker for CPT responded, "Maybe you can't afford *not* to go there more often."

~ ~ ~

It was my last week in Baghdad before leaving for the US. And what a full week it was! A week of more bombing and violence, but also a week of courageous and loving work that doesn't usually get reported. I was part of the hopeful vigil in Kerbala, the march to the CPA headquarters, and the last regular vigil at Tahrir Square. I went to our Iraqi friends, saying good-bye and "*Insha'alla*—I will be back again." And I had a last visit to the Holy Family school and the orphanage.

~ ~ ~

Several changes had taken place in the orphanage since September. Two new infants, Mustafa and Ziad, added to the melee of the playroom. New toys abounded and new chairs allowed these disabled children to sit more comfortably. A group of US soldiers came several afternoons a week to play with the them. While the soldiers were there, a Humvee and tank stood guard on the street in front of the door. But there was no change to the playful noises and sense of family. Because of my busy schedule, I had been able to join them only about once a week.

This day, while I sat among the children, singing and helping a large stuffed animal talk to them, a woman walked in hesitantly to greet them. She gently shook her head with a look of pity on her face and then left.

Her sentiment seemed out of place in this playful scene. Silently, my heart shouted, "No! You are mistaken. They are not things to be pitied. They are real people! They are Nurah and Amid and Nashua. When I see Dunia's mischievous smile as she grabs a handkerchief out of my pocket or watch Ziad's sparkling eyes and trusting look, I don't see them as a girl with cerebral palsy or a boy with brain damage. I see them as beautiful little people who have much to give."

Pity and love don't go together. Pity distances; love connects. With pity they are looked at and treated as a tragedy or as misfits. With love they are seen as fully human and good. Love stops seeing the deformity and watches for the beauty and uniqueness to emerge in a smile or twinkle of the eye, or even in the stormy cry of pain or anger.

I think of a similar kind of sentiment many have when they think of a group of people suffering war or poverty, as the Iraqi people are today. If pitied, we can distance ourselves from their humanity and can throw them some crumbs. We can feel generous because we are giving them something, rather than fully embracing them as deserving of every good thing that others in our world enjoy and as fully competent to decide how their country should be restored.

With pity, we can begrudgingly pull some money out of our pockets to rebuild what the US has destroyed, and then give that money to our companies who "know best how to do it right" (and in the process put large profits in their pockets). With pity we can believe that we need to guide the Iraqis into democracy, thinking we know what is best for their society. We can use pity to cover up all kinds of paternalistic, dominating, or oppressive policies.

In our CPT work among the Iraqi people, pity has no place. There's suffering, brokenness, anger, and pain, but we are privileged to be among them to see their strength, generosity, and creative spirit.

A newly arrived sister from India walked me to the door of the orphanage as I was ready to leave. As she thanked me, I said, "Thank you. I always receive more than I give." She responded, "Yes, that's the way it is with love."

～ ～ ～

Friday morning, March 19, I went to the Holy Family school to see my friend Ghalia. I felt bad turning her down when she invited me to visit her family over lunch. But I did accept going into her teens class to dialogue with them for about an hour.

First I asked them questions about how they saw things in Iraq, and then they asked me what I think as an American. The youth were animated. They spoke of the things I hear often from Iraqi adults, that security, building up from the destruction, and having their own elected government were top on the list. The girls spoke of not feeling safe on the streets. They asked me why the US hadn't repaired the electricity, why soldiers traveled through the streets on armed vehicles, pointing their guns at all the people, and why soldiers went into the homes and arrested people violently. These questions were hard to answer. They thought the US should leave as soon as there was enough security and there were elections. As with Iraqi adults, the longer we talked, the more open, honest, and critical they became. Their points of view were representative of the spectrum of Iraqi society.

Many said they didn't see any way to have gotten rid of Saddam other than the Americans coming in, and so this started a discussion about violence and nonviolence from a social-political and faith point of view. I told of other countries that had used nonviolent action to get rid of cruel dictators. They weren't ready to accept all I said, but listened intently. I shared about CPT and our willingness to take the same risks as soldiers to work for peace.

One boy suggested that we link them with American teenagers to form a joint peace club and work together for friendship and world peace. I told them this was a great idea that I would share with the rest of the team. I left with warm good-byes and was thankful for the gift I had received that morning with those youth.

I had one last meeting with Sa'ad Kadhim, the leader of the Committee of War Refusers. He said that twenty-six men had now had plastic surgery on their cut ears, and many more were scheduled in April. Most of this was granted through the Iraq Ministry of Health. They still had not received any compensation money.

As we said good-bye, I thought, "There goes one of the very

strong, sensitive leaders I have met among the Iraqi people. He has been wounded but he is channeling his pain to help encourage the Iraqi people, to build up rather than to continue the cycle of violence."

That weekend was also the anniversary of the beginning of the war in Iraq. Memories of that time kept emerging in my consciousness.

~ ~ ~

It was March 15, 2004, and our CPT Iraq team had gathered for worship. Jane read the Scripture from John 1:5: "The light shines in the darkness, and the darkness did not overcome it." She asked, "What does this Scripture passage say to us in this society torn by violence?"

In the time of quiet reflection I thought of one year earlier in the last days leading up to the war and during the bombing. The war seemed to be driven by the circle of decision makers in the Bush administration. With jets poised and an ultimatum given to Saddam, war seemed inevitable.

But some of us resisted this way of thinking to the very end. We found ourselves engaged in a kind of spiritual resistance. Some thought us unrealistic and impractical. It wasn't that we had any illusions about the Bush administration's capability of doing such a thing or thought it couldn't happen. We didn't want to get caught in a mindset that bought into it, got stuck in it, and could no longer see possibilities for creative action. We did not want the culture of fear and hopelessness to paralyze us and to swallow up the light in this intense unleashing of violence.

Do we make statements of faith and then let the darkness creep into our consciousness? Do we let the darkness take over and shape our worldview and lead us to believe that the answer to the world's problems lies with having superior force or that this war was the only way to deal with or get rid of an evil dictator? Christians even create theologies of how Jesus couldn't have really meant that we should love our enemy or that nonviolent, suffering love is more powerful than violence or evil. Some say, "We have to be practical in today's world."

One powerful way the Iraqi people defied the darkness

during the war was to start the call to prayer every time the bombing would start. Over the loud speakers of the mosques, we would hear, "*Allah Akbar!* (God is the greatest, or God is greater!)" God *is* more powerful than the greatest military power in the world. This call to prayer didn't stop the bombing, but it helped prevent the bombing from breaking the spirit of the people.

Some of it may have been our own craziness or stubbornness mixed in, but I couldn't help but think that our resisting the inevitably of war had some connection with the passage about the light triumphing over darkness.

In our CPT work today we resist getting caught in the mindset of the occupation system, which sees the Iraqi people through the eyes of fear and suspicion. We refuse to accept the mindset that anyone resisting the US occupation is a terrorist. We resist seeing either Iraqi or US soldiers as our enemies or believing that violence is the only way to combat terrorism. We chose to see things through the worldview of Jesus and the prophets, so we believe that the only way to solve the problems in Iraq is through turning around, changing directions (repentance), and establishing justice. But that means giving up US domination in Iraq.

Is it possible to walk, live, and work in a system of horrendous, overt structural violence without being overcome by it? How can we do it today here in Iraq, the US, or any other nation?

~ ~ ~

On Friday afternoon and evening, March 19, the eve of the anniversary of the war in Iraq, our team had two candlelight vigils in Baghdad. First we had a time of more personal sharing and prayer at the Al Dar Hotel, where we had stayed during the time of the bombing.

We read the same Scripture passages we had read in our worship gatherings in the evenings before and after the bombing had started, promises of God's care for the poor and oppressed who were being oppressed by "men who scheme to bring the poor and needy down." I told about our small group gathered together, reaffirming our commitment to follow Jesus and give our lives out of love for our brothers and sisters, even if that meant our own death. I had trouble getting the words out, with so many images and feelings coming back to me.

That same day, top Shi'a and Sunni clerics in Baghdad led large groups in a march from their mosques on opposite sides of the Tigris River to a bridge. There on the bridge they met together to form a large vigil, calling for unity and peace, calling on their people not to fight each other for political power.

Then in the evening, seven CPT members and a German friend gathered with candles around the flying carpet sculpture between the Palestine and Sheridan Hotels. This was the place of a peace vigil we had held on the eve of bombing a year earlier.

To get into the sculpture, within an area guarded by barricades, guards, and tanks, we had to go through a checkpoint and be searched. Cliff handed two US soldiers a flyer, which asked them to be responsible for human rights in their work. One got angry and said that this was demoralizing to the soldiers who were struggling to keep strong. One of their men had just been injured in an attack and was in the hospital in a coma. We expressed our sadness for him and carried this into our prayers.

When we lit our candles, people wandering by stared in disbelief to see a peace vigil in this place. We had a strong sense of truly bringing light into the darkness.

First we took time to remember the horrors of war and the consequences for all involved. We spoke about the pain we had felt. We read several verses from Isaiah that point to a new age of justice and peace. We expressed our hope. Our closing prayers for God's healing and care was for the soldiers and their families, as well as for the Iraqi people. Two tanks roared up alongside us, their gun barrels pointed at us as we walked away.

The soldiers found our presence there difficult. As three of us stopped to talk with the military commander on our way out of the checkpoint, he expressed his main concern: "It implies that my men are treating Iraqis badly, and I know that my men treat them with utmost respect." Cliff explained that the flyer was intended to encourage soldiers in ways that would increase their safety. The commander's words reminded us of how much fear and exhaustion US soldiers were carrying, how much it was affecting their actions.

For such a small group, we were well noticed, as light is noticed in darkness. We wanted to be light in the darkness of fear, suspicion, and pain. We wanted to be a sign of hope. Yet as Jane commented later, "We were a reminder to people, who didn't seem to want to be reminded, of the horrible suffering of the war and the necessity for peace." We pray that God's light of peace and of hope would shine through the prayers of thousands of people around the world.

~ ~ ~

The next morning we were sad to hear the sounds of mortars exploding in the Green Zone and were told that one mortar had struck a nearby residential area, killing an Iraqi civilian and wounding three. But we were also encouraged later to hear of the millions of people around the world who had come out on the streets that weekend to speak out against the US occupation.

So here it was, a year after the war had begun. Some Iraqis were still grateful for the United States' role in getting rid of Saddam Hussein. These were usually those who had personally been a victim of Saddam's regime and who had not suffered personal injuries or damage in the war or occupation. One year later, and the rebuilding of infrastructure, services, and social structures was still very meager. People felt unsafe and did not think that their lives were better. They were impatient and afraid that the occupation would be a long-term one. Increasing numbers felt betrayed and angry.

And one year later we were there recalling so much pain and suffering, tears and laughter, love and hope, remembering deeds of violence and greed, as well as deeds of love and courage. I found that love can at times be a "harsh and dreadful thing" when we let it move us to action. This had been the most difficult sixteen months I had ever experienced, but also one of the deepest, shaking me to the very core of my life. I was not the same person who had left home in October 2002 to come to Iraq. I had been challenged, humbled, and strengthened. *Humdillila!* Thanks be to God for this great gift.

~ ~ ~

So this is where love led me—into the fire. I walked through it and then back again into the ongoing struggles of a beautiful people with a beautiful land and culture that is besieged and wounded.

Now their struggle is also my struggle, and the struggle of thousands of international people who have put aside their own comfort and safety to resist an ongoing structure of violence in the form of an occupation. It is the work of those who have caught a vision of nonviolent intervention in situations of tension around the world, acting in the power of nonviolent, suffering love. It is the struggle of those who work to be channels of rebuilding and healing in Iraq.

I pray that love will again lead me there. *Insha'alla!*

Postscript of July 2004

An increase of violence erupted in Iraq one week after I returned to the US. On March 31, 2004, resistance fighters in Falluja mutilated the bodies of four American independent contractors. Four days later (April 4), the prominent Shi'a cleric, Moqtada Al-Sadr, launched a coordinated uprising with armed militia in the Baghdad neighborhood of Sadr City, in the holy city of Najaf, and several cities in southern Iraq. About that time a close Iraqi friend of the Christian Peacemaker Teams (CPT) team in Iraq, who had always spoken positively about US presence in Iraq, came to visit the team and breathlessly told how he had seen US helicopters flying over Sadr City spraying gunfire indiscriminately down on heavily populated areas. One of his personal friends was killed during that firing, and now he was outraged. He told the team, "I hate [Moqtada] Al-Sadr. Many people do not like him, but now I can say I hate what the American forces do too!"

On April 5, US forces surrounded and sealed off Falluja, trying to capture the men who committed the mutilations. This was followed by two weeks of fighting, including US bombing attacks. Non-American international human rights workers, and friends of CPT went into Falluja and helped medical workers. CPTers offered to go and help, but medical workers in Falluja did not want to take responsibility for having US citizens there. The team's friends reported that US soldiers bombed and destroyed a main hospital in Falluja, and took over another for a military base. Iraqi medical personnel created a makeshift medical clinic in a nearby garage to treat the over 1,200 wounded Iraqis. It was estimated that two-thirds of the wounded and the 900 killed were women and children. Once again, the US military responded with excessive violence.

In late April, the systematic abuse of Iraqi prisoners became more widely known when *The Washington Post* printed an article describing the abuses and CBS showed photographs of abuse on their March 28, "60 Minutes II" broadcast. We learned that General Sanchez requested administrative and criminal investigations of alleged physical and sexual abuse of Iraqi detainees in the US-run Abu Ghraib prison. The subsequent report, submitted on February 26 by Major General Antonio Taguba, stated that between October and December 2003 there were "numerous incidents of sadistic, blatant, and wanton criminal abuse inflicted," and showed photographs and video footage. In March, criminal charges were filed against six members of the 372nd Military Police Company. Sanchez was quoted by an aid as saying "this was more than one bad apple, one bad incident."

Later in June it was revealed that soon after the attacks of September 11, officials in the Bush Administration discussed how to disregard Geneva Conventions on torture and detention of prisoners. The prison at Guantanimo Bay soon became a place to put their ideas into practice.

Recently released memos from the White House, Justice Department, and Pentagon argued that the US did not need to follow Geneva Conventions prohibiting abuse of prisoners. In a 2002 memo from Alberto Gonzales, White House Counsel to President Bush, Gonzales argued that the war on terrorism "renders obsolete Geneva's strict limitations on questioning of enemy prisoners." In a 2002 Justice Department memo, approved by President Bush, torture was permitted if it did not result in organ failure or death.

When some internationals were taken hostage in early April, CPT team members began to take extra precautions. This meant not traveling far from our neighborhood, going out at night, going anywhere alone, congregating in public places, and that the women would wear headscarves in public. Iraqis close to the team expressed fear for their own safety as well as the team's, and advised them to leave temporarily. Because the team didn't want to endanger the lives of Iraqi friends and co-workers, the team flew to Amman on April 14. At that time they reported that militia controlled the main road from Baghdad to Amman, as well as all the main roads going into Baghdad.

CPTers Stewart Vriesinga and Le Anne Clausen returned to Baghdad on Monday, May 3, 2004, to check out the possibility of the whole team returning. On May 10, Sheila Provencher and Matthew Chandler also returned to Iraq. They were able to return to the same apartment and quickly became involved in media interviews and organizing a press conference for international media to meet with and interview released detainees who had been abused and "refugees" from the violence in Falluja. They continued visiting families of detainees in the Adopt-a-Detainee campaign, updating information about them, and interviewing released detainees.

Many friends of the team continued to call and stop by to see how the team was doing or to offer them rides around Baghdad. The team continued to consult with Iraqis who advised them not to travel outside of Baghdad, both for their own safety and because their visiting in villages and cities outside of Baghdad still might endanger Iraqi people relating close to the team.

By the end of May, the CPA and the Iraqi Governing Council (IGC) chose the leadership for the new interim government for Iraq, once more imposing a government on the Iraqi people. For prime minister they chose the secular Shi'a, Dr. Iyad Allawi, a man who had worked with the CIA and was widely believed to have raped an Iraqi woman while still working for Saddam Hussein. They chose for president, Sheik Ghazi al-Yawer, a Sunni who had been in exile in Saudi Arabia for two decades and a nephew to a Shammar tribal chief.

On June 9, the UN Security Council voted unanimously to adopt American and British resolution (1546) to officially end the occupation of Iraq and recognize this new interim government by June 30, 2004. The resolution called for elections of Iraqis to draw up a permanent constitution by January 31, 2005, for direct elections for a full-term government by December 31, 2005, and for an American-led multinational force to remain in Iraq to maintain security in partnership with Iraqi forces. In a secret ceremony on June 28 the CPA officially turned over the governing of Iraq to the new interim government and called it an exercise in democracy. Ambassador Paul Bremer left Iraq, and the new US Ambassador to Iraq, John D.

Negroponte, arrived to begin his duties in what is planned to become the largest US embassy in the world.

Before he left, Bremer signed an edict giving US and western defense contractors complete immunity from Iraqi law, created an electoral commission that can ban political parties, gave five-year terms to the new handpicked national security adviser and national intelligence chief, and appointed inspector-generals with five-year terms over every one of the twenty-six Iraqi ministries. It is not surprising that many Iraqi people are calling this another puppet government of the US, and many Middle East political analysts calling this new government a sham.

So, after fourteen months of occupation, how does one estimate the costs of the war and occupation of Iraq? According to a June 24, 2004, report by the Institute for Policy Studies and Foreign Policy in Focus, human costs include 982 (836 US military) deaths, more than 5,000 US soldiers injured, between 9,436 and 11,317 Iraqi civilian deaths, 40,000 Iraqis injured, and between 4,895 and 6,370 Iraqi soldiers and insurgents killed, between March 19, 2003 and June 16, 2004. International civilian workers deaths range from 50-90, and 30 international media workers, and an unknown cost of life and health because of exposure to DU.

Economic costs include $126.1 billion already approved by US Congress for Iraq, the $25 billion heading toward Congressional approval, (which would bring it to $151.1 billion), not to mention the increased cost to veteran physical and mental health care. All this takes away money that could go for meeting human needs.

For Iraqis, the costs include the rise in crime, lack of security, destruction of social institutions, the gouging of Iraqi economy from corporate war profiteering, unemployment, the reduction of oil revenues due to anti-occupation violence, a continued crippled health care and education infrastructure, human rights violations, uncertainty about regaining sovereignty of their country, and much more. The unilateral decision to go to war eroded international law, the credibility of the United Nations, set dangerous precedents for other countries, and increased anti-American sentiment.

On July 1, 2004, I saw Michael Moore's film, *Fahrenheit*

9/11. I was nodding as he laid out very skillfully the underlying connections of economic and political interests behind the war and humorously cut through the lies and deceptions of the Bush Administration. But then he began to show scenes of the horrific bombing, ripped up bodies, and the horror and pain the Iraqi people and US soldiers experienced.

Suddenly I was there once again, in the midst of the bombing at the water plant, hearing the explosions and watching the smoke erupting all along the horizon. I was once more at the Al Dar, trying to tune out the bomb explosions as I tried to sleep. I was at one of the bombed homes and at the hospital seeing the injured. It was real, and it was horrible. But as horrible as it was, it needed to be shown to help people see war for what it really was and is.

It is important that people see through the propaganda of the war, such as Bush's statement that this was a war to "save civilization." The longer I am back in the US, the more the US government's interpretations of what is happening in Iraq begins to creep into my own consciousness. Every so often I have to stop and say, no. I know that is not what is really happening. What was called the "turnover" is not an exercise in democracy. The Iraqi people have little more say over their lives now than before June 28. It is still an occupation and the control is still in the hands of the US, whose corporations continue to reap economic gain at the expense of Iraqi economy.

So what is our response? Do we try to defend and justify the war effort and US policies or acknowledge the wrong we have done and change course? Will America someday have the courage to repent of this tragedy and ask the Iraqi people for forgiveness? Can we allow the reality of this catastrophe in Iraq to awaken our hearts and minds to the basic injustice and violence in our world that our country perpetuates?

Will we allow for space in our hearts and lives for love to push us out of the nests of comfort and security we build for ourselves, and be present with those threatened or mistreated? Can we do it for Iraqis, Afghans, Palestinians, Sudanese, US military personnel, or those in power? What, if any, risks are we willing to take? Will we be willing to take on suffering or give our lives out of this love? And knowing how weak we each are, will we give up, or will we seek and allow God to give us the strength and hope we need to act in love?

The story of the people of Iraq doesn't end here. It has been part of my life and my story, but it is now also part of yours. What our nation chooses to do and what you choose to do in response could result in more suffering and death, or in reconciliation and life.

Timeline of Events in Iraq

September 19, 2002: President Bush urges US Congress to pass a resolution permitting force against Iraq, to change regime and remove weapons of mass destruction.

October 23—November 4, 2002: First Christian Peacemaker Teams (CPT) delegation to Iraq, arriving in Baghdad on October 28 and joins work with Iraq Peace Team (IPT).

November 9, 2002: UN Security Council passes Resolution 1441, resuming weapons inspection in Iraq.

November 18, 2002: First UN weapons inspectors arrive in Iraq.

December 1, 2002: First IPT affinity group moves to the Al Dar Hotel.

December 26, 2002—January 9, 2003: Second CPT delegation to Iraq.

January 11-25, 2003: Third CPT delegation to Iraq (university professors).

February 1-15, 2003: Fourth CPT delegation to Iraq.

February 24—March 10, 2003: Fifth CPT delegation to Iraq.

March 18—April 1, 2003: Sixth CPT delegation to Iraq.

March 20, 2003: Bombing of Baghdad. War on Iraq begins.

March 29, 2003: Several CPTers leave Iraq.

April 2, 2003: Remaining CPTers leave Iraq.

April 9, 2003: US troops enter Baghdad.

April 16, 2003: CPTers return to Iraq.

June 7-21, 2003: Seventh CPT delegation arrives in Iraq, first delegation after the war.

August 19, 2003: UN headquarters in Baghdad bombed.

October 27, 2003: Suicide bombings at Red Cross headquarters and police stations.

April 2, 2004: Major uprising begins in Falluja and Sadr City, Iraq.

June 9, 2004: UN Resolution 1546 passed recognizing the interim government and authorizing the ongoing presence of multinational force.

June 28, 2004: New Iraqi interim government established.

Glossary

Abu Ghraib Prison: Saddam Hussein's infamous prison west of Baghdad, now infamous for US atrocities.

Al Arabia: A major Arabic TV station based in Saudi Arabia.

Allah Akbar: "God is greater" or "God is greatest."

Appalachian Peace and Justice Network (APJN): Athens, Ohio-based nonprofit organization offering resources, training, and education for peacemaking.

Assyrian Democratic Party (ADP): A political party in Iraq representing the interests of Assyrian Christians.

Ba'ath Party: Iraqi political party of the former regime of Saddam Hussein.

Bucca Camp: A US run prison at Um Qasr, near Basra.

Call to prayer: A call to Muslims to pray, broadcast over loudspeakers from mosques five times a day.

Camp Cropper: A notorious US prison near the Baghdad Airport, housing most of the highest security prisoners.

Christian Peacemaker Teams (CPT): A Chicago/Toronto-based nonprofit organization sending violence prevention teams into international places of conflict.

Civil Military Operations Center (CMOC): Regional military offices in Iraq where Iraqis could go to get information, register complaints, or apply for permits. In early 2004, the name was changed to General Information Centers.

Coalition Provisional Authority (CPA): The civilian US and UK authorities, overseeing the governing and rebuilding of Iraq after the 2003 invasion (scheduled to dissolve June 30, 2004).

Committee of War Refusers: An Iraq organization, connected with NADHRI, working to help find compensation and corrective surgery for men whose ears have been cut by Saddam Hussein's regime for refusing to follow military orders.

Dar al Muhabha Orphanage: An orphanage in Baghdad run by the Sisters of Charity of Mother Teresa for severely handicapped children.

Depleted uranium (DU): Uranium 238, a highly radioactive and toxic byproduct of enriching natural uranium, with a half-life of 4.5 billion years, used in bullets and bombs, and to line military tanks in this and the first Gulf War (1991).

Economic sanctions on Iraq: UN Resolution 661, in August 1991, prohibited trade with Iraq. Later it was modified to allow (tightly restricted and monitored) limited purchases of humanitarian goods using revenues from sale of Iraqi oil.

General Information Center (GIC): (see Civil Military Operations Center)

Green Zone: Heavily fortified area in Central Baghdad, the former grounds of Saddam Hussein's Republican Palace, which became the headquarters for the US and UK Coalition Provisional Authority, and later the US embassy.

Gulf Peace Team: A group of international peace activists who camped out as a protest in the Iraqi desert, near the Saudi Arabian border before and during the first Gulf war (1990-91).

Human Rights Organization of Iraq (HROI): An Iraqi human rights organization with branches in many Iraqi cities. CPT worked with OHR branches in Baghdad, Balad, Najaf, and Ramadi since August 2003.

International Occupation Watch (IOW): An international coalition of peace and justice groups working with Iraqis to expose the impact of the military and economic occupation of Iraq.

Insha'allah: "God willing."

Iraqi Assistance Center (IAC): The agency that acts as the CPA's liaison to Iraqis and keeps lists of detainees.

Iraqi Civil Defense Corps (ICDC): The new Iraqi military forces established by the CPA since the 2003 invasion.

Iraq Peace Team (IPT): An organization of international peace activists living in and opposed to the war in Iraq and documenting conditions before, during, and after the invasion, formed by VITW and CPT.

Minders: Iraqi government representatives assigned to watch over the presence of international persons or groups in Iraq under Saddam Hussein's regime.

Oil for Food Program (OFP): A modification of the economic sanctions on Iraq, made in December 1996, which allowed Iraq to purchase humanitarian goods with a limited amount of revenue from oil sales.

Peaceful Tomorrows: Family members of September 11 victims who oppose using that tragedy as an excuse for war and seek nonviolent responses to terrorism. A group of four members visited Baghdad in January 2003.

Pledge of Resistance: A movement in the 1980s to oppose a US invasion of Nicaragua and revised in 2002, organizing people to resist the US invasion of Iraq.

National Association of Defense of Human Rights in Iraq (NADHRI): A Baghdad-based Iraqi human rights organization relating with CPT since August 2003.

Nonviolent Peaceforce: An international organization working to send trained civilians to be a "peace army" in international conflict areas.

Organization of Women's Freedom in Iraq (OWFI): One of the Iraqi women's organizations working for full participation of women in Iraqi society and against abuse of women.

Residence Office: The Iraqi immigration office in Baghdad under Saddam Hussein's regime, responsible for renewing Iraqi visas to foreigners.

Shi'a Muslims: One branch of Islam, with its most holy shrines located in Najaf and Kerbala, Iraq. Sixty percent of the Iraqi people are Shi'a.

Shock and Awe: A term used by the Bush Administration to warn of the massive bombing planned for Baghdad in March 2003.

Society for Human Rights in Iraq (SHRI): A Baghdad-based Iraqi human rights organization. CPT began relating with them in August 2003.

Sunni Muslims: The largest branch of Islam worldwide, but a minority in Iraq.

Union of the Unemployed of Iraq (UUI): An Iraqi organization established after the coalition invasion, seeking jobs and unemployment compensation.

UN Security Council Resolution 1441: Passed November 2002, it demanded Iraq's cooperation with UN weapons inspections using the threat of military action. The US used this resolution as its basis for invading Iraq in March 2003.

Voices in the Wilderness (VITW): Chicago-based nonprofit organization working since 1996 to end economic sanctions on Iraq, co-founder of IPT.

Weapons of mass destruction (WMD): Generally referring to chemical, biological, and nuclear weapons.

Witness For Peace (WFP): A nonprofit organization that began to send delegations of North Americans to Nicaragua in the 1980s to deter Contra attacks and oppose US foreign policy in the region. Currently sends delegations to several Central American countries.

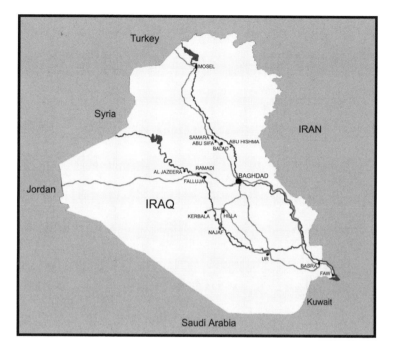

The Author

Peggy Gish is a mother, grandmother, farmer, and long-time peace and social justice activist from southern Ohio. She has served as a social worker in rural Indiana and inner city Chicago, as co-director of the Appalachian Peace and Justice Network, as a conflict management trainer, and a community mediator. Gish is a member of New Covenant Fellowship, a communal church affiliated with the Church of the Brethren. Since 1995, Gish has been involved with Christian Peacemaker Teams in the West Bank and Iraq.

Before 60 Minutes II, before the Red Cross Warnings, before the Taguba Report, there was The CPT Report, and it went to U.S. Ambassador L. Paul Bremer III and U.S. Lt. General Richard Sanchez.

—The Link, *June-July 2004*

By her presence, Peggy Gish accompanied the people of Iraq in their fear before the United States invasion of March 2003, and in their suffering during and after it. Thus she became what Monsignor Romero called a voice for the voiceless. This is a book to be savored and pondered by all practitioners of nonviolence.

—*Staughton Lynd, author*

This book gives new meaning to the adage, "The truth will make you free, but first it will make you uncomfortable." What if the price of peace and freedom turned out, not to be war, but to be uncomfortable? In *Iraq*, the reader is on-site with the nonviolent work of CPT. For anyone who ever wondered how nonviolence works, if it works, or what it looks like in a situation of great violence, Peggy Gish's *Iraq* addresses those questions.

—*John K. Stoner, Every Church A Peace Church*

I was glued to this fascinating diary. It reveals one so in love with a beautiful people and culture that pity of their suffering is not appropriate. Pity might diminish the privilege "to be among them to see their strength, generosity, and creative Spirit."

—*Dale W. Brown, Bethany Theological Seminary*

Peggy Gish is one of those people who live the reality of God's reign. In her book, readers will discover a new way to deal with "enemy." Peggy is both a dreamer and a realist. People of faith should read her book to be re-converted to a New Testament discipleship of love. Others should read the book to regain hope in human relationships and discover a new way to do politics. Peggy remains clear about the costliness of this route. She writes, "So this is where love led me—into the fire." Her book is a light, pointing toward that fire, inviting others into that circle of flaming love.

—*Cliff Kindy, Christian Peacemaker Teams*